Ramsey/Sleeper

ARCHITECTURAL Graphic STANDARDS

Eighth Edition

1991 Cumulative Supplement

JOHN RAY HOKE JR., AIA
Editor in Chief

ANTHONY LEWANDOWSKI
Managing Editor

JOHN WILEY & SONS, INC.

New York / Chichester / Brisbane / Toronto / Singapore

THE AMERICAN INSTITUTE OF ARCHITECTS

This book is dedicated to Lisa, Sara, Jake, and Janet.

NOTE TO *AGS* USERS

The next *AGS* supplement is scheduled for publication by March 1992. Supplements are cumulative. Users who wish to subscribe to the supplement service should contact Joseph Keenan, *AGS* Supplement Service, John Wiley & Sons, Inc., 605 Third Avenue, New York, NY 10158-0012.

Architecture firms and individual AIA members are invited to contribute to future supplements. Those interested should contact John Ray Hoke, Jr., AIA, The American Institute of Architects, 1735 New York Avenue, N.W., Washington, D.C. 20006.

ISBN 0 - 471 - 53031 - X

Printed in the United States of America

10 9 8 7 6 5 4 3 2 1

Contents

Publisher's Note

As publisher of Ramsey/Sleeper's *Architectural Graphic Standards* since 1932, John Wiley & Sons, Inc. feels a special kinship with the design professional community, as well as a deep and on-going commitment to provide it with superior architectural resources. Many distinguished professionals in the field have contributed to a wide range of expertise to *Architectural Graphic Standards* over the years. We have witnessed landmark changes in the field, from the design of buildings, to the materials used in the construction process, to the zoning and building code regulations governing the industry. The rapid pace of change in this area has prompted numerous requests from our readers for more frequent updates of information crucial to success in and a thorough understanding and knowledge of the building design and construction professions. It is in response to these requests and our own assessment of the field that we, in conjunction with the AIA, developed the *1991 Cumulative Supplement to Architectural Graphic*

Standards. The layout and format closely follow *Architectural Graphic Standards, Eighth Edition*. It is our intent to provide the design professional with the latest and most important innovations and information in an accessible format. The *Cumulative Supplement* will be revised and updated on an annual basis in order to keep it, and the professional community it serves, totally current and up-to-date.

We are proud to introduce the *1991 Cumulative Supplement* to *Architectural Graphic Standards* and welcome your comments and suggestions.

KENNETH R. GESSER
Publisher
Professional, Reference, and Trade Group
John Wiley & Sons, Inc.

Foreword

In this era of advanced communications, building industry information, fueled by high-speed processing of automated data, is constantly in flux. The dissemination of new technology through professional reference books, such as *Architectural Graphic Standards*, could easily lag behind without careful and frequent updates. Eero Saarinen eloquently expressed this sentiment in 1956 when he wrote in the foreword to the 5th edition of *AGS*: "the value of such a book depends basically on two things: One is the judgement as well as the thoroughness of its editors. The other is its contemporaneity."

In order to maintain the accuracy and completeness of this most popular and important reference text, the American Institute of Architects and John Wiley & Sons are launching a series of supplements to be published between major editions. As chairman of the AIA task group on *Architectural Graphic Standards*, I am honored to present to you this groundbreaking, first *AGS* supplement.

The walls of progress are built slowly but surely, for the concept of a regular supplement series has been considered since 1964 when the AIA assumed editorial responsibility for this valuable resource. I clearly recall during the final days of production of the 7th edition, the discussions between editor Robert T. Packard, AIA, and advisory board chairman Joseph A. Wilkes, FAIA, about the rapid rate of change in building technology and the subsequent need for the Institute to collect and distribute design practice information more quickly.

Following publication of the 8th edition, editor John Ray Hoke, Jr., AIA, with encouragement from advisory board chairman, Elliott Carroll, FAIA, and management support from AIA group vice president, Steven Etkin, began earnest negotiations with John Wiley & Sons to publish revisions and additions to *Architectural Graphic Standards* on a regular basis. They first explored the market for this venture by conducting an industry-wide survey, which confirmed the need for the supplements.

In the spring of 1989 a roundtable discussion between experts in architectural design, engineering, and construction produced a long list of significant topics and issues for inclusion in the supplement series. We are indeed indebted to this panel for contributing their unique insights and for raising our awareness of new developments in the building sciences. Security planning and design, concrete reinforcement, metal fastening, architectural woodwork, moisture protection, and building types such as offices, shops, animal shelters, greenhouses, and carwashes were identified as important new subject matter.

Momentum continued to grow as an advisory task group was formed to oversee the editorial process of the supplements to insure a high quality product. The first task group meeting was held in April 1990 with a formidable agenda: what new information should be included in the supplement; what existing pages should be revised; and what should the proper balance be between design criteria and technical data. The advisory task group studied a variety of formats before recommending a continuation of *AGS*'s traditional appearance. The use of the Masterformat indexing system was considered very important to maintaining logical and easy access to the information. Finally the task group heartily endorsed the planned use of automated drawing and publishing techniques to produce this and future *AGS* editions.

Very special thanks go to the men and women who volunteered their time and talents to serve on this first task group for the *Architectural Graphic Standards* supplement series. Norma Sklarek, FAIA, took charge of the early chapters, reviewing general planning and design data as well as technical reference material found in the Appendix. Edward Allen, AIA, examined pages on the basic building materials of concrete, masonry, metals, and wood. Darrel Rippeteau, AIA, checked information on thermal and moisture protection, windows, doors, and interior finishes. Jim Duda reviewed submissions on special construction, equipment, and furnishings. Fred Dubin, PE, looked over the material on mechanical and electrical engineering, while James Freehof, AIA, took on special topics such as energy, historic preservation, and recreation. Without the selfless contribution of dedicated task group members such as these, this high quality, practical, professional reference would not exist.

Ultimately credit for the successful completion of this supplement must go to members and associates of the American Institute of Architects who prepared specific reference pages. Since the publication of the 6th edition of *AGS* in 1970, the membership has accepted this responsibility and challenge, thus forming the backbone of *Architectural Graphic Standards*. We thank the individuals and organizations who cared enough to participate in the editorial process and look forward to working with them and others on future publications.

WILLIAM G. MINER, AIA
Chairman, AIA Task Force
Architectural Graphic Standards

Acknowledgments

THE AMERICAN INSTITUTE OF ARCHITECTS

STEVEN A. ETKIN
Group Vice President

JOHN RAY HOKE, JR., AIA
Editor in Chief

ANTHONY LEWANDOWSKI
Managing Editor

RUTHANN MACKEY
Production Assistant

LAIRD UEBERROTH
Production Manager

JAMES V. VOSE
Illustration Coordinator

JANET H. RUMBARGER
Senior Editor

NORA RICHTER GREER
Manuscript Editor

JOHN WILEY & SONS, INC.

KENNETH R. GESSER
Publisher

ROBERT J. FLETCHER IV
Production Director

EVERETT W. SMETHURST
Senior Editor

JOSEPH D. KEENAN
Marketing Manager

PAUL CONSTANTINE
Manager, Digital Production

TASK FORCE CHAIRMAN

WILLIAM G. MINER, AIA

TASK GROUP

EDWARD ALLEN, AIA

FRED DUBIN, PE

JAMES M. DUDA

JAMES FREEHOF, AIA

DARREL RIPPETEAU, AIA

NORMA SKLAREK, FAIA

COMPUTER GRAPHIC ILLUSTRATORS

JERRY L. SMITH

SCOTT PETERSON

STEVE DEHANAS, RIBA

JEFFERY MADSEN

TOM EPPS

ED RAHME

CONSULTING EDITORS

STEPHEN A. KLIMENT, FAIA

RICHARD J. VITULLO, RA

Preface

With the publication of the first supplement to the 8th edition, *Architectural Graphic Standards (AGS)* strikes out on a new course. Beginning with this issue, the many users of *AGS* will be offered annual supplements of technical information. Instead of having to wait for the 9th edition of this important reference work, subscribers will receive approximately 100 pages of new material each year until the new edition is published in 1994. The American Institute of Architects and John Wiley & Sons are proud to offer the Institute's members the most up-to-date information ever made available through the pages of *AGS*.

What will you find in these supplements? Our mission for this first supplement is to give readers a sampling of pages from throughout *AGS*, rather than featuring special sections or chapters. You will find at least one new or updated page for each chapter among the 40 revised 8th edition pages and 60 completely new pages of current information from the field. A new chapter entitled "Building Types" examines office buildings. Future supplements will feature zoos, museums, marketplaces, hospitals, housing, and institutional, ecclesiastical, and judicial facilities, among others.

Our milepost for this supplement to *AGS* is page 29, Masonry Arches. This classic page first appeared in the 1st edition. For this reissue it was composed and illustrated entirely on the computer. In preparing this material we have for the first time in *AGS*'s history relied heavily on computer technology. Over 90 percent of the technical material was produced on computer: the Intergraph and NeXT systems for drawings and labels, Apple and IBM-compatible computers for tables and text. My special thanks go to Christopher L. Barron, AIA, and Thomas A. Zurn of the Intergraph Company for helping us prepare illustrations of the fine quality you see here. For future supplements, creation and prepress production will be entirely electronic. Our continuing commitment to this method of preparation will make possible more timely and accurate production of this important work. Ultimately we expect to publish *AGS* in electronic format.

At Wiley, planning for the supplement service began in 1988 when Steve Kliment, FAIA, editor in architecture and construction, made a commitment to automating *AGS* using PC technology. In 1989, when Kliment left Wiley to accept the position of editor in chief of *Architectural Record*, Everett Smethurst was appointed editor. Robert J. Fletcher IV was, as for the 8th edition, in charge of all aspects of production for this project. My special thanks go to him

another time for his commitment to detail and for his professionalism. I would also like to acknowledge the good work performed by two other Wiley staff members, Joseph Keenan, marketing manager, and Paul Constantine, director of electronic publishing. They both have made major contributions of talent to this project.

In January 1990, when AIA began work on the supplement service, Anthony Lewandowski, formerly director of architectural computer services at Dewberry and Davis in Fairfax, Virginia, filled the position of managing editor for the project. Tony worked with a remarkable staff: Ruthann Mackey, production assistant, whose constant cheerfulness and dedication are greatly appreciated; Laird Ueberroth, architectural consultant, who served as production manager; Jim Vose, graphic coordinator, whose artistic talents breathed life into the computer graphics; Janet H. Rumbarger, senior editor; and Nora Richter Greer, manuscript editor.

I also want to thank others who made possible this first supplement. Rick Vitullo, who contributed extensively to the 8th edition, has once again used his gifted hand to make the pages of *AGS* come alive. I would also like to thank the following individuals for their contributions: June E. Morse, managing editor, Editorial Experts, Inc.; Jesse Oak, Anderson Cooper Georgelas; Steve DeHanas; Thomas Epps; Eric Gastier; Nancy Kilgore, O'Brien-Kilgore, Inc.; Stuart Knoop, Oudens + Knoop, Architects PC; Jeff Madsen; Scott Peterson; Eric Beach, Rippeteau Architects PC; and Jerry Smith.

In conclusion, a personal note: I wish to acknowledge my deep appreciation to a few key people who have given me their complete support and guidance throughout this project. They are Steve Etkin, group vice president for business centers at the American Institute of Architects; William G. Miner, AIA, chairman, *AGS* Task Force; Kenneth R. Gesser, publisher, professional, reference, and trade group, John Wiley & Sons; Robert J. Fletcher IV, production director at Wiley; Steve Kliment, editor in chief, *Architectural Record*; and, of course, Anthony Lewandowski, managing editor for *AGS*, whose remarkable effort has made the impossible possible.

JOHN RAY HOKE, JR., AIA
Editor in Chief
Architectural Graphic Standards
January 15, 1991

GENERAL

Closet systems can be assembled from prefabricated materials cut in the field to custom fit an existing closet. Closet systems are typically constructed of either solid particleboard covered in plastic laminate or steel wire coated with vinyl, polyvinyl chloride, or epoxy.

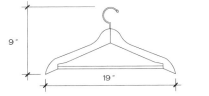

HANGER

TYPICAL LAYOUT DIMENSIONS

REFERENCE	DIMENSION	DESCRIPTION
A	96"	Minimum ceiling height (typical)
B	42"	Hanging storage for shirts, jackets, pants, and skirts for men and women
C	24"	Standard width for drawers and baskets; height for children's hanging clothes
D	36"	Storage for 3 pairs of men's shoes and 4 pairs of women's shoes
E	68"	Hanging storage for dresses and full length robes, evening gowns
F	14"	Standard shelf depth
G	12"	Distance rod is to be mounted from back of closet
H	3"	Distance from top of shelf above to centerline of rod
J	6"	Distance between shelves to allow for shoe storage.
K	24"	Minimum required inside clear depth for closet (typical)
L	12"	Shelf width for 1 stack of clothes
M	6"	Clearance from floor to allow for vacuuming
N	30"	Standard height for children's hanging clothes

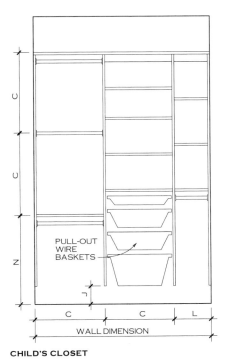

CHILD'S CLOSET

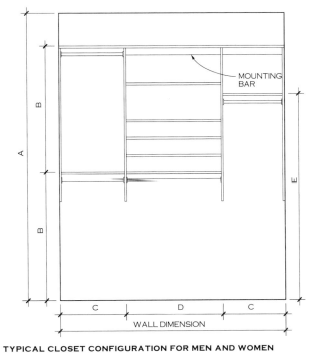

TYPICAL CLOSET CONFIGURATION FOR MEN AND WOMEN

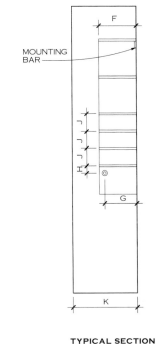

TYPICAL SECTION

SOLID SHELVING SYSTEMS

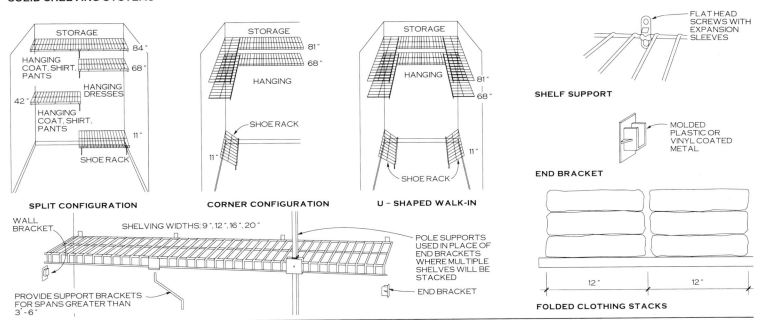

COATED STEEL WIRE SHELVING SYSTEMS

O'Brien - Kilgore, Inc.; Washington, D.C.

GENERAL

1. Typical height for work surface, desk, and credenza is 29 in. Return height is typically 27 in.
2. Universal work surface height is 28 in.
3. Minimum dimension between face of credenza and face of desk is 42 in.
4. Typical transaction counter is 12 to 15 in. deep and 42 to 48 in. high.
5. Freestanding credenzas may be used as computer work-surfaces by increasing depth from 20 in. to 24 in. and by adding a kneehole.
6. Chairman's office may also include an executive storage unit or bookcase.

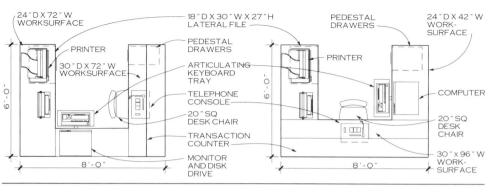

24" D X 72" W WORKSURFACE
PRINTER
30" D X 72" W WORKSURFACE
18" D X 30" W X 27" H LATERAL FILE
PEDESTAL DRAWERS
ARTICULATING KEYBOARD TRAY
TELEPHONE CONSOLE
20" SQ DESK CHAIR
TRANSACTION COUNTER
MONITOR AND DISK DRIVE
PEDESTAL DRAWERS
24" D X 42" W WORK-SURFACE
PRINTER
COMPUTER
20" SQ DESK CHAIR
30" x 96" W WORK-SURFACE

RECEPTIONIST – OPEN AREA

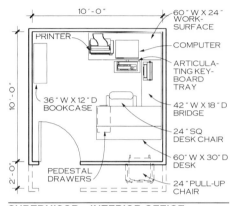

60" W X 24" WORK-SURFACE
PRINTER
COMPUTER
ARTICULATING KEY-BOARD TRAY
36" W X 12" D BOOKCASE
42" W X 18" D BRIDGE
24" SQ DESK CHAIR
60" W X 30" D DESK
PEDESTAL DRAWERS
24" PULL-UP CHAIR

SUPERVISOR – INTERIOR OFFICE

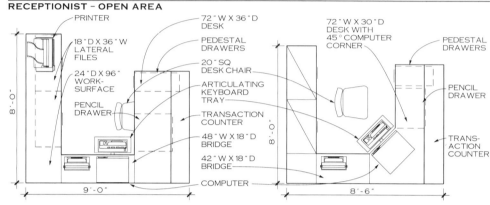

PRINTER
18" D X 36" W LATERAL FILES
24" D X 96" WORK-SURFACE
PENCIL DRAWER
72" W X 36" D DESK
PEDESTAL DRAWERS
20" SQ DESK CHAIR
ARTICULATING KEYBOARD TRAY
TRANSACTION COUNTER
48" W X 18" D BRIDGE
42" W X 18" D BRIDGE
COMPUTER
72" W X 30" D DESK WITH 45° COMPUTER CORNER
PEDESTAL DRAWERS
PENCIL DRAWER
TRANS-ACTION COUNTER

SECRETARY / CLERICAL

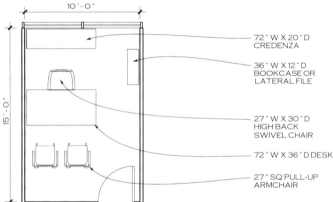

72" W X 20" D CREDENZA
36" W X 12" D BOOKCASE OR LATERAL FILE
27" W X 30" D HIGH BACK SWIVEL CHAIR
72" W X 36" D DESK
27" SQ PULL-UP ARMCHAIR

MANAGER – PERIMETER WINDOWED OFFICE

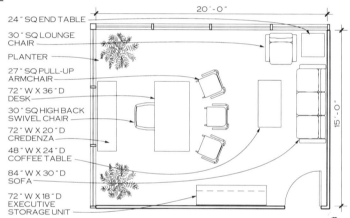

24" SQ END TABLE
30" SQ LOUNGE CHAIR
PLANTER
27" SQ PULL-UP ARMCHAIR
72" W X 36" D DESK
30" SQ HIGH BACK SWIVEL CHAIR
72" W X 20" D CREDENZA
48" W X 24" D COFFEE TABLE
84" W X 30" D SOFA
72" W X 18" D EXECUTIVE STORAGE UNIT

PRESIDENT – PERIMETER WINDOWED CORNER OFFICE

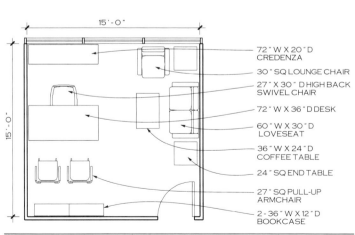

72" W X 20" D CREDENZA
30" SQ LOUNGE CHAIR
27" X 30" D HIGH BACK SWIVEL CHAIR
72" W X 36" D DESK
60" W X 30" D LOVESEAT
36" W X 24" D COFFEE TABLE
24" SQ END TABLE
27" SQ PULL-UP ARMCHAIR
2 - 36" W X 12" D BOOKCASE

VICE-PRESIDENT – PERIMETER WINDOWED OFFICE

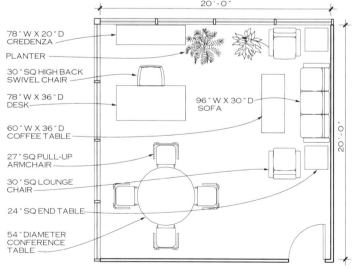

78" W X 20" D CREDENZA
PLANTER
30" SQ HIGH BACK SWIVEL CHAIR
78" W X 36" D DESK
60" W X 36" D COFFEE TABLE
27" SQ PULL-UP ARMCHAIR
30" SQ LOUNGE CHAIR
24" SQ END TABLE
54" DIAMETER CONFERENCE TABLE
96" W X 30" D SOFA

CHAIRMAN – PERIMETER WINDOWED CORNER OFFICE

O'Brien - Kilgore, Inc.; Washington, D.C.

1 SPACE PLANNING

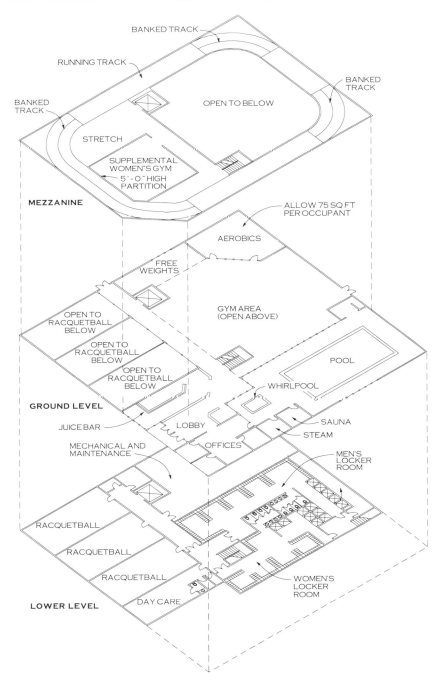

BANKED TRACK

RUNNING TRACK

BANKED TRACK

BANKED TRACK

OPEN TO BELOW

STRETCH

SUPPLEMENTAL WOMEN'S GYM
5'-0" HIGH PARTITION

MEZZANINE

ALLOW 75 SQ FT PER OCCUPANT

AEROBICS

FREE WEIGHTS

OPEN TO RACQUETBALL BELOW

GYM AREA (OPEN ABOVE)

OPEN TO RACQUETBALL BELOW

OPEN TO RACQUETBALL BELOW

POOL

GROUND LEVEL

WHIRLPOOL

JUICE BAR

LOBBY

SAUNA

STEAM

OFFICES

MECHANICAL AND MAINTENANCE

MEN'S LOCKER ROOM

RACQUETBALL

RACQUETBALL

RACQUETBALL

WOMEN'S LOCKER ROOM

LOWER LEVEL

DAY CARE

TYPICAL HEALTH CLUB LAYOUT

GENERAL

Health clubs combine many activities, services, and equipment types under one roof. The areas for each activity are usually open to each other. This promotes interaction and incentive for individuals to continue their participation. This layout visually exposes each member to other activities in which they may want to participate. The visual center of the plan is where the fitness and aerobic machines are located. Some uses are separated for privacy (e.g. locker rooms, supplemental women's gym, etc.) and for particularly high noise activities like aerobics and racquetball. Restaurants, juice bars, and lounges are also incorporated and are usually connected to the common areas.

Planning criteria for health clubs can be broken down into the following four main categories:

1. Aerobic/Cardiovascular
   a. Running track
   b. Treadmill/stair climbing machines
   c. Stationary bicycle
   d. Rowing machine
   e. Swimming pool
   f. Racquetball/squash
   g. Aerobic exercises
2. Anaerobic/Muscular Development
   a. Resistance and repetition fitness machines (includes weight, electronic, or air compression resistance)
   b. Free weights
3. Muscle and Blood Circulation Stimulation
   a. Whirlpool (hydrotherapy)
   b. Steam room (heat therapy)
   c. Sauna (heat therapy)
   d. Massage (direct muscle therapy)
4. Services and Support
   a. Fitness profile (check of weight, blood pressure, percentage of body fat, flexibility, grip strength, and cardiovascular endurance)
   b. Locker and shower rooms
   c. Restaurant and lounge
   d. Administration
   e. Day care
   f. Mechanical and maintenance

NOTES

1. Wet areas such as pools and saunas should be segregated from dry areas such as weight rooms .
2. Heavy traffic and wet areas should be finished with impervious floor materials such as ceramic tile. Wet areas should have a nonslip surface and slope to drains.
3. Open gym areas should be finished in a durable carpet with shock resistant padding.
4. Sound isolation systems should be used in all walls, ceilings, and floors that border occupied spaces. Of particular concern is impact noise from aerobic exercise, running, and free-weight training. Resiliency and mass should be built into the structure to reduce sound transmission.
5. Intense human activity, shower facilities, and the pool and sauna areas all contribute major concentrations of moisture that must be vented to the outside.
6. Lighting quality is an important issue for each activity. A diffuse or indirect system is preferred. However, moods can be created through the use of spot lighting, which can highlight activities. In water related spaces like pools and steam rooms, water resistant lighting is needed.

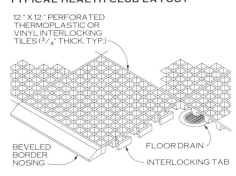

12" X 12" PERFORATED THERMOPLASTIC OR VINYL INTERLOCKING TILES (3/4" THICK, TYP.)

BEVELED BORDER NOSING

FLOOR DRAIN

INTERLOCKING TAB

NOTE

Used in pool areas, locker rooms, etc.

FLOORING FOR WET AREAS

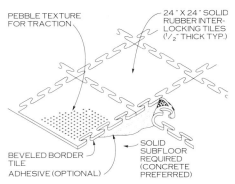

PEBBLE TEXTURE FOR TRACTION

24" X 24" SOLID RUBBER INTERLOCKING TILES (1/2" THICK TYP.)

BEVELED BORDER TILE

ADHESIVE (OPTIONAL)

SOLID SUBFLOOR REQUIRED (CONCRETE PREFERRED)

NOTE

Used in weight rooms and for aerobic classes.

FLOORING FOR HIGH-IMPACT AREAS

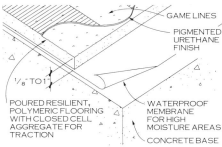

GAME LINES

PIGMENTED URETHANE FINISH

1/8" TO 1

POURED RESILIENT POLYMERIC FLOORING WITH CLOSED CELL AGGREGATE FOR TRACTION

WATERPROOF MEMBRANE FOR HIGH MOISTURE AREAS

CONCRETE BASE

NOTE

Used on running tracks.

POURED RESILIENT FLOORING DETAIL

Brosso, Wilhelm, & McWilliams; Baltimore, Maryland
Richard J. Vitullo, Oak Leaf Studio; Crownsville, Maryland

SPACE PLANNING 1

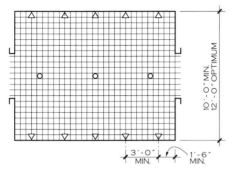

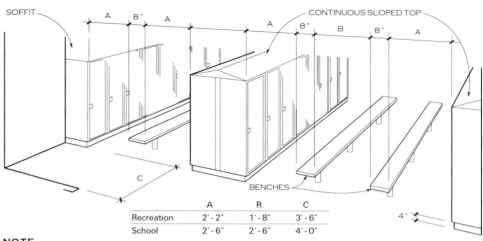

NOTE

Educational facilities with time constraints should have 10 shower heads for the first 30 persons and one shower head for every four additional persons. In recreational facilities one shower head for each 10 dressing lockers is a minimum. Temperature controls are necessary to keep water from exceeding 110° F. Both individual and master controls are needed for group showers.

NOTE

Bench should be minimally 8 in. wide and 16 in. high. Traffic breaks of 3 ft minimum width should occur at maximum intervals of 12 ft. Main traffic aisle should be wider. Avoid lockers that meet at 90° corner.

	A	B	C
Recreation	2'-2"	1'-8"	3'-6"
School	2'-6"	2'-6"	4'-0"

GROUP SHOWERS

LOCKER ROOM

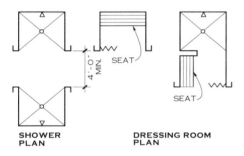

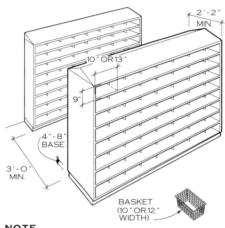

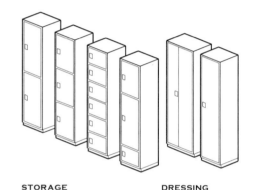

	MINIMUM	OPTIMUM
Showers	3'-0" x 3'-6"	3'-6" x 3'-6"
Dressing Rooms	3'-0" x 3'-6"	3'-6" x 4'-0"

NOTE

Individual dressing rooms and showers can be combined in a variety of configurations to obtain 1:1, 2:1, 3:1, and 4:1 ratios.

INDIVIDUAL SHOWERS AND DRESSING ROOMS

STORAGE   **DRESSING**

STANDARD SIZES (IN.)

Width	9	12	15	18
Depth	12	15	18	
Height	60	72 (overall)		

NOTE

For schools, standard storage locker is 9 in. or 12 in. x 12 in. x 12 in. to 24 in. Standard dressing lockers are 12 in. x 12 in. x 60 in. or 72 in. Number of dressing lockers should be equal to the peak period load plus 10 to 15% for expansion.

NOTE

Basket racks vary from 7 to 10 tiers in height. Wide baskets require 1 ft shelf space, small baskets 10 in. shelf space; both fit 1 ft to 1 1/2 ft deep shelf. Back-to-back shelving is 2 ft 3 in. wide. Height is 9 1/4 in.

BASKET ROOM AND BASKET RACK

LOCKER TYPES

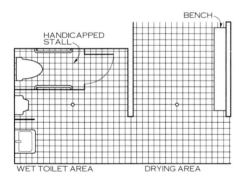

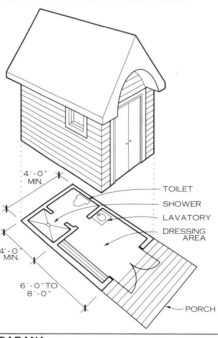

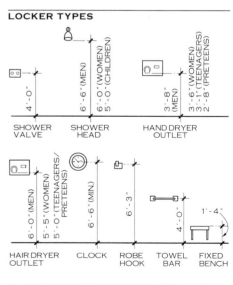

NOTE

The drying room should have about the same area as the shower room. Provision for drainage should be made. Heavy duty towel rails, approximately 4 ft from the floor, are recommended. A foot drying ledge, 18 in. high and 8 in. wide as shown in the drawing, is desirable. An adjacent wet toilet is suggested. Avoid curbs between drying room and adjacent space. Size of towel service area (which can be used for distributing uniforms) varies. Size of area varies with material to be stored, with 200 sq ft usually being sufficient.

DRYING ROOM AND WET TOILET

Richard J. Vitullo; Oak Leaf Studio; Crownsville, Maryland

CABANA

RECOMMENDED MOUNTING HEIGHTS

LOCKER ROOM FACILITIES CHECKLIST

1. Fixed benches 16 in. high.
2. Lockers on raised base.
3. Locker numbering system.
4. Hair dryers—one per 20 lockers.
5. Mirrors at lavatory.
6. Makeup mirror and shelf.
7. Drinking fountain (height as required).
8. Bulletin board.
9. Dressing booths, if required.
10. Full - length mirror.
11. Clock.
12. Door signs.
13. Sound system speaker, if required.
14. Lighting at mirrors for grooming.
15. Lighting located over aisles and passages.
16. Adequate ventilation for storage lockers.
17. Windows located with regard to height and arrangement of lockers.
18. Visual supervision from adjacent office.

GENERAL NOTES

1. The most widely used arrangement of lockers is the bay system, with a minimum 4 ft circulation aisle at each end of the bays. Ordinarily, the maximum number of lockers in a bay is 16. Locate dry (shoe) traffic at one end of the bays and wet (barefoot) traffic at the other end. For long bays with a single bench, make 3 ft breaks at 15 ft intervals.
2. Supervision of school lockers is the easiest if they are located in single banks along the two walls, providing one or more bays that run the length of the room.
3. The number of lockers in a locker room depends on the anticipated number of members and/or size of classes. For large numbers separate locker areas should be encouraged. In small buildings interconnecting doors provide flexibility and allow for the handling of peak loads.
4. Individual dressing and shower compartments and a shower stall for the handicapped may be required.
5. Basket storage, if included, generally is self-service. Maximum height is 8 tiers. A dehumidifying system should be provided to dry out basket contents overnight. Separate auxiliary locker rooms for teams, part-time instructors, faculty, or volunteer leaders may be required. A small room for the coach's use may be desirable.
6. The shower room should be directly accessible to the drying room and locker room that it serves. When a shower room is designed to serve a swimming pool, the room should be located so that all must pass through showers before reaching the pool deck.
7. Separate wet and dry toilet areas are recommended. Wet toilets should be easily accessible from the shower room. When designed for use with a swimming pool, wet toilets should be located so that users must pass through the shower room after use of toilets.
8. Locker room entrance and exit doors should have vision barriers.
9. All facilities should be barrier-free.
10. Floors should be of impervious material, such as ceramic or quarry tile, with a Carborundum impregnated surface, and should slope toward the drains. Concrete floors (nonslip surface), if used, should be treated with a hardener to avoid the penetration of odors and moisture.
11. Walls should be of materials resistant to moisture and should have surfaces that are easily cleaned. All exterior corners in the locker rooms should be rounded.
12. Heavy duty, moisture resistant doors at locker room entrances and exits should be of sufficient size to handle the traffic flow and form natural vision barriers. Entrance/exit doors for the lockers should be equipped with corrosion resistant hardware.
13. Ceilings in shower areas should be of ceramic tile or other material impervious to moisture. Locker room ceilings should be acoustically treated with a material impervious to moisture and breakage. Floor drains should be kept out of the line of traffic, where possible.

Richard J. Vitullo; Oak Leaf Studio; Crownsville, Maryland

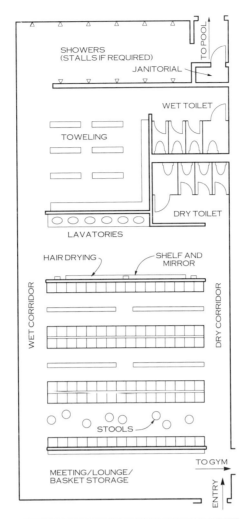

GYMNASIUM AND POOL LOCKER ROOM

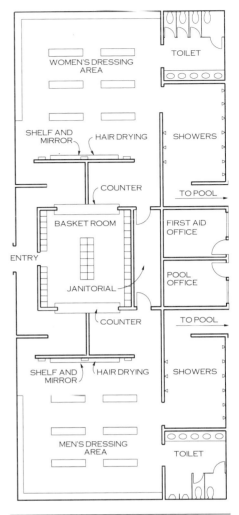

POOL LOCKER ROOM

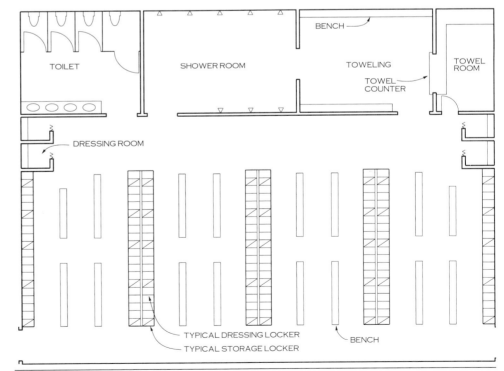

GYMNASIUM LOCKER ROOM

SPACE PLANNING   1

SITE SELECTION

The development of an effective protection for a building site begins with identification of five issues:

1. The potential target(s): persons, goods, information.
2. The potential adversaries: amateur or professional individuals; criminal or political organizations; unstructured groups acting together in an episode.
3. The potential means: human body; commonly available tools; specialized tools; weapons; explosives; vehicles.
4. The availability and types of response personnel.
5. The balance between the cost of deterrence or resistance and the level of acceptable risk.

RESCUE   PARKING   FIRE   HOSPITAL   POLICE

SYMBOL LEGEND

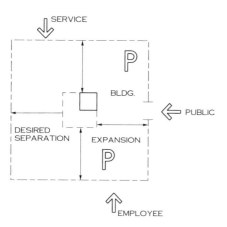

CONSIDERATIONS

1. Sufficient for desired separation between building and perimeter.
2. Sufficient to maintain separation with future expansion.
3. Sufficient for segregation of parking and access.

SITE SIZE

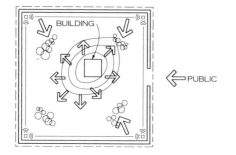

CONSIDERATIONS

1. Allows for siting building out of sight of adjacent uses.
2. Allows economical perimeter protection.
3. Allows good surveillance and intrusion detection sightlines.
4. Allows needed elevations for antennae.

SITE TOPOGRAPHY

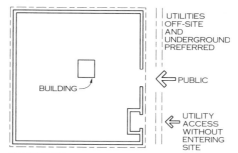

UTILITIES OFF-SITE AND UNDERGROUND PREFERRED

PUBLIC

UTILITY ACCESS WITHOUT ENTERING SITE

CONSIDERATIONS

1. No easements through site.
2. Utility suppliers' access to site can be controlled.
3. Reliable utility services.
4. Utility services not vulnerable to sabotage.

SITE UTILITIES

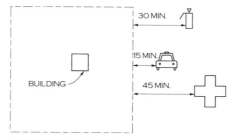

CONSIDERATIONS

1. Public fire protection.
   a. Max. 30 minute response.
   b. Well-trained and equipped.
   c. Acceptable for secure area fire control.
2. Public law enforcement.
   a. Max. 15 minute response.
   b. Well-trained and equipped.
   c. Willing to work with owner's security personnel.
3. Medical care.
   a. 30-45 minute response time.
   b. Well-trained and equipped.

SITE EMERGENCY SERVICES

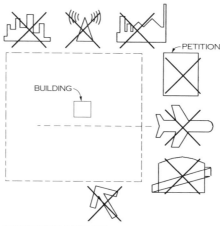

CONSIDERATIONS

1. Compatibility of permitted uses.
2. Acceptability of adjacent structures.
   a. No intruding visual sightlines.
   b. No hostile occupancies.
   c. No radio interference.
   d. No nearby aircraft pathways.
   e. No congested adjacent arterial roads.

SITE SURROUNDING USES

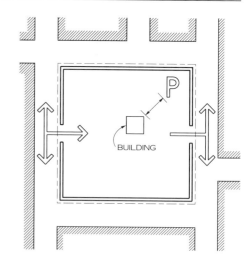

ACCESS TO SITE CONSIDERATIONS

1. Parking needs can be met in controlled areas on site at desired distance from building.
2. Parking needs can be met off site.
3. Public transportation available.
4. Alternative routes available to potential target personnel.
5. Adjacent streets not congested, and not preventing access by emergency vehicles and rapid evacuation.
6. No unimpeded high-speed approaches to site perimeter.

COMMUNITY CONSIDERATIONS

1. Not hostile toward proposed use.
2. Will accept well-designed, visible security measures (perimeter enclosures, lighting, etc.).

SITE ACCESS

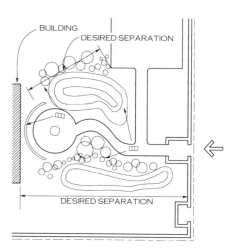

The vehicular approach to sensitive buildings should be contained by landscape. Berms and plantings can shield sensitive areas from vision as well as denying direct off-roadway access to building. Indirect or curving approach toward a building minimizes speed of vehicular approach. All drop-off access to a building should be limited access, and desired separations from parking and site perimeter should be maintained.

SITE APPROACH DIAGRAM

Stuart L. Knoop, W. David Owen, Brian J. F. Baer, Oudens + Knoop Architects P.C.; Washington, D.C.

1   SECURITY PLANNING

SITE PERIMETER SECURITY

The design of the defensive measures consists of three interrelated factors:

1. Detection systems sensitive to intrusion attempts or other hostile acts must alert response personnel promptly and with minimal false alarms.
2. Delay systems, barriers, or distances must impede the intruder sufficiently to allow time for action by response personnel.
3. Whether public law enforcement or on-site forces, response personnel must be able to take the required neutralizing action in the time afforded by the detection and delay systems.

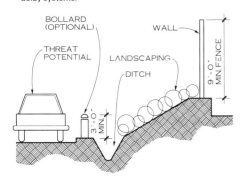

DITCH AND WALL PERIMETER SECURITY

RATES OF PENETRATION

TYPE	PENETRATION MODE TIME IN MINUTES		
	OVER	THROUGH	UNDER
8' high chain link fence	4-12	8-24	3-9
Same with barbed top concertina	5-15	-	-
Same with cable or rail	-	9-27	5-27
Same with mesh buried 2'	-	-	75
Same with concrete security sill	-	-	75
8' high reinforced 8" concrete wall	15-30	7-21	N/A

NOTE

Selected rates in minutes for penetration activities using commonly available articles or tools.

VEHICLE BARRIER EFFECTIVENESS

TYPE	ADVANTAGES	DISADVANTAGES
Earth ditch 13-20' wide and 5' deep	Penetrated but stops and damages vehicle	Can be bridged
Chain-link fence with 3/4" cable	Penetrated but stops and damages vehicle	Personnel can follow through
Concrete vehicle barrier	Penetrated but demolishes vehicle	Second vehicle or personnel can follow through
8" high reinforced concrete antiram wall	Vehicle does not penetrate	Costly

NOTES

Comparative effectiveness of generic, nonproprietary vehicle barriers. Vehicle used is a 3/4 ton pickup traveling at 50 mph.

Proprietary active barriers, such as ramp barricades, crash beams, pop-up bollards, tire traps, specially reinforced gates, etc., are rated by each manufacturer by specific model. These devices have been in widespread use for some years.

Stuart L. Knoop, W. David Owen, Brian J. F. Baer, Oudens + Knoop Architects P.C.; Washington, D.C.

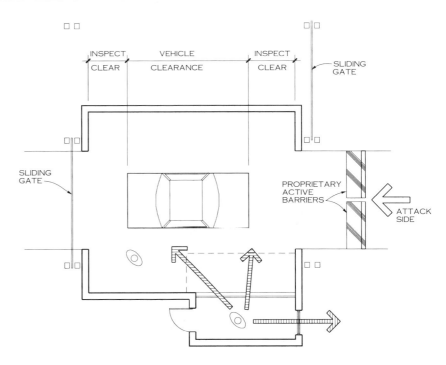

NOTE

In areas of high risk a screening facility is needed to detect guns, explosives, or other threats. A sally-port detains a vehicle for inspection and prevents access by tailgating.

A typical sally-port consists of a detainment area of size sufficient for vehicle clearance and space to operate inspection equipment. The entry and exit of the sally-port is operated from an adjacent guard booth. The entry to the sally-port is often guarded by an active barrier. In areas of extreme sensitivity a secondary guard is needed to perform the vehicle inspection.

SITE ACCESS— SALLY-PORTS

PROTECTION TECHNIQUE EVALUATION:
(ON A SCALE OF 1 AS MOST TO 5 AS LEAST)

	DEPENDABILITY[1]	ACCURACY[2]	SPEED OF PROCESS	SKILLED LABOR INTENSITY[3]	TECHNOLOGICAL INTENSITY[4]	RESISTANCE TO DEFEAT	USER CONVENIENCE
IDENTIFICATION							
Visual/oral	4	4	3	1	5	4	1
Badge	4	4	3	3	2	5	2
Card	2	2	1	2	4	3	2
Card and P.I.N.	1	1	1	2	5	1	3
Biometric	2	2	3	2	5	1	4
Card and Biometric	1	1	4	3	5	1	5
SCREENING							
Visual/oral	5	5	5	1	5	2	4
Body search	1	2	5	1	5	3	5
Walk-through detector	3	3	2	2	3	4	3
X-ray	4	4	3	2	2	2	4
Parcel inspection	2	2	5	2	5	2	5
SEGREGATION							
Oral/graphic	5	5	1	5	5	5	1
Guard/controller	3	3	2	4	2	4	3
Key	5	-	1	5	5	4	2
Card access	2	3	1	2	4	4	2
Digital combination	4	4	3	4	5	4	4
DUAL DIGITAL							
Combinations	5	5	2	4	5	2	5
Biometric	2	2	3	3	1	2	4
Two or more techniques	1	1	4	4	5	1	4

NOTES

1. Dependability refers to performance reliability with least maintenance and repair.

2. Accuracy refers to precision of task performance.

3. Skilled labor intensity refers to quality and number of experienced personnel needed.

ACCESS CONTROL

The illustrations on this page are intended to show a range of access control spaces and techniques that, in practice, could take any number of combined forms; for instance, within the same point of control, such as a lobby, several techniques might be applied depending on the nature and volume of the persons being screened. In Diagram A, the control is a little more than one encounters in the waiting room of a physician's office; in Diagram D, the control is such as might be used at a nuclear facility.

In any situation, the following must be defined:

1. The potential target(s): persons, goods, information.
2. The potential adversaries: amateur or professional individuals; criminal or political organizations; unstructured groups acting together in an episode.
3. The potential means: human body; commonly available tools; specialized tools; weapons; explosives; vehicles.
4. The availability and types of response personnel.
5. The balance between the cost of deterrence or resistance and the level of acceptable risk.

CARD KEY   GUARD   BADGE   BUTTON PAD

BIOMETRIC   WALK THROUGH METAL DETECTOR   BAG X-RAY   RECEPTION

TURNSTILE   SECURE WHEN ACTIVATED   ALWAYS SECURE

SYMBOL LEGEND

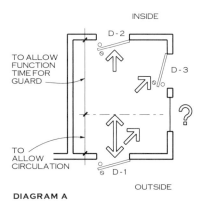

DIAGRAM A

FEATURES

1. Identification: visual, oral
2. Screening: visual
3. Segregation: oral or graphic instructions
4. Traffic handling: same for all persons; entrance and exit combined
5. Operation: all doors normally operable for entry and exit; doors secured by receptionist as needed

BASIC ACCESS CONTROLS

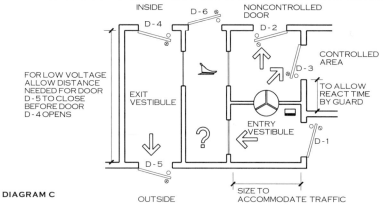

DIAGRAM B

FEATURES

1. Identification: visual/oral, except door D-5 to limited access area requires card and personal ID number (PIN).
2. Screening: visual/oral for employees; walk-through metal detector, parcel X-ray, visual/oral for pass issuance by receptionist.
3. Segregation: separated employee and visitor control. Visitors admitted by guard after identification, pass issuance, and screening. Employees segregated by card, key, PIN, code.
4. Traffic handling: visitors issued passes, screened, exit on surrender of pass. Employees enter and exit using card at turnstile.
5. Operation: exterior entrance doors D-1, D-3, and D-4 usually operable both directions; locked after hours. Door D-2 always locked; unlocked by guard after screening. Door D-6 normally locked; locked by guard in emergency. Door D-5 always locked, unlocked by card, key, PIN, guard, or combination. All doors operable in exit direction.

LOW VOLUME VISITOR ENTRY/EXIT AND HIGH VOLUME EMPLOYEE ENTRY/EXIT

DIAGRAM C

FEATURES

1. Identification: visual, oral
2. Screening: visual
3. Segregation: oral or graphic instructions
4. Traffic handling: same for all persons; entrance and exit separated

5. Operation: Door D-1 normally operable, secure after hours; turnstile card operated by employees, released by guard or receptionist for visitors. Door D-2 normally operable to noncontrolled area, can be locked by guard in emergency. Door D-3 to controlled area always locked, unlocked by guard. Doors D-4 and D-5 always locked on outside; unlocked for exit. Distance needed to allow D-4 to close before D-5 opened. Doors can be interlocked, but not recommended for high volume.

SEPARATE EXIT AND ENTRANCE

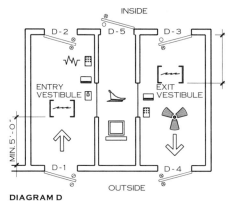

DIAGRAM D

FEATURES

1. Identification: visual, magnetic card, PIN, biometric combination.
2. Screening: walk-through metal detectors, radioactive and explosive materials "sniffers" etc. in and out.
3. Segregation: by identification.
4. Traffic handling: one person at a time.
5. Operation: all doors except D-1 locked from outside. D-1 locks when entry vestibule in use. Door D-2 unlocks only after successful screening and identification. D-1 locks for containment by guard; D-4 unlocks after successful exit screening and log-out.

HIGH SECURITY ENTRY/EXIT SALLY-PORT

Stuart L. Knoop, W. David Owen, Brian J. F. Baer, Oudens + Knoop Architects P.C.; Washington, D.C.

BUILDING SYSTEMS
THREAT ANALYSES AND RESPONSE

The illustration on this page exemplifies a building in which information or processes might be the threatened targets. The intention is to screen the public and to segregate employees as to their access to certain parts of the building.

In any building, the threat must be determined preferably before a site is selected. Threat analysis consists of five considerations:

1. The potential targets: persons, goods, information.
2. The potential adversaries: amateur or professional individuals; criminal or political organizations; unstructured groups acting together in an episode.
3. The potential means: human body; commonly available tools; specialized tools; weapons; explosives; vehicles.
4. The availability and types of response personnel: public law enforcement; military; contract security forces; owner personnel. Use of force as a response governed by law.
5. The balance between the cost of deterrence or resistance and the level of acceptable risk.

As the threats are determined, the means of countering them must be evaluated.

1. Visibility of security measures and the inconvenience of them to the public may be an unacceptable public image or may have a desirable deterrent effect.
2. The skill and legal authority of response personnel varies widely. At best, physical security design affords time to take action such as by force, to defuse a situation by negotiation or to escape peril. No physical measures are undefeatable by determined, skilled, and well-financed adversaries.
3. Designs to counter response to security threats must be tempered by life safety and access needs for persons with disabilities. These are often in conflict, especially in cases where emergency egress must be through an access-controlled lobby or where heavy ballistic doors must be operated by elderly or wheelchair-confined persons. Usually alternative assisted access is preferable to attempting to reconcile the demands of security with those of easy accessibility.

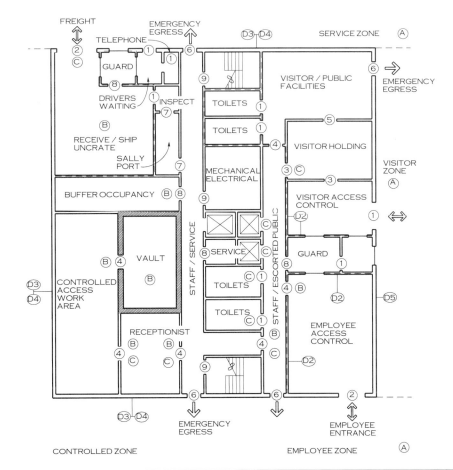

BUILDING SECURITY DIAGRAM

NOTES

1. Exterior zones separated from each other; access to each from public rights-of-way controlled.
2. Employees controlled by monitored selective access system such as access control cards. Coded for level of permitted access.
3. Visitors must have escorted access by employees in access control system.
4. Wall construction depends on threat:
   - D-1 Blast
   - D-2 Ballistic
   - D-3 Forced entry
   - D-4 Surreptitious entry
   - D-5 All of the above.

DOOR FUNCTIONS FOR BUILDING SECURITY DIAGRAM

DOOR FUNCTION	1	2	3	4	5	6	7	8	9
No control function					•				
Outside normally locked			•	•		•	•	•	•
Inside normally operable			•	•	•	•	•	•	•
Outside locked by guard/controller	•	•							
Outside unlocked by guard/controller				•			•	•	
Outside unlocked by card, key, I.D., etc.					•		•	•	
Inside locked under emergency						•			
Outside unlocked under emergency									•
Outside locked after hours only			•	•					
After hours unlocked by guard/controller				•					
Doors interlocked						•			

BUILDING SYSTEMS MEAN PENETRATION TIME

4 IN. THICK, 3,000 PSI CONCRETE WITH ONE LAYER 1/2 IN. - 6 X 6 MESH

Sledge, hand bolt-cutters	3.2 min.	1 person
Sledge, cutting torch	3.3 min.	2 persons

6 IN. THICK, 3,000 PSI CONCRETE WITH ONE LAYER #5 – 6 IN. X 6 IN.

Sledge, hand hydraulic bolt-cutters	4.7 min.	1 person
Sledge, cutting torch	4.0 min.	2 persons

8 IN. THICK 3000 PSI CONCRETE WITH TWO LAYERS #5 - 6 IN. X 6 IN.

Rotohammers, sledge, punch, hand-held power hydraulic bolt-cutters, generator	30 min.	2 persons

4 IN. THICK CMU, UNFILLED, NO REBAR

Sledge	0.4 min.	1 person

8 IN. THICK CMU VOL. #8 REBAR IN MORTAR-FILLED CORES

Sledge, cutting torch	2.7 min.	2 persons

8 IN. HOLLOW CMU FILLED WITH MORTAR, 1 IN. X 9 GAUGE EXPANDED STEEL MESH BONDED TO BLOCK, 4 IN. SOLID CMU

Sledge, punch, wrecking bar, rotohammer, drill, cutting torch, generator	4.9 min.	2 persons
Bolt-cutters, battering ram	10 min.	3 persons

NOTE

1. Explosives not included.

Stuart L. Knoop, W. David Owen, Brian J. F. Baer, Oudens + Knoop Architects P.C.; Washington, D.C.

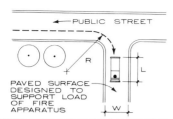

FIRE APPARATUS ACCESS

Fire apparatus (i.e., pumpers, ladder trucks, tankers) should have unobstructed access to buildings. Check with local fire department for apparatus turning radius (R), length (L), and other operating characteristics. Support systems embedded in lawn areas adjacent to the building are acceptable.

RESTRICTED ACCESS

Buildings constructed near cliffs or steep slopes should not restrict access by fire apparatus to only one side of the building. Grades greater than 10 percent make operation of fire apparatus difficult and dangerous. Avoid parking decks abutted to buildings. Consider pedestrian bridge over instead.

FIRE DEPARTMENT RESPONSE TIME FACTOR

Site planning factors that determine response time are street accessibility (curbs, radii, bollards, T-turns, culs-de-sac, street and site slopes, street furniture and architectural obstructions, driveway widths), accessibility for firefighting (fire hydrant and standpipe connection layouts, outdoor lighting, identifying signs), and location (city, town, village, farm). Check with local codes, fire codes, and fire department for area regulations.

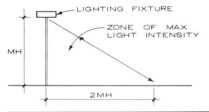

OUTDOOR LIGHTING

Streets that are properly lighted enable fire fighters to locate hydrants quickly and to position apparatus at night. Avoid layouts that place hydrants and standpipe connections in shadows. In some situations, lighting fixtures can be integrated into exterior of buildings. All buildings should have a street address number on or near the main entrance.

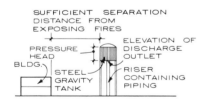

GRAVITY TANK

Gravity tanks can provide reliable source of pressure to building standpipe or sprinkler systems. Available pressure head increases by 0.434 psi/ft increase of water above tank discharge outlet. Tank capacity in gallons depends on fire hazard, water supply, and other factors. Tanks require periodic maintenance and protection against freezing during cold weather. Locations subject to seismic forces or high winds require special consideration. Gravity tanks also can be integrated within building design.

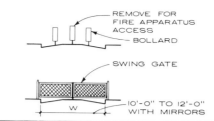

ACCESS OBSTRUCTIONS

Bollards used for traffic control and fences for security should allow sufficient open road width (W) for access by fire apparatus. Bollards and gates can be secured by standard fire department keyed locks (check with department having jurisdiction).

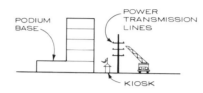

STREET FURNITURE AND ARCHITECTURAL OBSTRUCTIONS

Utility poles can obstruct use of aerial ladders for rescue and fire suppression operations. Kiosks, outdoor sculpture, fountains, newspaper boxes, and the like can also seriously impede fire fighting operations. Wide podium bases can prevent ladder access to the upper stories of buildings. Canopies and other nonstructural building components can also prevent fire apparatus operations close to buildings.

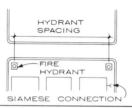

FIRE HYDRANT AND STANDPIPE CONNECTION LAYOUT

Locate fire hydrants at street intersections and at intermediate points along roads so that spacing between hydrants does not exceed capability of local fire jurisdiction. Hydrants should be placed 2 to 10 ft from curb lines. Siamese connections for standpipes should be visible, marked conspicuously, and be adjacent to the principal vehicle access point to allow rapid connection by fire fighters to the pumping engine.

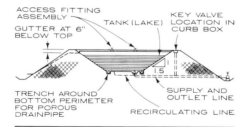

ON-SITE LAKES

Man-made and natural on-site lakes are used for private firefighting in suburbs, on farms, and at resorts. A piped supply system to a dry hydrant is preferred for its quantity flexibility, better maintenance, and accessibility. Man-made lakes with reservoir liners can be berm-supported or sunk in the ground. Lakes and ponds are natural water supplies dependent on the environment. See local codes, fire codes, and fire departments for on-site lake regulations.

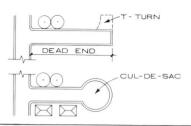

DRIVEWAY LAYOUTS

Long dead ends (greater than 150 ft) can cause time consuming, hazardous backup maneuvers. Use t-turns, culs-de-sac, and curved driveway layouts to allow unimpeded access to buildings.

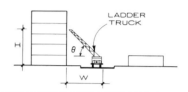

DRIVEWAY WIDTHS

For full extension of aerial ladders at a safe climbing angle (θ), sufficient driveway width (W) is required. Estimate the required width in feet by: $W = (H - 6) \cot \theta + 4$, where preferred climbing angles are 60 to 80°. Check with local fire department for aerial apparatus operating requirements, including width of aerial device with stabilizing outriggers extended.

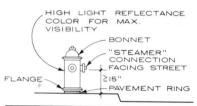

FIRE HYDRANT PLACEMENT

Fire hose connections should be at least 15" above grade. Do not bury hydrants or locate them behind shrubs or other visual barriers. Avoid locations where runoff water and snow can accumulate. Bollards and fences used to protect hydrants from vehicular traffic must not obstruct fire fighters' access to hose connections. "Steamer" connection should usually face the side of arriving fire apparatus.

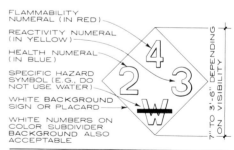

NFPA 704 DIAMOND SYMBOLS

Standard diamond symbols provide information fire fighters need to avoid injury from hazardous building contents. 0 numeral is the lowest degree of hazard, 4 is highest. Locate symbols near building entrances. Correct spatial arrangement for two kinds of diamond symbols are shown. Consider integrating symbols with overall graphics design of building. (Refer to "Identification of the Fire Hazards of Materials," NFPA No. 704, available from the National Fire Protection Association.)

D. L. Collins and M. David Egan, P.E.; College of Architecture, Clemson University; Clemson, South Carolina
Nicholas A. Phillips, AIA; Lockwood Greene; New York, New York
National Fire Protection Association, see data sources

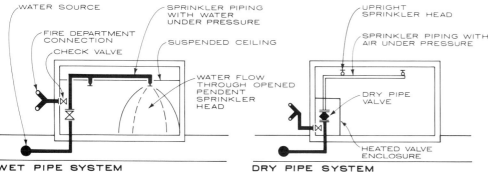

WET PIPE SYSTEM

DRY PIPE SYSTEM

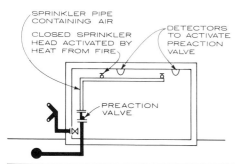

PREACTION SYSTEM

DELUGE SYSTEM

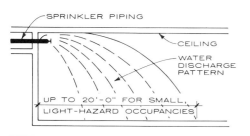

SIDEWALL SPRINKLER HEAD
(HORIZONTAL SIDEWALL SHOWN)

Piping can be unobtrusively installed along sides of exposed ceiling beams or joists. In small rooms, sidewall heads provide water discharge coverage without overhead piping.

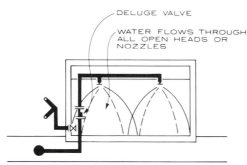

PENDENT SPRINKLER HEAD

Can be recessed in ceiling (e.g., coffered, modeled) or hidden above flat metal cover plate. (Flush sprinkler heads are also available.)

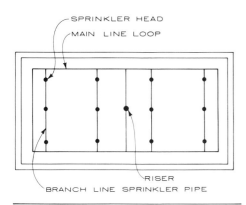

HYDRAULICALLY DESIGNED SPRINKLER SYSTEM LAYOUT

Loop provides water flow from two directions to operating sprinkler heads so pipe sizes will be small. Hydraulic calculations can assure delivery of adequate water flow and pressure throughout piping network to meet design requirements.

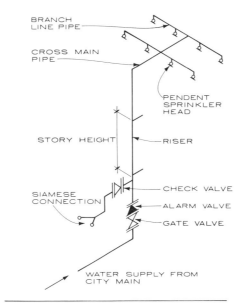

SPRINKLER SYSTEM RISER

M. David Egan, P.E.; College of Architecture, Clemson University; Clemson, South Carolina

TYPES OF SYSTEMS

WET PIPE: Piping network contains water under pressure at all times for immediate release through sprinkler heads as they are activated by fire. Wet pipe system is the most widely used system, since water delivery is faster than with a dry pipe system.

DRY PIPE: Piping network contains air (or nitrogen) under pressure. Following loss of air pressure through opened sprinkler head, dry pipe valve opens allowing water to enter piping network and to flow through opened sprinkler head (or heads). Used where piping is subject to freezing.

PREACTION: Closed head, dry system containing air in piping network. Preaction valve is activated by heat or smoke detection system more sensitive than sprinkler heads. The opened preaction valve allows water to fill piping network and to flow through sprinkler heads, as they are activated by heat from fire. Used where leakage or accidental discharge would cause water damage.

DELUGE: Sprinkler heads (or spray nozzles) are open at all times and normally there is no water in piping network. Mechanical or hydraulic valves, operated by heat or flame detection systems, are used to control water flow to heads by opening water control deluge valve. Deluge systems are special use systems, as water discharges from all heads (or nozzles) at the same time.

STANDPIPE AND HOSE: Dry standpipes are empty water pipes used by fire fighters to connect hoses in buildings to fire department pumpers. Wet standpipes are water filled pipes permanently connected to public or private water mains for use by industrial fire brigades or by fire fighters.

FOAM: Used to suppress flammable liquid fires. Foam can be distributed by piping network to nozzles or other discharge outlets (e.g., tubes, troughs, monitors) depending on the hazard.

HALON (haloginated hydrocarbon): previously used where water damage to building contents would be unacceptable. The use of halon systems is being phased out due to environmental concerns, and new installations are not allowed in many areas. Piping network connects fixed supply of halon to nozzles that discharge uniform, low concentration throughout room. To avoid piping network, discharge cylinders may be installed throughout room or area. Though generally nontoxic, delayed discharge can cause problems by allowing decomposition of halon. Rapid detection is necessary.

CO_2 (carbon dioxide): Does not conduct electricity and leaves no residue after its use. Piping network connects fixed supply of CO_2 to nozzles that discharge CO_2 directly on burning materials where location of fire hazard is known (called "local application") or discharge CO_2 uniformly throughout room (called "total flooding"). In total flooding systems, safety requirements dictate advance alarm to allow occupants to evacuate area prior to discharge.

DRY CHEMICAL: Can be especially useful on electrical and flammable liquid fires. Powdered extinguishing agent, under pressure of dry air or nitrogen, commonly discharged over cooking surfaces (e.g., frying).

PREPARATION FOR SPRINKLER SYSTEMS

1. Begin planning sprinkler system at the very earliest design stages of project.
2. Determine hazard classification of building and type of system best suited for suppression needs.
3. Refer to national standards (NFPA), state and local codes.
4. Check with authority having jurisdiction:
   a. State and local fire marshals.
   b. Commercial risk services.
   c. Insurance underwriting groups such as IRI, or FM (if they have jurisdiction).
5. Use qualified fire protection engineers to design system. Be sure water supply is adequate (e.g., by water flow tests). Integrate system with structural, mechanical, and other building services.
6. Check space requirements for sprinkler equipment. Sprinkler control room must be heated to prevent freezing of equipment.
7. Consider possible future alterations to building.

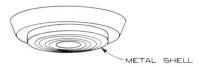

HEAT DETECTOR

METAL SHELL

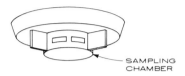

IONIZATION SMOKE DETECTOR

SAMPLING CHAMBER

PHOTOELECTRIC SMOKE DETECTOR

SAMPLING CHAMBER

FIRE AND SMOKE DETECTORS

OUTER LENS

INFRARED OR ULTRAVIOLET FLAME DETECTOR

HEAT DETECTOR

Fixed temperature heat detectors (e.g., those rated at 135 to 197°F) use low melting point solder or metals that expand when exposed to heat to detect fire. Rate-of-rise heat detectors alarm when rate of temperature change exceeds about 15°F/min. Expansion of air in chamber with calibrated vent is used to detect rapidly developing fires. Devices are available with both rate-of-rise and fixed temperature detection features.

IONIZATION SMOKE DETECTOR

Ionization detectors use the interruption of small current flow between electrodes by smoke in ionized sampling chamber to detect fire. Dual chamber (with reference chamber exposed only to air temperature, pressure, and humidity) and single chamber detectors are available. Ionization detectors can be used in rooms and, when designed for use in air ducts, to detect smoke in air distribution systems.

PHOTOELECTRIC SMOKE DETECTOR

Photoelectric smoke detectors use the scattering of light by smoke into view of photocell. Light source is light emitting diode (LED). Photoelectric detectors can be used in rooms and, when designed for use in air ducts, to detect smoke in air distribution systems.

INFRARED OR ULTRAVIOLET FLAME DETECTOR

Infrared (IR) and ultraviolet (UV) flame detectors respond to the UV and IR radiant energy from flames. Alarm is only triggered when IR (or UV) energy flickers at a rate that is characteristic of flames. Flame detectors can be used in large open areas where rapid development of flaming conditions could occur (e.g., flammable liquids fire hazards).

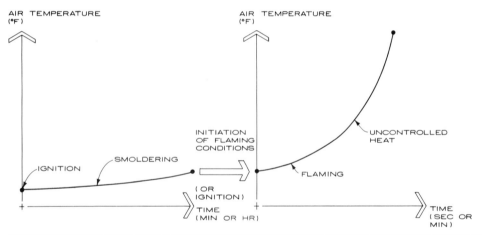

STAGES OF FIRE

STAGES OF FIRE

Carefully match fire detectors to anticipated fire hazard (e.g., photoelectric smoke detectors for smoldering fires, ionization smoke detectors for flaming fires, flame detectors for flash fires). The time-temperature curves show growth to hazardous conditions for smoldering, flaming, and uncontrolled heat stages of fire.

CHECKLIST FOR RESIDENTIAL FIRE DETECTION

1. Use smoke detectors to protect the following (in decreasing order of importance):
   a. Every occupied floor and basement.
   b. Sleeping areas and basement near stairs.
   c. Sleeping areas only.
2. Use heat detectors to protect remote areas (e.g., basement shops, attics) where serious fires could develop before smoke would reach smoke detector or in areas such as garages or kitchens where smoke detectors would be exposed to high smoke levels during normal conditions.
3. Locate smoke detectors on ceilings near center of rooms (or on the upper walls 6 to 12 in. from ceiling) where smoke can collect. In long corridors, consider using two or more detectors.
4. Use closer spacing between detectors where ceiling beams, joists, and the like will interrupt flow of smoke to detector.
5. Do not place smoke detectors near supply air registers or diffusers.
6. For guidelines on fire detection for residences, refer to ''Household Fire Warning Equipment,'' NFPA No. 74, available from the National Fire Protection Association.

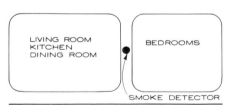

RESIDENTIAL OCCUPANCY (WITH SINGLE SLEEPING AREA)

RESIDENTIAL OCCUPANCY (WITH SPLIT SLEEPING AREAS)

ANNUNCIATOR DISPLAY PANEL

HARD COPY PRINTOUT

AUTOMATED CONTROL CONSOLE

NOTE

When fire is detected (e.g., by smoke, heat, flame detectors or water flow indicators in sprinkler system piping), automated control systems immediately summon the fire department. Floor plans of fire area can be projected on annunciator display panel to pinpoint trouble spots. Controls can be designed to automatically shut down fan systems or active fans and dampers for smoke removal and control. In addition, remote firefighter control panel, with telephone communication to control console and to each floor in building, can be used to control and monitor status of elevators, pumps and emergency generators, fans, dampers, and the like.

M. David Egan, P.E.; College of Architecture, Clemson University; Clemson, South Carolina
John L. Bryan; Fire Protection Engineering, University of Maryland; College Park; Maryland

FIRE PROTECTION

MINIMUM UNIFORMLY DISTRIBUTED LIVE LOADS

OCCUPANCY OR USE	LIVE LOAD (PSF)
Armories and drill rooms	150
Assembly halls and other places of assembly	
Fixed seats	50
Movable seats	100
Platforms (assembly)	100
Attics	
Nonstorage	25
Storage	30[5]
Bakeries	150
Balconies	
Exterior	60
Interior (fixed seats)	50
Interior (movable seats)	100
Bowling Alleys, poolrooms, and similar recreational areas	75
Broadcasting studios	100
Catwalks	25
Cold storage rooms	
Floor	150
Roof	250
Corridors	
First floor	100
Other floors, same as occupancy served except as indicated	
Dance halls and ballrooms	100
Dining rooms and restaurants	100
Dormitories	
Nonpartitioned	80
Partitioned	40
File rooms	
Card	125[1]
Letter	80[1]
High-density storage	150[5]
Fire escapes on multifamily or single family residential buildings only	100
Foundries	600[2]
Fuel rooms, framed	400[2]
Garages (passenger cars only). For trucks and buses use AASHO[3] lane load	50
Grandstands	100[6]
Greenhouses	150
Gymnasiums, main floor and balconies	100
Hospitals	
Operating rooms and laboratories	60
Private rooms	40
Wards	40
Corridors, above first floor	80
Hotels (see residential)	
Kitchens, other than domestic	150[2]
Laboratories, scientific	100
Laundries	150[2]
Libraries	
Reading rooms	60
Stack rooms (books and shelving at 65 pcf) but not less than indicated	150
Corridors, above first floor	80
Manufacturing	
Light	75
Heavy	125
Ice	300
Marquees	60
Morgues	125
Office buildings	
Office	50
Business machine equipment	100[2]
Lobbies	100
Corridors, above first floor	80
File and computer rooms require heavier loads based on anticipated occupancy	
Penal Institutions	
Cell blocks	40
Corridors	100
Printing plants	
Composing rooms	100
Linotype rooms	100
Paper storage rooms	[4]
Pressrooms	150[2]
Public rooms	100

OCCUPANCY OR USE	LIVE LOAD (PSF)
Residential	
Multifamily houses	
Private apartments	40
Public rooms	100
Corridors	80
Dwellings	
First floor	40
Second floor and habitable attics	30
Inhabitable attics	20
Hotels	
Guest rooms	40
Public rooms	100
Corridors serving public rooms	100
Rest rooms and toilet rooms	40
Schools	
Classrooms	40
Corridors	80
Sidewalks, vehicular driveways, and yards subject to trucking	250
Skating rinks	100
Stairs and exit-ways	100
Storage warehouses	
Light	125
Heavy	250
Hay or grain	300
Stores	
Retail	
First floor, rooms	75
Upper floors	75
Wholesale	60
Telephone exchange rooms	150[2]
Theaters	
Aisles, corridors, and lobbies	100
Orchestra floors	50
Balconies	50
Stage floors	100
Dressing rooms	40
Grid iron floor or fly gallery grating	60
Projection room	100
Transformer rooms	200[2]
Vaults, in offices	250[1]
Yards and terraces, pedestrians	100

NOTES

1. Increase when occupancy exceeds this amount.
2. Use weight of actual equipment when greater.
3. American Association of State Highway Officials.
4. Paper storage 50 lb/ft of clear story height.
5. Verify with design criteria.
6. Additional loads—120 lb/linear ft vertical, 24 lb/ft parallel lateral, and 10 lb/ft perpendicular to seat and footboards.

LIVE LOAD

Live load is the weight superimposed by the use and occupancy of the building or other structure, not including the wind, snow, earthquake, or dead load.

The live loads to be assumed in the design of buildings and other structures shall be the greatest loads that probably will be produced by the intended use or occupancy, but in no case less than the minimum uniformly distributed unit load.

THRUSTS AND HANDRAILS

Stairway and balcony railing, both exterior and interior, shall be designed to resist a vertical and a horizontal thrust of 50 lb/linear ft applied at the top of the railing. For one- and two-family dwellings, a thrust of 20 lb/linear ft may be used instead of 50.

CONCENTRATED LOADS

Floors shall be designed to support safely the uniformly distributed live load or the concentrated load in pounds given, whichever produces the greater stresses. Unless otherwise specified, the indicated concentration shall be assumed to occupy an area of $2\frac{1}{2}$ sq ft (6.26 ft²) and shall be located so as to produce the maximum stress conditions in the structural members.

PARTIAL LOADING

The full intensity of the appropriately reduced live loads applied only to a portion of the length of a structure or member shall be considered if it produces a more unfavorable effect than the same intensity applied over the full length of the structure or member.

IMPACT LOADS

The live loads shall be assumed to include adequate allowance for ordinary impact conditions. Provision shall be made in structural design for uses and loads that involve unusual vibration and impact forces.

1. ELEVATORS: All elevator loads shall be increased 100% for impact, and the structural supports shall be designed within limits of deflection prescribed by American National Standard Safety Code for elevators and escalators, A17.1 - 1981, and American National Standard Practice for the Inspection of Elevators, Escalators, and Moving Walks (Inspector's Manual) A17.2 - 1979.
2. MACHINERY: For the purpose of design, the weight of machinery and moving loads shall be increased as follows to allow for impact:
   a. Elevator machinery, 100%.
   b. Light machinery, shaft or motor driven, 20%.
   c. Reciprocating machinery or power driven units, 50%.
   d. Hangers for floors or balconies, 33%.
   All percentages to be increased if so recommended by the manufacturer.
3. CRANEWAYS: All craneways, except those using only manually powered cranes, shall have their design loads increased for impact as follows:
   a. A vertical force equal to 25% of the maximum wheel load.
   b. A lateral force equal to 20% of the weight of trolley and lifted load only, applied one-half at the top of each rail.
   c. A longitudinal force of 10% of the maximum wheel loads of the crane applied at top of rail.
4. PARKING GARAGE GUARDRAILS: Guardrails and walls acting as impact rails in parking structures shall be designed for a minimum horizontal ultimate load of 10,000 lb applied 18 in. above the floor at any point of the guardrail.

MINIMUM ROOF LOADS

1. FLAT, PITCHED, OR CURVED ROOFS: Ordinary roofs — flat, pitched, or curved — shall be designed for the live loads or the snow load, whichever produces the greater stress.
2. PONDING: For roofs, care shall be taken to provide drainage or the load shall be increased to represent all likely accumulations of water. Deflection of roof members will permit ponding of water accompanied by increased deflection and additional ponding.
3. SPECIAL PURPOSE ROOFS: When used for promenade purposes, roofs shall be designed for a maximum live load of 60 psf; 100 psf when designed for roof garden or assembly uses. Roofs used for other special purposes shall be designed for appropriate loads, as directed or approved by the building official.

LIVE LOAD REDUCTION

In general, design live loads should not be in excess of 100 psf on any member, supporting an area of 150 sq ft or more, except for places of public assembly, repair garages, parking structures, and roofs. The reduction shall not exceed the value of R from the following formulas:

$$R = .08(A-150)$$
$$R = 23(1+D/L)$$

where   R = reduction (%)
   D = dead load per square foot of area supported by the member
   L = live load per square foot of area supported by the member
   A = area supported by the member

In no case should the reduction exceed 60% for vertical members, nor 40 to 60% for horizontal members.

For live loads in excess of 100 psf, some codes allow a live load reduction of 20% for columns only.

CODES AND STANDARDS

The applicable building code should be referred to for specific uniformly distributed live loads, movable partition load, special and concentrated load requirements.

In addition to specific code requirements, the designer must consider the effects of special loading conditions, such as moving loads, construction loads, roof top planting loads, and concentrated loads from supported or hanging equipment (radiology, computer, heavy filing, or mechanical equipment)

The live loads given in this table are obtained by reference to ASCE, UBC, BOCA, and SBCCI.

Charles W. Vanderlinden, PE; Hansen Lind Meyer, Inc.; Orlando, Florida

RECOMMENDED AND MAXIMUM AIR VELOCITIES FOR DUCTS

DESIGNATION	RESIDENCES	SCHOOLS, THEATERS, PUBLIC BUILDINGS	INDUSTRIAL BUILDINGS
RECOMMENDED VELOCITIES (FPM)			
Outdoor air intakes (a)	500	500	500
Filters (a)	250	300	350
Heating coils (a), (b)	450	500	600
Cooling coils (a)	450	500	600
Air washers (a)	500	500	500
Fan outlets	1000-1600	1300-2000	1600-2400
Main ducts (b)	700-900	1000-1300	1200-1800
Branch ducts (b)	600	600-900	800-1000
Branch risers (b)	500	600-700	800
MAXIMUM VELOCITIES (FPM)			
Outdoor air intakes (a)	800	900	1200
Filters (a)	300	350	350
Heating coils (a), (b)	500	600	700
Cooling coils (a)	450	500	600
Air washers (a)	500	500	500
Fan outlets	1700	1500-2200	1700-2800
Main ducts (b)	800-1200	1100-1600	1300-2200
Branch ducts (b)	700-1000	800-1300	1000-1800
Branch risers (b)	650-800	800-1200	1000-1600

(a) These velocities are for total face area, not the net free area; other velocities in table are for net free area.

(b) For low velocity systems only.

DUCT AREA PER SQUARE FOOT OF FLOOR AREA (IN SQ. IN.)

VELOCITY (FT PER MINUTE)
NEARLY SQUARE DUCTS LESS THAN 1000 CFM
FRICTION ALLOWANCE = 1.10

CUBIC FT PER HOUR/ SQ FT	400	600	800	1000	1200	1400	1600
30	0.198	0.132	0.099	0.079	0.069	0.057	0.050
35	0.231	0.154	0.116	0.092	0.077	0.066	0.058
40	0.264	0.176	0.132	0.106	0.088	0.075	0.066
45	0.297	0.198	0.149	0.119	0.099	0.085	0.074
50	0.330	0.220	0.165	0.132	0.110	0.094	0.083
55	0.363	0.242	0.182	0.145	0.121	0.104	0.091
60	0.396	0.264	0.198	0.158	0.132	0.113	0.099
65	0.429	0.286	0.215	0.172	0.143	0.123	0.107
70	0.462	0.308	0.231	0.185	0.154	0.132	0.116
75	0.495	0.330	0.248	0.198	0.165	0.141	0.124
80	0.528	0.352	0.264	0.211	0.176	0.151	0.132
85	0.561	0.374	0.281	0.224	0.187	0.160	0.140
90	0.594	0.396	0.297	0.238	0.198	0.170	0.149
95	0.627	0.418	0.314	0.251	0.209	0.179	0.157
100	0.660	0.440	0.330	0.264	0.220	0.189	0.165
105	0.693	0.462	0.347	0.277	0.231	0.198	0.173
110	0.726	0.484	0.363	0.290	0.242	0.207	0.182
115	0.759	0.506	0.380	0.304	0.253	0.217	0.190
120	0.792	0.528	0.396	0.317	0.264	0.226	0.198
130	0.858	0.572	0.429	0.343	0.286	0.245	0.215
140	0.924	0.616	0.462	0.370	0.308	0.264	0.231
150	0.990	0.660	0.495	0.396	0.330	0.283	0.248

DUCT AREA PER SQUARE FOOT OF FLOOR AREA (IN SQ. IN.)

VELOCITY (FT PER MINUTE)
NEARLY SQUARE DUCTS MORE THAN 1000 CFM
FRICTION ALLOWANCE = 1.05

CUBIC FT PER HOUR/ SQ FT	400	600	800	1000	1200	1400	1600
150	0.945	0.630	0.473	0.378	0.315	0.270	0.236
160	1.008	0.672	0.504	0.403	0.336	0.288	0.252
170	1.071	0.714	0.536	0.428	0.357	0.306	0.268
180	1.134	0.756	0.567	0.454	0.378	0.324	0.284
200	1.260	0.840	0.630	0.504	0.420	0.360	0.315
220	1.386	0.924	0.693	0.554	0.462	0.396	0.347
240	1.512	1.008	0.756	0.605	0.504	0.432	0.378
260	1.638	1.092	0.819	0.655	0.546	0.468	0.410
280	1.764	1.176	0.882	0.706	0.588	0.504	0.441
300	1.890	1.260	0.945	0.756	0.630	0.540	0.473
320	2.016	1.344	1.008	0.806	0.672	0.576	0.504
340	2.142	1.428	1.071	0.857	0.714	0.612	0.536
360	2.268	1.512	1.134	0.907	0.756	0.648	0.567
380	2.394	1.596	1.197	0.958	0.798	0.684	0.599
400	2.520	1.680	1.260	1.008	0.840	0.720	0.630

DUCT AREA PER SQUARE FOOT OF FLOOR AREA

VELOCITY (FT PER MINUTE)
ROUND DUCTS
FRICTION ALLOWANCE = 1.00

CUBIC FT PER HOUR/ SQ FT	400	600	800	1000	1200	1400	1600
30	0.180	0.120	0.090	0.072	0.060	0.051	0.045
35	0.210	0.140	0.105	0.084	0.070	0.060	0.053
40	0.240	0.160	0.120	0.096	0.080	0.069	0.060
45	0.270	0.180	0.135	0.108	0.090	0.077	0.068
50	0.300	0.200	0.150	0.120	0.100	0.086	0.075
55	0.330	0.220	0.165	0.132	0.110	0.094	0.083
60	0.360	0.240	0.180	0.144	0.120	0.103	0.090
65	0.390	0.260	0.195	0.156	0.130	0.111	0.098
70	0.420	0.280	0.210	0.168	0.140	0.120	0.105
75	0.450	0.300	0.225	0.180	0.150	0.129	0.113
80	0.480	0.320	0.240	0.192	0.160	0.137	0.120
85	0.510	0.340	0.255	0.204	0.170	0.146	0.128
90	0.540	0.360	0.270	0.216	0.180	0.154	0.135
95	0.570	0.380	0.285	0.228	0.190	0.163	0.143
100	0.600	0.400	0.300	0.240	0.200	0.171	0.150
105	0.630	0.420	0.315	0.252	0.210	0.180	0.158
110	0.660	0.440	0.330	0.264	0.220	0.189	0.165
115	0.690	0.460	0.345	0.276	0.230	0.197	0.173
120	0.720	0.480	0.360	0.288	0.240	0.206	0.180
130	0.780	0.520	0.390	0.312	0.260	0.223	0.195
140	0.840	0.560	0.420	0.336	0.280	0.240	0.210
150	0.900	0.600	0.450	0.360	0.300	0.257	0.225
160	0.960	0.640	0.480	0.384	0.320	0.274	0.240
170	1.020	0.680	0.510	0.408	0.340	0.291	0.255
180	1.080	0.720	0.540	0.432	0.360	0.309	0.270
190	1.140	0.760	0.570	0.456	0.380	0.326	0.285
200	1.200	0.800	0.600	0.480	0.400	0.343	0.300
220	1.320	0.880	0.660	0.528	0.440	0.377	0.330
240	1.440	0.960	0.720	0.576	0.480	0.411	0.360
260	1.560	1.040	0.780	0.624	0.520	0.446	0.390
280	1.680	1.120	0.840	0.672	0.560	0.480	0.420
300	1.800	1.200	0.900	0.720	0.600	0.514	0.450
320	1.920	1.280	0.960	0.768	0.640	0.549	0.480
340	2.040	1.360	1.020	0.816	0.680	0.583	0.510
360	2.160	1.440	1.080	0.864	0.720	0.617	0.540
380	2.280	1.520	1.140	0.912	0.760	0.651	0.570

DUCT AREA PER SQUARE FOOT OF FLOOR AREA (IN SQ IN.)

VELOCITY (FT PER MINUTE)
THIN RECTANGULAR DUCTS (W TO D 1:5)
FRICTION ALLOWANCE = 1.25

CUBIC FT PER HOUR/ SQ FT	400	600	800	1000	1200	1400	1600
30	0.225	0.150	0.113	0.090	0.075	0.064	0.056
35	0.263	0.175	0.131	0.105	0.088	0.075	0.066
40	0.300	0.200	0.150	0.120	0.100	0.086	0.075
45	0.338	0.225	0.169	0.135	0.113	0.096	0.084
50	0.375	0.250	0.188	0.150	0.125	0.107	0.094
55	0.413	0.275	0.206	0.165	0.138	0.118	0.103
60	0.450	0.300	0.225	0.180	0.150	0.120	0.113
65	0.488	0.325	0.244	0.195	0.163	0.139	0.122
70	0.525	0.350	0.263	0.210	0.175	0.150	0.131
75	0.563	0.375	0.281	0.225	0.188	0.161	0.141
80	0.600	0.400	0.300	0.240	0.200	0.171	0.150
85	0.638	0.425	0.319	0.255	0.213	0.182	0.159
90	0.675	0.450	0.338	0.270	0.225	0.193	0.169
95	0.713	0.475	0.356	0.285	0.238	0.204	0.178
100	0.750	0.500	0.375	0.300	0.250	0.214	0.188
105	0.788	0.525	0.394	0.315	0.263	0.225	0.197
110	0.825	0.550	0.413	0.330	0.275	0.236	0.206
115	0.863	0.575	0.431	0.345	0.288	0.246	0.216
120	0.900	0.600	0.450	0.360	0.300	0.257	0.225
130	0.975	0.650	0.488	0.390	0.325	0.279	0.244
140	1.050	0.700	0.525	0.420	0.350	0.300	0.263
150	1.125	0.750	0.563	0.450	0.375	0.321	0.281
160	1.200	0.800	0.600	0.480	0.400	0.343	0.300
170	1.275	0.850	0.638	0.510	0.425	0.364	0.319
180	1.350	0.900	0.675	0.540	0.450	0.386	0.338
190	1.425	0.950	0.713	0.570	0.475	0.407	0.356
200	1.500	1.000	0.750	0.600	0.500	0.429	0.375
220	1.650	1.100	0.825	0.660	0.550	0.471	0.413
240	1.800	1.200	0.900	0.720	0.600	0.514	0.450
260	1.950	1.300	0.975	0.780	0.650	0.557	0.488
280	2.100	1.400	1.050	0.840	0.700	0.600	0.525
300	2.250	1.500	1.125	0.900	0.750	0.643	0.563
320	2.400	1.600	1.200	0.960	0.800	0.686	0.600
340	2.550	1.700	1.275	1.020	0.850	0.729	0.638
360	2.700	1.800	1.350	1.080	0.900	0.771	0.675
380	2.850	1.900	1.425	1.140	0.950	0.814	0.713

1   BUILDING LOADS AND CALCULATIONS

GENERAL

When a public sewer system is not available to treat and dispose of a building's sewage wastes, a private sewage system is required. The most common system used today is the septic tank. This simple mechanical system treats waste water through anaerobic (not dependent on oxygen) bacteria digesting human waste into a thick sludge, which settles to the bottom and is periodically pumped out. The solid sludge is taken and dumped into the sewer system of a modern treatment plant where it is dried and hauled away to a special landfill dump. Only water—the effluent—is treated and returned to the soil through a leach field. This water, about 70% purified by the septic tank, is further purified by aerobic (dependent on oxygen) bacteria in the leach field.

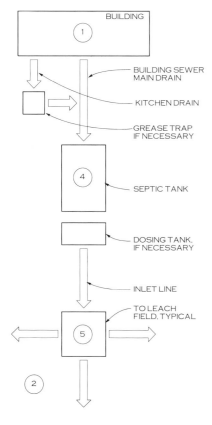

The following is a procedure for planning a private sewage disposal system:

1. Determine quantity of sewage flow (see Table A).
2. Soil and topography study.
   a. Determine type and permeability of soil; make a percolation test (see Table B).
   b. Examine site topography to help choose proper effluent disposal system.
   c. Determine elevation of watertable (groundwater).
   d. Determine proximity of wells and streams (see Table C).
3. Determine requirements of local codes.
4. Design septic tank (see Septic Tank Volume Determination).
5. Choose and layout an effluent disposal system.

NOTES

1. Since various health environmental departments have other standards, consult with them before preparing final designs.
2. Since a septic system is naturally gravity fed, when below-grade toilet fixtures are present a lift pump (which pumps sewage up and out to the septic tank) is needed.
3. Groundwater level shall be at least 2 ft below any effluent disposal system.
4. Package sewage treatment plants are recommended for flows greater than 3500 gallons/day when adequate percolation is not possible.
5. Septic tank and disposal system shall be at least 100 feet from shallow wells and 50 feet from deep wells.

L. James Cooke, Jr., P.E.; Department of Veteran Affairs; Washington, D.C.
Richard J. Vitullo, Oak Leaf Studio; Crownsville, Maryland

TABLE A.   QUANTITIES OF SEWAGE FLOWS

TYPE OF ESTABLISHMENT	GALLONS PER PERSON PER DAY
Airports (per passenger)	5
Bathhouses and swimming pools	10
Camps	
Campground with central comfort stations	35
Day camps (no meals served)	15
Resort camp (night and day) with limited plumbing	50
Cottages and small dwelling with seasonal occupancy[1]	50
Country clubs (per resident member)	100
Country clubs (per nonresident member present)	25
Dwellings	
Boardinghouses[1]	50
Multiple family dwellings (apartment)	60
Single family dwellings[1]	75
Factories (gallons per person, per shift, exclusive of industry wastes)	35
Hospitals (per bed space)	240
Hotels with private baths (2 persons per room)[2]	60
Institutions other than hospitals (per bed)	100
Laundries, self-service (gallons per wash, i.e., per customer)	50
Mobile home parks (per space)	250
Picnic parks (toilet wastes only, per picnicker)	5
Picnic parks with bathhouses, showers, and flush toilets	10
Restaurants (toilets and kitchen wastes per patron)	10
Restaurants (kitchen wastes per meal served)	3
Restaurants (additional for bars and cocktail lounges)	2
Schools	
Boarding	100
Day, with gyms, cafeteria, and showers	25
Service station (per vehicle served)	10
Theaters	
Movie (per auditorium seat)	5
Drive-in (per car space)	5
Travel trailer parks with individual water and sewer hookups	100
Workers	
Day, at schools and offices (per shift)	15

NOTES

1. Two people per bedroom.
2. Use also for motel.

TABLE C.   EFFLUENT DISPOSAL SYSTEM LOCATION

MINIMUM DISTANCES (FEET)

FROM TO	LEACH FIELD	SEPTIC TANK
Wells (shallow)	100	100
Wells (deep)	50	50
Streams	25	50
Building	10	20
Property line	10	10

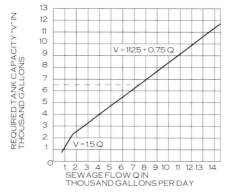

SEPTIC TANK VOLUME DETERMINATION

TABLE B.   ALLOWABLE RATE OF SEWAGE APPLICATION TO A SOIL ABSORPTION SYSTEM

PERCOLATION RATE—TIME (MIN) FOR WATER TO FALL 1 IN.	MAXIMUM RATE OF SEWAGE APPLICATION (GAL/SQ FT/DAY) FOR ABSORPTION TRENCHES,[1] SEEPAGE BEDS, AND SEEPAGE PITS[2]
1 or less	5.0
2	3.5
3	2.9
4	2.5
5	2.2
10	1.6
15	1.3
30 [3]	0.9
45 [3]	0.8
60 [3,4]	0.6

NOTES

1. Absorption area for drainage field is figured as trench bottom width and length and 12 in. of side wall and includes a statistical allowance for vertical sidewall area.
2. Absorption area for seepage pits is effective sidewall area.
3. Over 30 is unsuitable for seepage pits.
4. Over 60 is unsuitable for absorption systems. If permissible, use sand filtration system. For subsurface sand filters use 1.15 gal/sq ft/day.

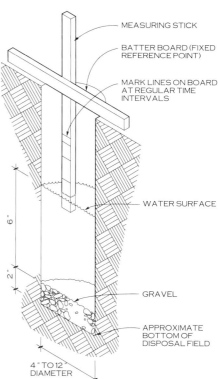

PROCEDURE

First soak hole by filling at least 12 in. over gravel with water and continue to refill with water so that hole is soaked for 24 hours. After 24 hours adjust the depth of water over the gravel to approximately 6 in. Now measure the drop in water level over a 30 minute period.

1. The location and elevation of the test hole are approximately the same as disposal field.
2. This test is recommended by the Environmental Protection Agency; check local requirements for other test conditions.

PERCOLATION TESTS

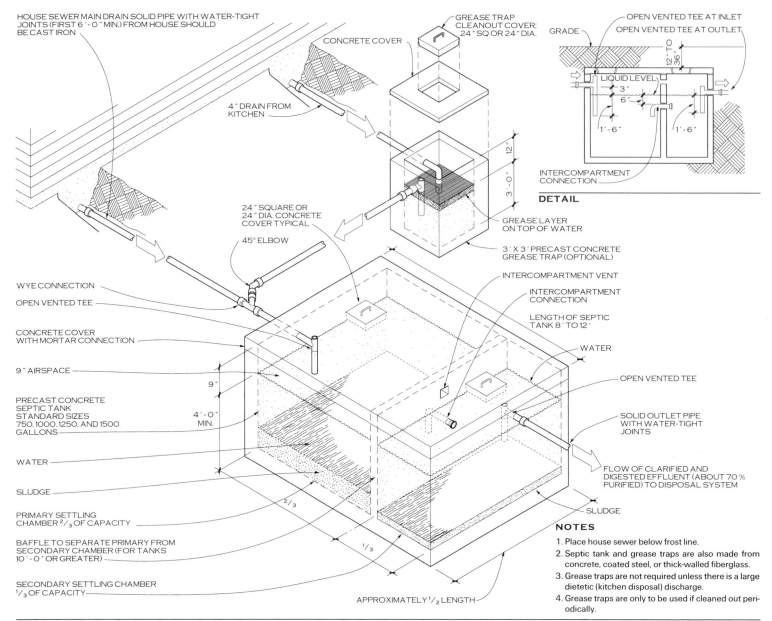

HOUSE SEWER MAIN DRAIN SOLID PIPE WITH WATER-TIGHT JOINTS (FIRST 6'-0" MIN.) FROM HOUSE SHOULD BE CAST IRON

CONCRETE COVER

4" DRAIN FROM KITCHEN

GREASE TRAP CLEANOUT COVER; 24" SQ OR 24" DIA.

GRADE

OPEN VENTED TEE AT INLET

OPEN VENTED TEE AT OUTLET

12" TO 36"

LIQUID LEVEL

3"

6"

1'-6"   1'-6"

INTERCOMPARTMENT CONNECTION

DETAIL

24" SQUARE OR 24" DIA. CONCRETE COVER TYPICAL

45° ELBOW

12"

3'-0"

GREASE LAYER ON TOP OF WATER

3' X 3' PRECAST CONCRETE GREASE TRAP (OPTIONAL)

WYE CONNECTION

OPEN VENTED TEE

CONCRETE COVER WITH MORTAR CONNECTION

9" AIRSPACE

9"

PRECAST CONCRETE SEPTIC TANK STANDARD SIZES 750, 1000, 1250, AND 1500 GALLONS

4'-0" MIN.

WATER

SLUDGE

2/3

PRIMARY SETTLING CHAMBER 2/3 OF CAPACITY

BAFFLE TO SEPARATE PRIMARY FROM SECONDARY CHAMBER (FOR TANKS 10'-0" OR GREATER)

SECONDARY SETTLING CHAMBER 1/3 OF CAPACITY

1/3

APPROXIMATELY 1/2 LENGTH

INTERCOMPARTMENT VENT

INTERCOMPARTMENT CONNECTION

LENGTH OF SEPTIC TANK 8' TO 12'

WATER

OPEN VENTED TEE

SOLID OUTLET PIPE WITH WATER-TIGHT JOINTS

FLOW OF CLARIFIED AND DIGESTED EFFLUENT (ABOUT 70% PURIFIED) TO DISPOSAL SYSTEM

SLUDGE

NOTES

1. Place house sewer below frost line.
2. Septic tank and grease traps are also made from concrete, coated steel, or thick-walled fiberglass.
3. Grease traps are not required unless there is a large dietetic (kitchen disposal) discharge.
4. Grease traps are only to be used if cleaned out periodically.

SEPTIC TANK

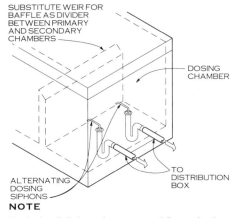

SUBSTITUTE WEIR FOR BAFFLE AS DIVIDER BETWEEN PRIMARY AND SECONDARY CHAMBERS

DOSING CHAMBER

ALTERNATING DOSING SIPHONS

TO DISTRIBUTION BOX

NOTE

Used primarily in larger (e.g., commercial) capacity situations that have large leach fields, effluent is collected in specific amounts, 500 to 1000 gallons at a time. Then it is released quickly to the distribution box in order to flood the leach field intermittently and evenly. Also used in conjunction with sand filter disposal systems.

DOSING OR SIPHON CHAMBER

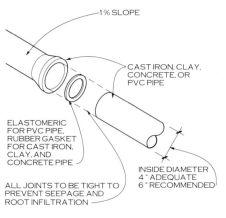

1% SLOPE

CAST IRON, CLAY, CONCRETE, OR PVC PIPE

ELASTOMERIC FOR PVC PIPE, RUBBER GASKET FOR CAST IRON, CLAY, AND CONCRETE PIPE

INSIDE DIAMETER 4" ADEQUATE 6" RECOMMENDED

ALL JOINTS TO BE TIGHT TO PREVENT SEEPAGE AND ROOT INFILTRATION

NOTE

Use cast iron or PVC pipe at first 6 ft minimum from house for main drain (inlet); areas near wells or other natural water supplies; areas near trees or shrubs that may cause root stoppage in clay pipes.

SOLID DRAIN AND OUTLET PIPE

REMOVABLE COVER

INLET PIPE FROM SEPTIC TANK

CAST CONCRETE DISTRIBUTION BOX

TO LEACH FIELD

TYPICAL OPEN VENTED TEE OUTLET

TO LEACH FIELD

TO LEACH FIELD

NOTE

Purpose is to distribute effluent from septic tank equally to each leach line and thereby to the whole leach field.

DISTRIBUTION BOX

L. James Cooke, Jr., P.E.; Department of Veteran Affairs; Washington, D.C.
Richard J. Vitullo, Oak Leaf Studio; Crownsville, Maryland

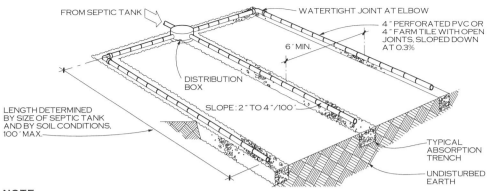

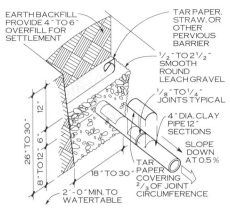

NOTE

A leach field or seepage bed replaces the typical absorption trench with an entirely excavated leach field filled with gravel. This type of installation requires more gravel but allows freer lateral movement for effluent and better aerobic breakdown and is often cheaper and faster to build.

NOTE

Perforated PVC may be used in place of farm tile.

OPEN-ENDED LEACH LINES LAYOUT (SLIGHTLY SLOPED GRADE)

ABSORPTION TRENCH DETAIL

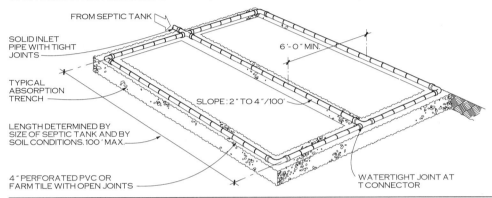

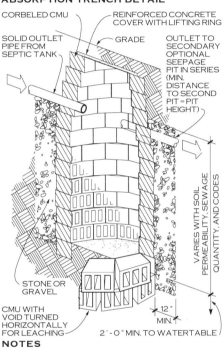

INTERCONNECTED (SERIAL) LEACH LINES LAYOUT (FLAT GRADE)

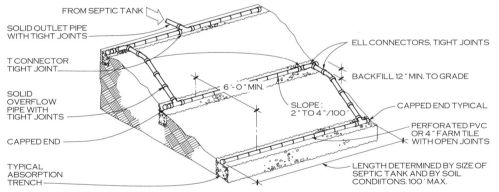

NOTES

1. Seepage pits may be made from precast concrete with slots for leaching.
2. For proper installation, soil must be absorbent.

SEEPAGE PIT

INTERCONNECTED (SERIAL) LEACH LINES LAYOUT (HIGHLY SLOPED GRADE)

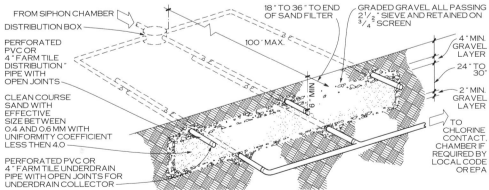

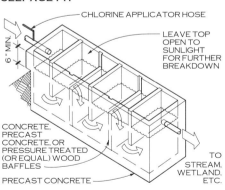

NOTES

1. Due to cost, sand filters should be used only where other systems are not feasible, such as the soil having a precolation rate of 1 in. in 30 minutes or above.
2. Use this system in conjuction with a siphon chamber.

NOTES

1. Local codes may require use of chlorine contact chamber to further treat effluent that may run too closely to wetlands, streams, etc. Use with sand filter system.
2. Provide 20 minutes of detention at average flow. Minimum size is 50 gallons.

SAND FILTER LAYOUT

CHLORINE CONTACT CHAMBER

L. James Cooke, Jr., P.E; Department of Veteran Affairs; Washington, D.C.
Richard J. Vitullo, Oak Leaf Studio; Crownsville, Maryland

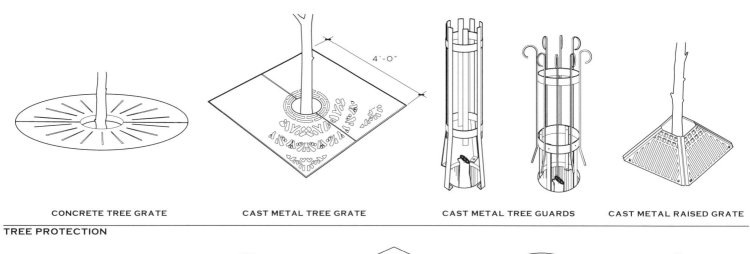

CONCRETE TREE GRATE   CAST METAL TREE GRATE   CAST METAL TREE GUARDS   CAST METAL RAISED GRATE

TREE PROTECTION

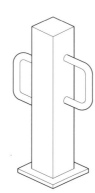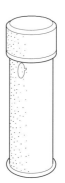

CONCRETE   CONCRETE (WITH LIGHT)   STEEL (WITH BIKE RACK)   STEEL   CAST METAL

BOLLARDS

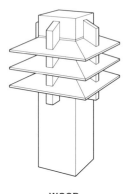

WOOD   METAL   METAL   METAL   METAL   CAST METAL

LANDSCAPE LIGHTS

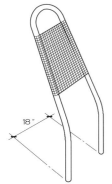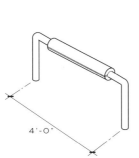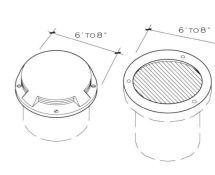

STEEL LEANING POST   STEEL LEANING PIPE   CAST METAL DRAIN COVERS   METAL (PROJECTED)   METAL (FLUSH)

MISCELLANEOUS   **DRIVE / WALKOVER LIGHTS**

Richard J. Vitullo, Oak Leaf Studio; Crownsville, Maryland
Scott Peterson; Falls Church, Virginia

2   SITE IMPROVEMENTS

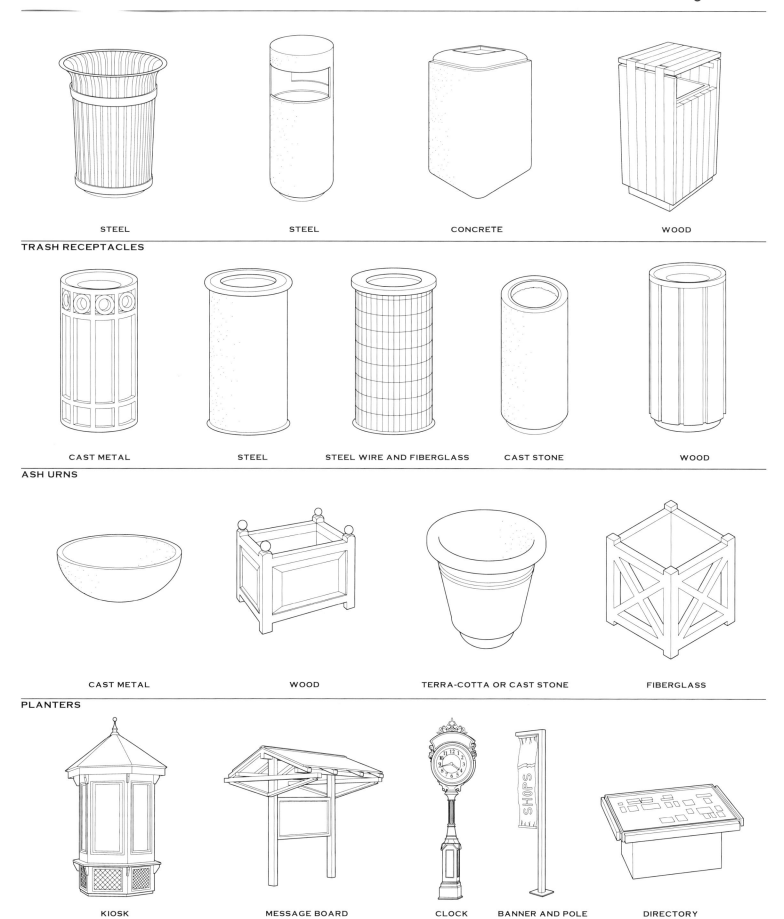

STEEL STEEL CONCRETE WOOD

TRASH RECEPTACLES

CAST METAL STEEL STEEL WIRE AND FIBERGLASS CAST STONE WOOD

ASH URNS

CAST METAL WOOD TERRA-COTTA OR CAST STONE FIBERGLASS

PLANTERS

KIOSK MESSAGE BOARD CLOCK BANNER AND POLE DIRECTORY

INFORMATION-RELATED FURNISHINGS

Richard J. Vitullo, Oak Leaf Studio; Crownsville, Maryland
Jerry Smith; Arlington, Virginia

SITE IMPROVEMENTS 2

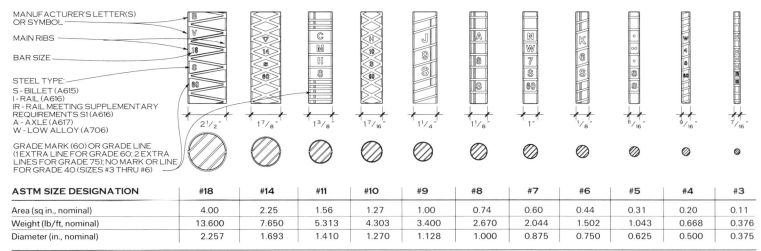

ASTM SIZE DESIGNATION	#18	#14	#11	#10	#9	#8	#7	#6	#5	#4	#3
Area (sq in., nominal)	4.00	2.25	1.56	1.27	1.00	0.74	0.60	0.44	0.31	0.20	0.11
Weight (lb/ft, nominal)	13.600	7.650	5.313	4.303	3.400	2.670	2.044	1.502	1.043	0.668	0.376
Diameter (in., nominal)	2.257	1.693	1.410	1.270	1.128	1.000	0.875	0.750	0.625	0.500	0.375

ASTM STANDARD REINFORCING BAR SIZES

GENERAL

Steel reinforcement for concrete consists of reinforcing bars and welded wire fabric. Bars are manufactured by hot-roll process as round rods with lugs, or deformations, which inhibit longitudinal movement of the bar in the surrounding concrete. Bar sizes are indicated by numbers. For sizes #3 through #8, they are the number of eighths of an inch in the nominal diameter of the bars. Sizes #9 through #11 are round and correspond to the former 1 in., 1 1/8 in., and 1 1/4 in. square sizes. Sizes #14 and #18 correspond to the former 1 1/2 in. and 2 in. square sizes respectively. The nominal diameter of a deformed bar is equal to the actual diameter of a plain bar with the same weight per foot as the deformed bar. Epoxy-coated and zinc-coated (galvanized) reinforcing bars are used when corrosion protection is needed. In some instances, a fiber-reinforced plastic (FRP) rebar has been used for concrete reinforcement because of its high tensile strength and light weight, corrosion resistant and dielectric (nonconductive) properties. It is manufactured in the same sizes as steel rebars and also has deformations on its surface. Consult manufacturers for further information.

Welded wire fabric is used in thin slabs, shells, and other designs where the available space is too limited to give proper cover and clearance to deformed bars. Welded wire fabric, also called mesh, consists of cold drawn wire (smooth or deformed) in orthogonal patterns and is resistance welded at all intersections.

Wires in the form of individual wire or group of wires are used in the fabrication of prestressed concrete.

STRUCTURAL CONCRETE REINFORCEMENT SHRINKAGE

REINFORCEMENT		% OF CROSS SECTIONAL AREA OF CONCRETE, ONE WAY
GRADE	TYPE	
40/50	Deformed bars	0.20
—	Welded wire fabric	0.18
60	Deformed bars	0.18

STANDARD STEEL WIRE SIZES AND GAUGES

SMOOTH WIRE NUMBER	DEFORMED WIRE NUMBER	ASW GAUGE NUMBER	FRACTIONAL DIA., IN. (NOM.)	DECIMAL DIA., IN (NOM.)	AREA (SQ. IN.)	WEIGHT (LB/LIN. FT)
W20	D20	—	1/2	.505	.200	.680
—	—	7/0	31/64	.490	.189	.642
W18	D18	—	15/32	.479	.180	.612
—	—	6/0	5/32	.462	.168	.571
W16	D16	—	29/64	.451	.160	.544
—	—	5/0	7/16	.431	.146	.496
W14	D14	—	13/32	.422	.140	.476
—	—	4/0	13/32	.394	.122	.415
W12	D12	—	25/64	.391	.120	.408
W11	D11	—	3/8	.374	.110	.374
W10.5	—	—	3/8	.366	.105	.357
—	—	3/0	23/64	.363	.103	.350
W10	D10	—	23/64	.357	.100	.340
W9.5	—	—	11/32	.348	.095	.323
W9	D9	—	11/32	.338	.090	.306
—	—	2/0	11/32	.331	.086	.292
W8.5	—	—	21/64	.329	.085	.289
W8	D8	—	21/64	.319	.080	.272
W7.5	—	—	5/16	.309	.075	.255
—	—	1/0	5/16	.307	.074	.251
W7	D7	—	19/64	.299	.070	.238
W6.5	—	—	19/64	.288	.065	.221
—	—	1	19/64	.283	.063	.214
W6	D6	—	9/32	.276	.060	.204
W5.5	—	—	17/64	.265	.055	.187
—	—	2	17/64	.263	.054	.183
W5	D5	—	1/4	.252	.050	.170
—	—	3	15/64	.244	.047	.160
W4.5	—	—	15/64	.239	.045	.153
W4	D4	4	7/32	.226	.040	.136
W3.5	—	—	7/32	.211	.035	.119
—	—	5	13/64	.207	.034	.115
W3	—	—	3/16+	.195	.030	.102
W2.9	—	6	3/16+	.192	.029	.098
W2.5	—	7	3/16	.178	.025	.085
W2.1	—	8	11/64	.162	.021	.071
W2	—	—	5/32	.160	.020	.068
—	—	9	5/32	.148	.017	.058
W1.4	—	—	9/64	.124	.014	.048

COMMON STOCK STYLES OF WELDED WIRE FABRIC

NEW DESIGNATION (W-NUMBER)	OLD DESIGNATION (WIRE GAUGE)	STEEL AREA (IN./FT²)		WEIGHT (LB/100 SQ FT)
		LONG.	TRANS.	
SHEETS + ROLLS				
6 x 6 - W1.4 x W1.4	6 x 6 - 10 x 10	.028	.028	21
6 x 6 - W2.0 x W2.0	6 x 6 - 8 x 8	.040	.040	29
6 x 6 - W2.9 x W2.9	6 x 6 - 6 x 6	.058	.058	42
6 x 6 - W4.0 x W4.0	6 x 6 - 4 x 4	.080	.080	58
4 x 4 - W1.4 x W1.4	4 x 4 - 10 x 10	.042	.042	31
4 x 4 - W2.0 x W2.0	4 x 4 - 8 x 8	.060	.060	43
4 x 4 - W2.9 x W2.9	4 x 4 - 6 x 6	.087	.087	62
4 x 4 - W4.0 x W4.0	4 x 4 - 4 x 4	.120	.120	85

Spacing   Wire Size
6 x 12 - W16 x W8
LONGITUDINAL WIRE   TRANSVERSE WIRE

METHOD OF DESIGNATION FOR WELDED WIRE FABRIC

REINFORCING STEEL GRADES AND STRENGTHS

ASTM SPEC	YIELD STRENGTH (PSI)	ULTIMATE STRENGTH (PSI)	STEEL TYPE
New billet ASTM A-615			S
Grade - 40	40,000	70,000	
Grade - 60	60,000	90,000	
Rail steel ASTM A-616			R
Grade - 50	50,000	80,000	
Grade - 60	60,000	90,000	
Axle steel ASTM A-617			A
Grade - 40	40,000	70,000	
Grade - 60	60,000	90,000	
Deformed wire ASTM A-496			-
Welded fabric	70,000	80,000	
Cold drawn wire ASTM A-82			-
Welded fabric W 1.2	56,000	70,000	
Size W 1.2	65,000	75,000	

Richard J. Vitullo, Oak Leaf Studio; Crownsville, Maryland

3 CONCRETE REINFORCEMENT

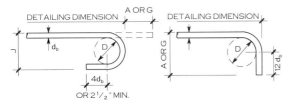

STANDARD HOOK

BAR SIZE	180° HOOK			90° HOOK	
	A OR G	J	D	A OR G	D
# 3	5"	3"	2¹/₄"	6"	2¹/₄"
# 4	6"	4"	3"	8"	3"
# 5	7"	5"	3³/₄"	10"	3³/₄"
# 6	8"	6"	4¹/₂"	12"	4¹/₂"
# 7	10"	7"	5¹/₄"	14"	5¹/₄"
# 8	11"	8"	6"	16"	6"
# 9	15"	11³/₄"	9¹/₂"	19"	9¹/₂"
#10	17"	13¹/₄"	10³/₄"	22"	10³/₄"
#11	19"	14³/₄"	12"	24"	12"
#14	27"	21³/₄"	18¹/₄"	31"	18¹/₄"
#18	36"	28¹/₂"	24"	41"	24"

STANDARD REINFORCING BAR HOOK DETAILS

STIRRUP HOOKS AND TIES

BAR SIZE	90° HOOK/TIE		135° HOOK/TIE			135° SEISMIC HOOK/TIE		
	A OR G	D	A OR G	D	H	A OR G	D	H
#3	4"	1¹/₂"	4"	1¹/₂"	2¹/₂"	4¹/₄"	1¹/₂"	3"
#4	4¹/₂"	2"	4¹/₂"	2"	3"	4¹/₂"	2"	3"
#5	6"	2¹/₂"	5¹/₂"	2¹/₂"	3³/₄"	5¹/₂"	2¹/₂"	3³/₄"
#6	12"	4¹/₂"	7³/₄"	4¹/₂"	4¹/₂"	7³/₄"	4¹/₂"	4¹/₂"
#7	14"	5¹/₄"	9"	5¹/₄"	5¹/₄"	9"	5¹/₄"	5¹/₄"
#8	16"	6"	10¹/₄"	6"	6"	10¹/₄"	6"	6"

COMPRESSION SPLICES AND ANCHORAGES FOR REINFORING BARS

STEEL GRADE (FY-KSI)	CONCRETE COMPRESSION STRENGTH (F'C)	LAP SPLICE IN d_b ≥12 IN.	DOWELS, IN d_b
40	3000	20	15
	4000	20	13
	5000	20	12
50	3000	25	18
	4000	25	16
	5000	25	15
60	3000	30	22
	4000	30	19
	5000	30	18
75	3000	44	28
	4000	44	24
	5000	44	23

NOTES

1. d_B = reinforcing bar diameter.
2. Reinforcing bars #14 and #18 may not be used in lap splices except when lapped to #11 bars or smaller. To find the lap dimension, take the larger figure of either 22 d_B of the larger bar or 30 d_B of the smaller bar.
3. Consult Concrete Reinforcing Steel Institute (CRSI) for tension splices and anchorages.

TENSION SPLICES AND ANCHORAGE
F'c = 3,000 PSI, NORMAL WEIGHT

BAR SIZE	LAP CLASS	TOP BARS CATEGORY						OTHER BARS CATEGORY					
		1	2	3	4	5	6	1	2	3	4	5	6
# 3	A	16	16	16	16	16	16	13	13	13	13	13	13
	B	21	21	21	21	21	21	16	16	16	16	16	16
# 4	A	23	22	22	22	22	22	18	17	17	17	17	17
	B	30	28	28	28	28	28	23	22	22	22	22	22
# 5	A	36	29	27	27	27	27	27	22	21	21	21	21
	B	46	37	35	35	35	35	36	29	27	27	27	27
# 6	A	50	40	35	32	32	32	39	31	27	25	25	25
	B	65	52	46	42	42	42	50	40	35	32	32	32
# 7	A	69	55	48	39	38	38	53	42	37	30	29	29
	B	89	71	63	50	49	49	69	55	48	39	38	38
# 8	A	90	72	63	51	45	43	70	56	49	39	35	33
	B	117	94	82	66	59	56	90	72	63	51	45	43
# 9	A	114	91	80	64	57	48	88	70	62	49	44	37
	B	148	119	104	83	74	63	114	91	80	64	57	48
#10	A	145	116	102	81	73	58	112	89	78	63	56	45
	B	188	151	132	106	94	76	145	116	102	81	73	58
#11	A	178	142	125	100	89	71	137	110	96	77	69	55
	B	231	185	162	130	116	93	178	142	125	100	89	71
#14	N/A	242	242	170	170	121	121	187	187	131	131	93	93
#18	N/A	356	356	250	250	178	178	274	274	192	192	137	137

NOTES

1. Lap splice lengths are multiples of tension development lengths; Class A - 1.0 I_D (ACI 12.15.1) Values of I_D for bars in beams or columns are based on transverse reinforcement meeting minimum requirements for stirrups in ACI 11.5.4 and 11.5.5.3, or meeting tie requirements in ACI 7.10.5; and are based on minimum cover specified in ACI 7.7.1.
2. Conditions that require Category 1 or Category 2 lap splice lengths should be avoided if at all possible for the larger bar sizes. These inordinately long lengths present possible construction problems due to placing, congestion, etc. Options available in trying to avoid Category 1 or 2 conditions include:
   a. Increasing the concrete cover to more than one bar diameter and/or increase the bar c.-c. spacing to more than three bar diameters.
   b. Utilizing the A_{TR} allowance in ACI 12.2.3 (b) for beams or columns. Note that if ties or stirrups meet the minimum A_{TR} requirement, Category 1 lengths are reduced to Category 5 lengths and Category 2 lengths are reduced to Category 6 lengths.
3. The ACI 318-89 code does not allow lap splices of #14 or #18 bars. The values tabulated for those bar sizes are the tension development lengths.
4. Top bars are horizontal bars with more than 12 in. of concrete cast below the bars.
5. #11 and smaller edge bars with c.-c. spacing not less than 6d_b are assumed to have a side cover not less than 2.5d_b. Otherwise, Category 5 applies rather than Category 6.
6. For lightweight aggregate, multiply the values above by 1.3.
7. For epoxy-coated reinforcing bars, multiply the values above by one of the following factors:
   a. Cover < 3d_b or c.-c. spacing < 7d_b multiply top bars by 1.31 and all other bars by 1.50.
   b. Cover > 3d_b and c.-c. spacing > 7d_b multiply top bars and all other bars by 1.20.
8. See CRSI's *Reinforcement: Anchorages, Lap Splices and Connections* manual for tables of tension development and lap splices for other concrete strengths and epoxy-coated rebars.

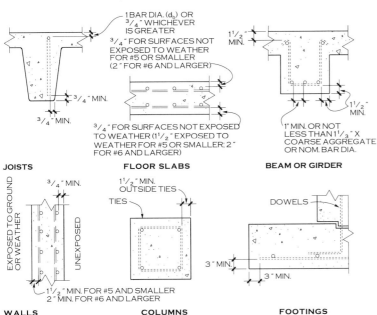

JOISTS   FLOOR SLABS   BEAM OR GIRDER

WALLS   COLUMNS   FOOTINGS

PROTECTION FOR REINFORCEMENT

Richard J. Vitullo, Oak Leaf Studio; Crownsville, Maryland
Concrete Reinforcing Steel Institute; Schaumburg, Illinois

GENERAL

Lally columns are prefabricated structural units that consist of a load-bearing steel column, filled with concrete. This creates a column with increased load-bearing capacity in a space no larger than a standard column. Fireproof lally columns have a thin steel shell and a layer of insulating material between the shell and the structural steel. Fire ratings range from two to four hours depending on the thickness of the insulating material. The protective steel shell allows fireproof lally columns to be left exposed in either interior or exterior applications.

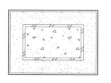

TYPICAL LALLY COLUMN SHAPES

CONCRETE FILLED STEEL TUBING

OUTER DIMENSION OF TUBING	WALL THICK-NESS	WEIGHT PER FT	ALLOWABLE SAFE LOADS IN KIPS EFFECTIVE LENGTH IN FEET KL WITH RESPECT TO RADIUS OF GYRATION										U.L. RATED/ FIREPROOFED COLUMN SQUARE SHELL SIZES		
			6	8	10	12	14	16	18	20	22	24	2 HR	3 HR	4 HR
3 x 3	1/2	15	62	53	40								6 x 6	7 x 7	8 x 8
3 1/2 x 3 1/2	1/4	20	77	68	55	42							6 x 6	7 x 7	8 x 8
4 x 4	1/4	25	98	89	78	65	51	40					6 x 6	7 x 7	8 x 8
	3/8	28	132	119	102	85	64								
5 x 5	1/4	36	137	128	118	107	94	80	64						
	3/8	40	185	172	158	141	124	103	82				7 x 7	8 x 8	9 x 9
	1/3	44	229	212	194	173	150	124							
6 x 6	1/4	49	178	169	160	150	138	125	110	95	79				
	3/8	55	241	228	215	200	183	165	145	124	101		8 x 8	9 x 9	10 x 10
	1/2	60	299	283	267	248	226	204	177	151					
7 x 7	1/4	65	221	213	204	194	183	171	158	143	128	111			
	3/8	72	297	285	273	259	243	227	208	189	168	146	9 x 9	10 x 10	11 x 11
	1/2	78	369	354	337	320	301	279	255	230	204	176			
8 x 8	1/4	82	266	259	251	240	231	218	206	193	178	163			
	3/8	90	357	346	334	321	306	291	272	254	236	215	10 x 10	11 x 11	12 x 12
	1/2	98	440	427	412	395	377	355	334	311	286	259			
10 x 10	1/4	122	364	357	349	340	330	320	308	296	282	267			
	3/8	132	482	471	460	448	435	419	404	388	369	350	11 x 11	13 x 13	14 x 14
	1/2	142	592	579	566	550	533	515	495	474	453	428			

CONCRETE FILLED STEEL PIPE

OUTER DIAMETER OF PIPE (IN.)	WALL THICKNESS	WEIGHT PER FT	ALLOWABLE SAFE LOADS IN KIPS EFFECTIVE LENGTH IN FEET KL WITH RESPECT TO RADIUS OF GYRATION											U.L. RATED/FIREPROOFED COLUMNS SQUARE SHELL SIZES			ROUND SHELL SIZES		
			6	8	10	12	14	16	18	20	22	24	26	2 HR.	3 HR.	4 HR.	2 HR.	3 HR.	4 HR.
3 1/2	.216	15	45	40	32														
	.300	17	58	49	39									6 x 6	7 x 7	8 x 8	6 5/8	6 5/8	8 5/8
	.600	23	94	79	60														
4	.226	20	58	53	45	36													
	.318	22	75	66	56	46								6 x 6	7 x 7	9 x 9	6 5/8	8 5/8	8 5/8
4 1/2	.237	24	73	66	59	51	41												
	.337	27	93	86	76	65	52							7 x 7	8 x 8	9 x 9	6 5/8	8 5/8	8 5/8
	.674	36	155	139	122	102													
5 1/2	.258	36	106	99	92	85	75	66	54										
	.375	39	139	130	120	110	98	84	69					8 x 8	9 x 9	10 x 10	8 5/8	8 5/8	10 3/4
	.750	52	230	215	198	178	156	132											
6 5/8	.280	49	144	139	132	123	114	104	93	81	68								
	.432	56	197	188	178	166	153	140	125	109				9 x 9	10 x 10	11 x 11	8 5/8	10 3/4	10 3/4
	.864	73	327	312	293	272	249	225	198	169									
8 5/8	.322	81	232	225	218	210	201	190	179	167	154	141	127						
	.500	91	314	305	295	283	270	257	242	226	209	191	171	11 x 11	12 x 12	13 x 13	10 3/4	12 3/4	12 3/4
	.875	111	475	460	444	425	404	383	359	334	307	278	248						
10 3/4	.365	123	342	336	328	320	311	300	289	277	264	251	237						
	.500	133	423	415	406	394	383	370	356	342	326	309	291	13 x 13	14 x 14	15 x 15	14	14	16
12 3/4	.375	169	442	437	429	421	412	402	391	380	368	355	341						
	.500	178	534	526	517	507	496	484	470	457	442	426	409	15 x 15	16 x 16	17 x 17	16	16	18

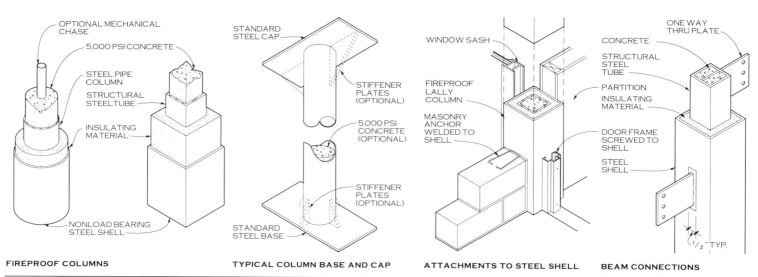

FIREPROOF COLUMNS

TYPICAL COLUMN BASE AND CAP

ATTACHMENTS TO STEEL SHELL   BEAM CONNECTIONS

TYPICAL LALLY COLUMN ASSEMBLIES

Eric Gastier; Alexandria, Virginia

CAST - IN - PLACE CONCRETE

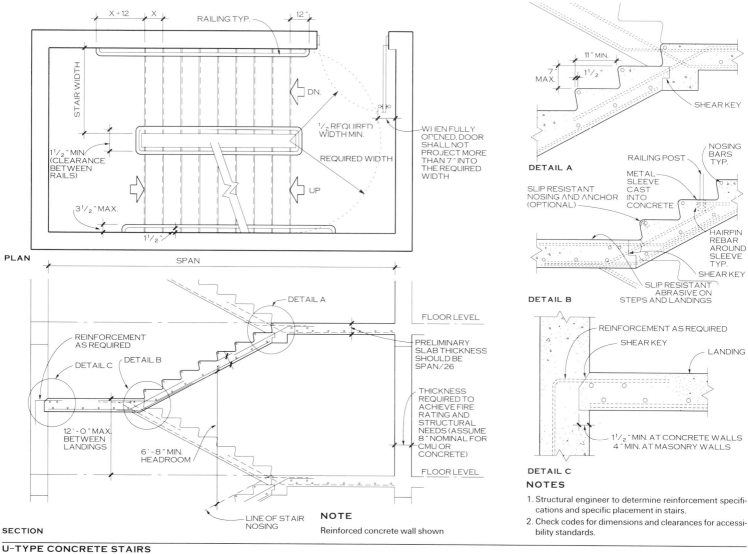

PLAN

SECTION

NOTE

Reinforced concrete wall shown

U-TYPE CONCRETE STAIRS

DETAIL A

DETAIL B

DETAIL C

NOTES

1. Structural engineer to determine reinforcement specifications and specific placement in stairs.
2. Check codes for dimensions and clearances for accessibility standards.

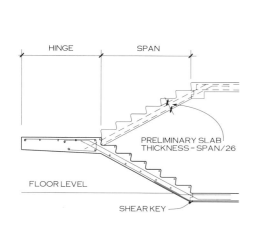

NOTE

Extend hinge only as required by stair width, unless otherwise permitted by structural engineer.

FREESTANDING CONCRETE STAIR

Richard J. Vitullo, Oak Leaf Studio; Crownsville, Maryland

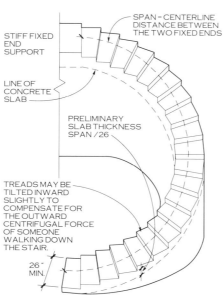

NOTE

Use of helicoidal concrete stairs depends on very stiff fixed end support and small support deflection.

HELICOIDAL CONCRETE STAIR

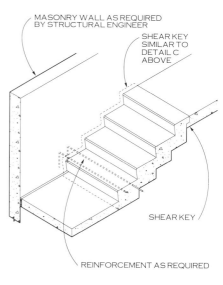

NOTE

Reinforcement must develop full bond in masonry walls and have full development length in concrete walls.

CANTILEVER CONCRETE STAIR

CAST - IN - PLACE CONCRETE   3

DEFINITION

Wall tie refers to wire or sheet metal devices used to connect two or more masonry wythes or used to connect masonry veneers to masonry backup systems.

GENERAL FUNCTION

Wall ties perform three primary functions:
1. Provide a connection.
2. Transfer lateral loads.
3. Permit inplane movement to accommodate or restrain differential material movements.

Metal ties may also be required to serve as horizontal joint reinforcement or provide longitudinal continuity.

TYPES OF WALL TIES

1. Unit ties.
2. Continuous horizontal joint reinforcement.
3. Adjustable ties (unit and continuous).
4. Re-anchoring systems.

TIE SELECTION

Building codes and standards have typically required minimum tie size and maximum tie spacing limits to control tie loading and deformation.

Corrosion problems associated with the use of wire ties and metal stud backup systems are currently being debated among building professionals, brick masonry associations, and manufacturers.

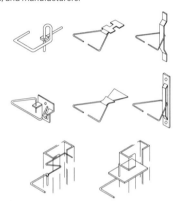

TIES FOR STEEL AND CONCRETE

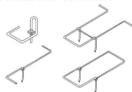

TIES FOR MASONRY BACKUP

ADJUSTABLE UNIT MASONRY TIES

NOTE

Tie must extend a minimum of $^5/_8$ in. into the brick veneer and a maximum of $^1/_2$ the width of the brick.

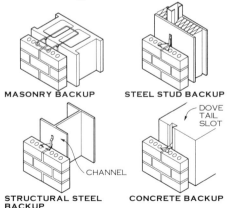

MASONRY BACKUP   STEEL STUD BACKUP   STRUCTURAL STEEL BACKUP   CONCRETE BACKUP

ADJUSTABLE UNIT TIE DETAILS

Eric K. Beach, Rippeteau Architects, PC; Washington, D.C.

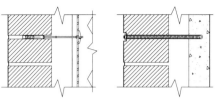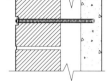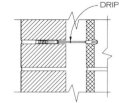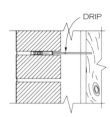

STEEL STUD BACKUP   CONCRETE BACKUP   MASONRY BACKUP   WOOD STUD BACKUP

MASONRY RE-ANCHORING SYSTEMS

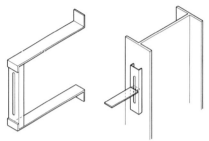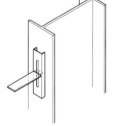

MASONRY TYPE CHANNEL SLOT   WELD - ON TYPE CHANNEL SLOT (ANCHOR SHOWN)

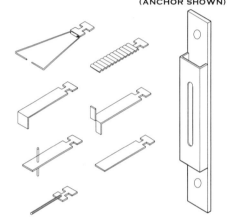

ANCHOR CONFIGURATIONS   FACE TYPE CHANNEL SLOT

CHANNEL SLOTS AND ANCHORS

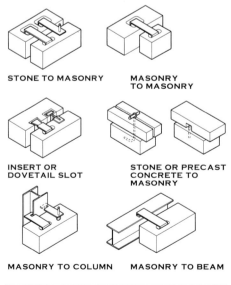

STONE TO MASONRY   MASONRY TO MASONRY
INSERT OR DOVETAIL SLOT   STONE OR PRECAST CONCRETE TO MASONRY
MASONRY TO COLUMN   MASONRY TO BEAM

ANCHOR DETAILS

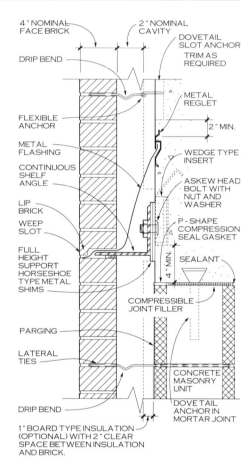

CAVITY WALL SHELF ANCHOR DETAIL

NOTE

Alter shelf angle size and corresponding wall dimensions if insulation is used.

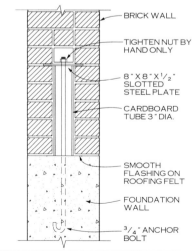

WALL TO FOUNDATION ANCHORAGE

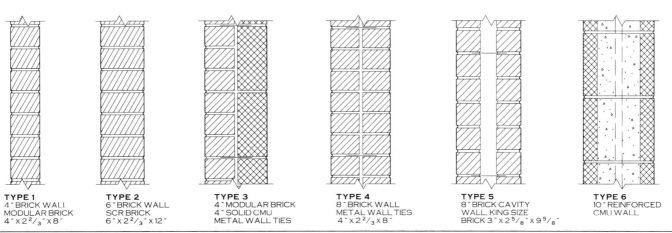

| | TYPE 1
4" BRICK WALL
MODULAR BRICK
4" x 2²/₃" x 8" | TYPE 2
6" BRICK WALL
SCR BRICK
6" x 2²/₃" x 12" | TYPE 3
4" MODULAR BRICK
4" SOLID CMU
METAL WALL TIES | TYPE 4
8" BRICK WALL
METAL WALL TIES
4" x 2²/₃" x 8" | TYPE 5
8" BRICK CAVITY
WALL, KING SIZE
BRICK 3" x 2⁵/₈" x 9⁵/₈" | TYPE 6
10" REINFORCED
CMU WALL |

PROPERTIES OF MASONRY WALLS

WALL TYPE NUMBER		1	2	3	4	5	6
Allowable compressive load (lb/linear ft)[6]	Type M mortar	[9]	25,200[2]	11,040[2,3]	33,600[2,3]	11,520[2,3]	[9]
	Type S mortar		25,200[2]	11,040[2,3]	33,600[2,3]	11,520[2,3]	
	Type N mortar		21,600[2]	9,600[2,3]	28,800[2,3]	10,080[2,3]	
Lateral support spacing (ft-in.)[5]	Bearing walls		9'-0"	12'-0"	12'-0"	9'-0"	
Material quantity (per 100 sq ft)[7]	Mortar (cu ft)	5.5	7.9	11	14.1	7.8	
	Brick/CMU	675	450	675/113	1350	960	
U value (Btu/sq ft/hr/F°)	Uninsulated	0.78	0.66	0.30-0.49[8]	0.58	0.40	
U value with 1 in. rigid insulation	(Polystyrene)	0.15	0.15	0.11-0.13[8]	0.14	0.13	
Wall weight (lb/sq ft)	Unplastered	40	60	52-69[8]	80	60	
Average sound resistance (STC)	Unplastered	45	51	45-50[8]	52	49 (est.)	
Fire resistance (hr)	Unplastered	1	2	4	2-4[8]	3	

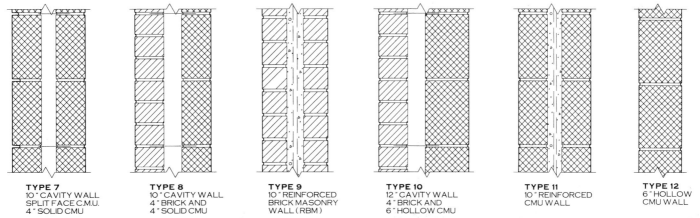

| | TYPE 7
10" CAVITY WALL
SPLIT FACE C.M.U.
4" SOLID CMU | TYPE 8
10" CAVITY WALL
4" BRICK AND
4" SOLID CMU | TYPE 9
10" REINFORCED
BRICK MASONRY
WALL (RBM) | TYPE 10
12" CAVITY WALL
4" BRICK AND
6" HOLLOW CMU | TYPE 11
10" REINFORCED
CMU WALL | TYPE 12
6" HOLLOW
CMU WALL |

PROPERTIES OF MASONRY WALLS

WALL TYPE NUMBER		7[1]	8[1]	9	10[1]	11	12
Allowable compressive load (lb/linear ft)[6]	Type M mortar	11,040[2]	11,040[2]	[9]	9,000[2]	[9]	8,280[2]
	Type S mortar	11,040[2]	11,040[2]		9,000[2]		8,280[2]
	Type N mortar	9,600[2]	9,600[2]		8,400[2]		7,200[2]
Lateral support spacing (ft-in.)[5]	Bearing walls	12'-0"	12'-0"		15'-0"		9'-0"
Material quantity (per 100 sq ft)	Mortar/grout (cu ft)	12	15	11/18.8	15		6
	Brick/CMU	113/113	675/113	1350	675/113		113
U value (Btu/sq ft /hr/ F°)	Uninsulated	0.23-0.33[8]	0.23-0.33[8]	0.44	0.22-0.32[8]		0.32-0.59[8]
U value with 1 in. rigid insulation	(Polystyrene)	0.11-0.12[8]	0.11-0.12[8]	0.13	0.11-0.12[8]		0.12-0.14[8]
Wall weight (lb/sq ft)	Unplastered	52-69[8]	52-69[8]	94.2	58-84[8]		20-46[8]
Average sound resistance (STC)	Unplastered	55	55	59	55		30-45[8]
Fire resistance (hr)	Unplastered	4	4	4	4		1-2[8]

NOTES

1. Use straight metal wire ties – no drips.
2. Brick compressive strength is 8000 psi plus; CMU compressive strength is 1500 psi plus.
3. Collar joints filled with mortar (¹/₂ in).
4. If loads bear only on one wythe, area is based on one wythe only.
5. Lateral support is based on h/t = 18.
6. Load bearing strengths are based on allowable compressive stresses taken from ACI 530/ASCE 5 Building Code Requirements for Masonry Structures.

7. Waste is not included, as this will vary with job. A waste factor of 2 to 5% is frequently applied for masonry units and 10 to 20% for mortar.
8. A range of values is shown for several categories because of aggregate type and density of units.
9. Rational design engineered masonry should be used in order to handle all variables under load bearing conditions. See ACI 530/ASCE 5 Building Code Requirements for Masonry Structures.

Brian E. Trimble, EIT; Brick Institute of America, Reston, Virginia.

PREASSEMBLED MASONRY PANELS

Prefabrication of brick masonry was first developed in the 1950s in France, Switzerland, and Denmark. Prefabrication began in the U.S. in the early 1960s.

FABRICATION METHODS

1. Hand laying. Methods used are the same as for conventional in-place masonry, except the panels are made either at an off-site or on-site plant.
2. Casting. Masonry units and grout are combined similarly to precast concrete. Usually units are placed, either by hand or machine, horizontally or vertically in a form or mold. The form is filled with a grout at atmospheric pressure or under moderate pressure.
3. Equipment. Equipment varies from simple hand tools to highly sophisticated automated machinery.
4. Masonry units. Both solid and hollow brick can be used in prefabrication. Solid brick masonry units are those that have coring of less than 25 percent of the bedding area. Hollow brick units are cored in excess of 25 percent but less than 40 percent of the bedding area. Faces larger than the standard modular unit are usually $2 \frac{1}{4}$ x $7 \frac{5}{8}$ in.
5. Mortar and grout. Conventional mortar or mortar with high-bond can be used. Prefabricated panels usually are subjected to higher stresses during handling than when in service in a structure. Drawings below show connection to steel frame; connections to concrete frame are also available.

NOTES

1. Incorporated in most panel designs are structural steel frames anchored to the back of the panel to create a clear span panel with a two-point gravity bearing on the structure.
2. Complex shapes can be made without the need for falsework and shoring. Complicated shapes with returns, soffits, arches, etc., are made by using jigs and forms.

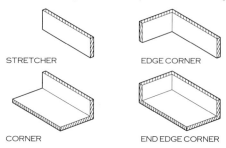

THIN BRICK UNITS

STRETCHER

EDGE CORNER

CORNER

END EDGE CORNER

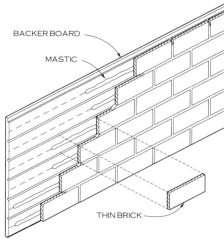

BACKER BOARD

MASTIC

THIN BRICK

MODULAR THIN BRICK PANEL

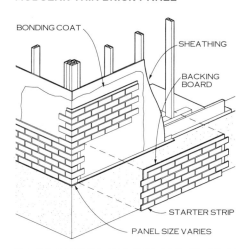

BONDING COAT

SHEATHING

BACKING BOARD

STARTER STRIP

PANEL SIZE VARIES

MODULAR PANELS OVER WOOD FRAME CONSTRUCTION

Eric K. Beach, Rippeteau Architects, PC; Washington, D.C.

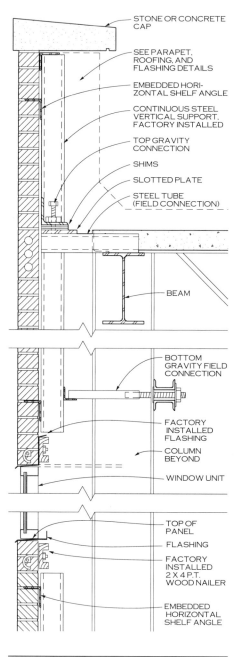

STONE OR CONCRETE CAP

SEE PARAPET, ROOFING, AND FLASHING DETAILS

EMBEDDED HORIZONTAL SHELF ANGLE

CONTINUOUS STEEL VERTICAL SUPPORT, FACTORY INSTALLED

TOP GRAVITY CONNECTION

SHIMS

SLOTTED PLATE

STEEL TUBE (FIELD CONNECTION)

BEAM

BOTTOM GRAVITY FIELD CONNECTION

FACTORY INSTALLED FLASHING

COLUMN BEYOND

WINDOW UNIT

TOP OF PANEL

FLASHING

FACTORY INSTALLED 2 X 4 P.T. WOOD NAILER

EMBEDDED HORIZONTAL SHELF ANGLE

SECTION THROUGH TYPICAL PREASSEMBLED MASONRY PANEL WITH GRAVITY CONNECTIONS

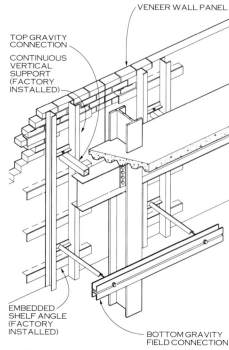

VENEER WALL PANEL

TOP GRAVITY CONNECTION

CONTINUOUS VERTICAL SUPPORT (FACTORY INSTALLED)

EMBEDDED SHELF ANGLE (FACTORY INSTALLED)

BOTTOM GRAVITY FIELD CONNECTION

NOTE

Prefabricated brick panels may be installed on concrete frames.

PANEL CONNECTION TO STRUCTURAL FRAME

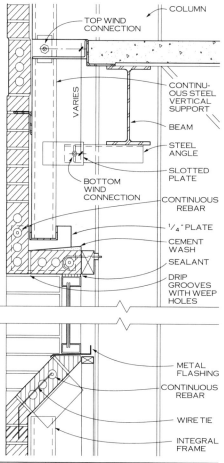

TOP WIND CONNECTION

COLUMN

VARIES

CONTINUOUS STEEL VERTICAL SUPPORT

BEAM

STEEL ANGLE

SLOTTED PLATE

BOTTOM WIND CONNECTION

CONTINUOUS REBAR

$\frac{1}{4}$" PLATE

CEMENT WASH

SEALANT

DRIP GROOVES WITH WEEP HOLES

METAL FLASHING

CONTINUOUS REBAR

WIRE TIE

INTEGRAL FRAME

SECTION THROUGH NONVERTICAL PREASSEMBLED MASONRY PANEL WITH WIND CONNECTIONS

TERRA-COTTA

Terra-cotta is a high grade of weathered or aged clay, which, when mixed with sand or with pulverized fired clay, can be molded to a hardness and compactness not obtainable with other materials. Used extensively until the 1930s, terra-cotta has been largely replaced with ceramic veneer.

Terra-cotta was usually hollow cast in blocks, open to the back to reveal internal webbing.

Ceramic veneer is not hollow cast but is a veneer of glazed ceramic tile that is ribbed on the back. It is frequently attached to metal ties that are anchored to the building.

Other types of terra-cotta are:

1. Brownstone terra-cotta. A dark red or brown block, which is hollow cast. Used extensively in the mid- to late-19th century.
2. Fireproof construction terra-cotta. Inexpensive and lightweight, these rough-finished hollow building blocks span beams. The blocks are available but not used widely today.
3. Glazed architectural terra-cotta. Hollow units were hand cast in molds or carved in clay and heavily glazed. Sometimes called architectural ceramics, this terra-cotta type was used until the 1930s.

NOTES

Ceramic veneer can be anchored or adhered to masonry .

The ceramic veneer manufacturer should provide scale shop drawings as detailed from the architect's drawings. To be used for setting, the shop drawings should indicate all dimensions and sizes of joints, and all anchors, hangers, expansion, and control or pressure-relieving joints.

Nonferrous metal anchors should be embedded in the masonry and encased for protection from corrosion.

The minimum thickness of anchored-type ceramic veneer, exclusive of ribs, should be 1 in.

Ceramic veneer should be set true to line in setting mortar. Spaces between anchored ceramic veneer and backing walls should be filled with grout: spaces $3/4$ in. or more in width with pea gravel and spaces $3/4$ in. with mortar.

The minimum thickness of adhesion-type ceramic veneer, including ribs, should be $1/4$ in. with ribbed or scored backs.

An evenly spread coat of neat portland cement and water should be applied to the wall and the entire back of the ceramic veneer panel about to be set. Then one half of the setting mortar coat should be immediately applied on the chosen wall area and the other on the ceramic veneer piece's entire back. Tap the piece into place on the wall to completely fill all voids, with the total thickness of the mortar averaging $3/4$ in. There should be some excess mortar forced out at the joints and edge of the ceramic veneer.

MOLD-PRESSED CERAMIC VENEER

The minimum thickness of the exposed faces of mold-pressed ceramic veneer is 1 in. Backs of special shapes should be open and ribbed.

For placement, turn all units bottom-side up and fill solidly with grout filler for mold-pressed ceramic veneer. When the fill has set sufficiently to permit handling, set the units.

When applied to soffits, each piece of ceramic veneer, in addition to the usual centers and wooden wedges, shall be supported by bent and vertical wooden shores. A constant upward pressure is needed until the mortar coat has set.

Adhesion can be tested with a 1 x 1 x 4 in. vitrified test bar. First dissolve vinyl acetate in methyl iso-butyl keytone. Apply to the ceramic veneer surface and text bar. The adhesive is heated by means of an infrared lamp until bubbling ceases. Press the two surfaces together until cool. Then knock or pry off test bar.

TERRA-COTTA VENEER PRECAST PANEL

Terra-cotta precast panels have a keyback design, which allows each piece to easily become an integral part of the precast unit through a mechanical bond. No fasteners are needed.

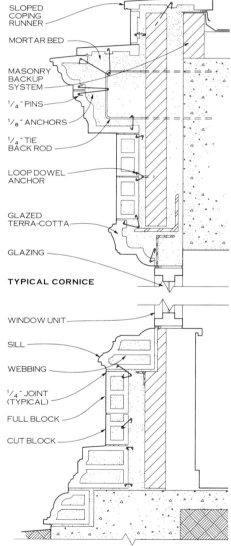

TYPICAL CORNICE

TYPICAL BASE

DESIGN OF BEST PRODUCTS CORPORATE HEADQUARTERS

TERRA-COTTA WALL SECTION

Eric K. Beach, Rippeteau Architects, PC; Washington, D.C.

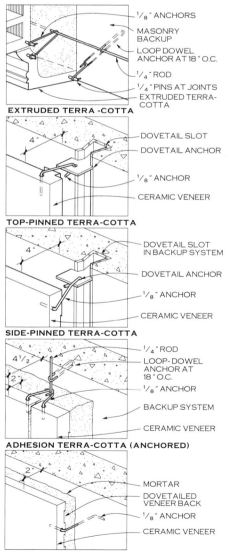

EXTRUDED TERRA -COTTA

TOP-PINNED TERRA-COTTA

SIDE-PINNED TERRA-COTTA

ADHESION TERRA-COTTA (ANCHORED)

ADHESION TERRA-COTTA (ANCHORED)

ANCHORING SYSTEMS

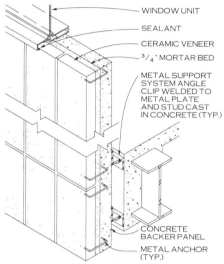

TERRA-COTTA PRECAST PANEL

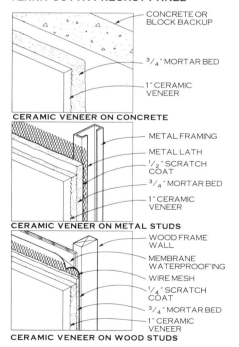

CERAMIC VENEER ON CONCRETE

CERAMIC VENEER ON METAL STUDS

CERAMIC VENEER ON WOOD STUDS

GROUT-ADHERED CERAMIC VENEER

GENERAL

Brick veneer construction consists of a nominal 3 in.- or 4 in.- thick exterior brick tied to a backup system with metal ties in such a way that a 1 in. minimum clear space is provided between the veneer and backup system. The brick veneer is supported on the foundation and is designed to carry no vertical loads, other than its own weight. There are five requirements for satisfactory performance of brick veneer:

1. An adequate foundation
2. A sufficiently strong, rigid, well-braced backup system
3. Proper attachment of the veneer to the backup system
4. Proper detailing, materials, and workmanship.
5. Thorough cleanup of the wall cavity after construction to ensure proper wall drainage.

DESIGN AND CONSTRUCTION

1. Foundations: It is recommended that the foundation or foundation wall be at least equal to the total thickness of the brick veneer wall assembly. Many building codes permit a nominal 8 in. foundation wall under single-family dwellings constructed of brick veneer, provided the wall is corbeled as shown in the detail, below right.
2. Anchors and ties: Refer to page 24 for a description of the types of anchors and ties. There should be one brick veneer tie for every 2 $\frac{2}{3}$ sq ft of wall area, with a maximum spacing of 24 in. o.c. For one- and two-family wood frame construction, the tie spacing may be modified to one tie for each $3\frac{1}{4}$ sq ft of wall area with a maximum spacing of 24 in. o.c. With metal stud backing 1 tie for every 2 sq ft of wall is required .

3. Flashing and weepholes: Flashing and weepholes should be located above and as near to grade as possible at the bottom of the wall and at all openings for proper wall drainage. Weepholes should be spaced no more than 24 in. o.c. and located in the head joints immediately above all flashing. Flashing should be securely fastened to the backup system and extend through the face of the brick veneer.
4. Lintels, sills, and jambs: Typical construction details are shown below. The advantages of using reinforced brick lintels are efficient use of materials, built-in fireproofing, elimination of differential movement, and no required painting or maintenance.

EMPIRICAL HEIGHT LIMITATIONS FOR BRICK VENEER

NOMINAL THICKNESS OF BRICK (IN.)	(MM)	STORIES	HEIGHT AT PLATE (FT)	(M)	HEIGHT AT GABLE (FT)	(M)
3	75	2	20	6.10	28	8.53
4	100	3	30	9.14	38	11.58

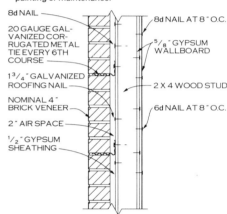

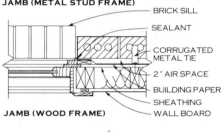

2-HOUR RATED BRICK VENEER ASSEMBLY

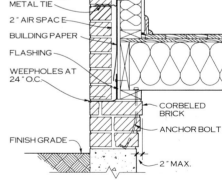

CORBELED FOUNDATION

The total projection of the corbel should not exceed 2 in. (50 mm), with individual corbels projecting not more than one third the thickness of the unit nor one half the height of the unit. The top corbel course should not be higher than the bottom of the floor joist and shall be a full header course.

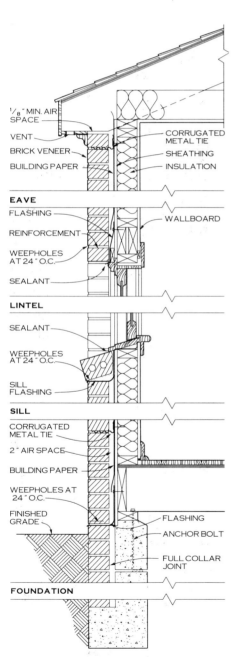

BRICK VENEER ON WOOD FRAME

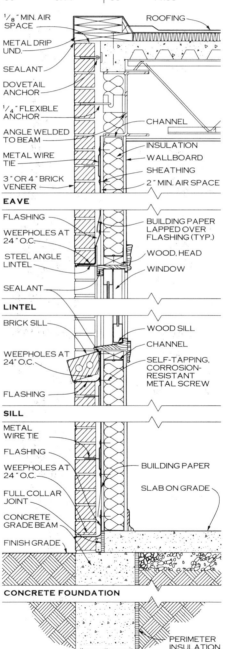

BRICK VENEER ON STEEL STUDS

SELECTED DETAILS

Eric K. Beach, Rippeteau Architects, PC; Washington, D.C.
Brick Institute of America; Reston, Virginia

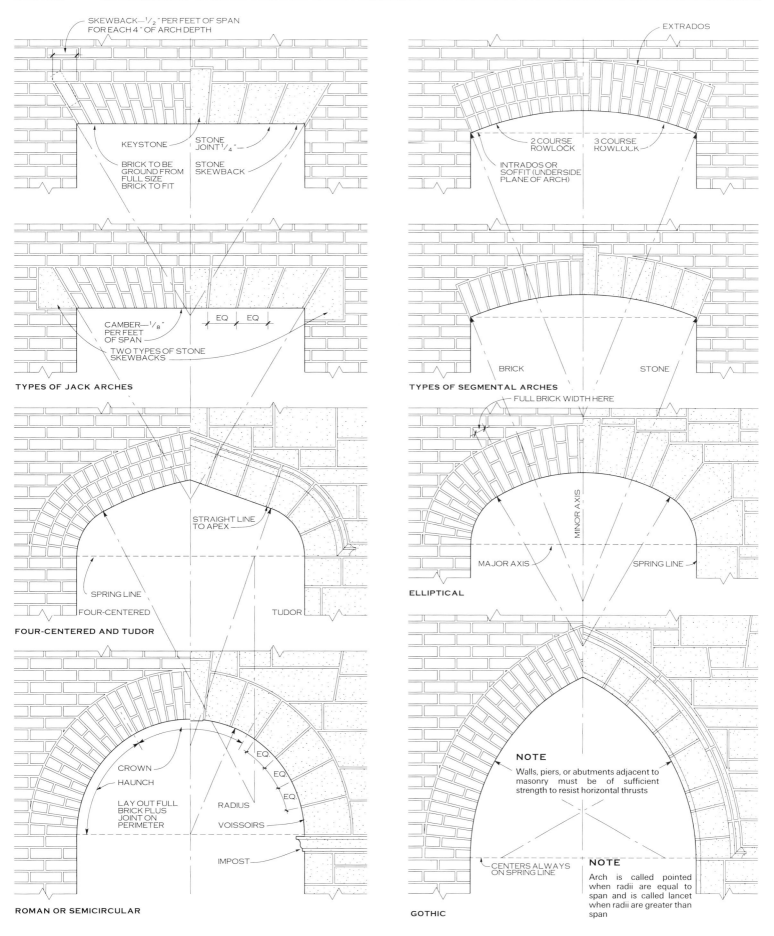

SKEWBACK—1/2" PER FEET OF SPAN FOR EACH 4" OF ARCH DEPTH

EXTRADOS

KEYSTONE

STONE JOINT 1/4"

BRICK TO BE GROUND FROM FULL SIZE BRICK TO FIT

STONE SKEWBACK

2 COURSE ROWLOCK

3 COURSE ROWLOCK

INTRADOS OR SOFFIT (UNDERSIDE PLANE OF ARCH)

CAMBER—1/8" PER FEET OF SPAN

EQ   EQ

TWO TYPES OF STONE SKEWBACKS

BRICK

STONE

TYPES OF JACK ARCHES

TYPES OF SEGMENTAL ARCHES

FULL BRICK WIDTH HERE

STRAIGHT LINE TO APEX

MINOR AXIS

SPRING LINE

FOUR-CENTERED

TUDOR

MAJOR AXIS

SPRING LINE

FOUR-CENTERED AND TUDOR

ELLIPTICAL

CROWN

HAUNCH

EQ

EQ

EQ

LAY OUT FULL BRICK PLUS JOINT ON PERIMETER

RADIUS

VOISSOIRS

NOTE

Walls, piers, or abutments adjacent to masonry must be of sufficient strength to resist horizontal thrusts

IMPOST

CENTERS ALWAYS ON SPRING LINE

NOTE

Arch is called pointed when radii are equal to span and is called lancet when radii are greater than span

ROMAN OR SEMICIRCULAR

GOTHIC

Richard J. Vitullo, Oak Leaf Studio; Crownsville, Maryland

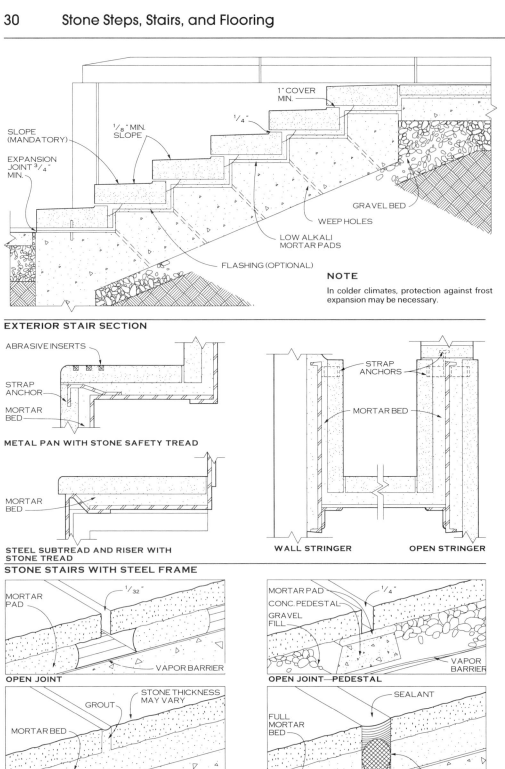

EXTERIOR STAIR SECTION

1" COVER MIN.

1/4"

1/8" MIN. SLOPE

SLOPE (MANDATORY)

EXPANSION JOINT 3/4" MIN.

GRAVEL BED

WEEP HOLES

LOW ALKALI MORTAR PADS

FLASHING (OPTIONAL)

NOTE

In colder climates, protection against frost expansion may be necessary.

ABRASIVE INSERTS

STRAP ANCHOR

MORTAR BED

METAL PAN WITH STONE SAFETY TREAD

MORTAR BED

STEEL SUBTREAD AND RISER WITH STONE TREAD

STONE STAIRS WITH STEEL FRAME

STRAP ANCHORS

MORTAR BED

WALL STRINGER   **OPEN STRINGER**

MORTAR PAD

1/32"

VAPOR BARRIER

OPEN JOINT

MORTAR PAD

CONC. PEDESTAL

GRAVEL FILL

1/4"

VAPOR BARRIER

OPEN JOINT—PEDESTAL

GROUT

STONE THICKNESS MAY VARY

MORTAR BED

THICK SET—CLOSED JOINT

SEALANT

FULL MORTAR BED

BACKUP ROD

VAPOR BARRIER

CONTROL JOINT AND FULL MORTAR BED

1/4" MARBLE OR GRANITE

FIBERGLASS

VERMICULITE BOARD

STEEL BACKING

SETTING BED (1/4" - 3/8")

CONCRETE OR WOOD FLOOR

STONE SANDWICH FLOOR PANEL (PREFAB)

MORTAR BED WITH REINFORCING

GROUT

ROOFING FELT OR POLYETHYLENE FILM

WOOD SUBFLOOR

STONE OVER WOOD FLOOR

STONE FLOORING

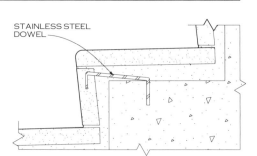

STAINLESS STEEL DOWEL

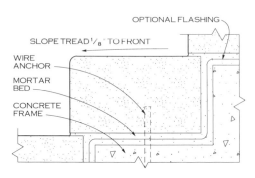

OPTIONAL FLASHING

SLOPE TREAD 1/8" TO FRONT

WIRE ANCHOR

MORTAR BED

CONCRETE FRAME

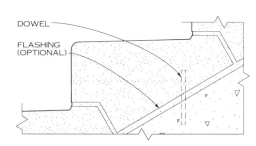

DOWEL

FLASHING (OPTIONAL)

STONE STAIRS WITH CONCRETE FRAME

DESIGN FACTORS FOR STONE STAIRS

Stone used for steps should have an abrasive resistance of 10 (measured on a scale from a minimum of 6 to a maximum of 17). When different varieties of stone are used, their abrasive hardness should be similar to prevent uneven wear.

Dowels and anchoring devices should be noncorrosive.

If a safety tread is used on stairs, a light bush hammered soft finish or nonslip finish is recommended.

To prevent future staining, dampproof the face of all concrete or concrete block, specify low alkali mortar, and provide adequate drainage (slopes and weep holes).

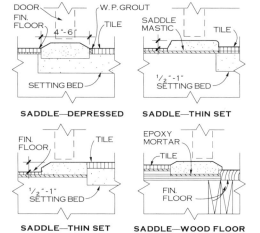

DOOR

FIN. FLOOR

W. P. GROUT

4" - 6"

TILE

SETTING BED

SADDLE—DEPRESSED

SADDLE MASTIC

TILE

1/2" - 1" SETTING BED

SADDLE—THIN SET

FIN. FLOOR

TILE

1/2" - 1" SETTING BED

SADDLE—THIN SET

EPOXY MORTAR

TILE

FIN. FLOOR

SADDLE—WOOD FLOOR

STONE THRESHOLDS

Eric K. Beach, Rippeteau Architects, PC; Washington, D.C.

HISTORY OF MARBLE

Marble is one of the oldest and finest building materials. It is also one of the most versatile quality building finishes. It is used on the exterior and interior of buildings as a cladding for both horizontal and vertical surfaces. It is used in residential, commercial, and institutional buildings. Marble is also used to create adornments for buildings and in building furnishings as table and countertops.

Marble is composed of the minerals calcite or dolomite with trace amounts of other minerals. These other minerals stain the calcite or dolomite and give the marble its color or veining. The purest marbles are white.

Most marble began as the shells of sea creatures; the shells were deposited in sedimentary layers on the bottom of the ocean and compressed under great weight to form limestone.

Limestone is also a popular building material and can be used in many of the same applications as marble. Marble can be defined for building purposes as any limestone capable of taking a polish. Most limestones, however, are too soft and coarse to take a polish, because they have not undergone a geologic process called metamorphosis.

Metamorphosis is the result of the compaction and melting of limestone by tremendous pressure and heat deep within the earth. This process removes inconsistencies and bonds the resulting crystallized base minerals into a uniform, hard, dense material that can be shaped and polished.

Travertine and onyx are two marbles that are formed differently. Travertine is dissolved calcite precipitated from the water in hot springs. It is characterized by many irregular cavities. Onyx is dissolved calcite precipitated from cold water solutions in caves. It is characterized by smooth, even veining.

CLASSIFICATION OF MARBLE

Marble is classified into groups depending on its working qualities. The groups are as follows:

Group A	Sound stone with uniform and favorable working qualities.
Group B	Stone similar to group A but with less favorable working qualities. May have natural faults.
Groups C and D	Stone with variations in its working qualities, containing geologic flaws, voids, and veins. Group D includes many of the highly colored decorative marbles.

IMPORTANT TERMS

Igneous Rock : Sometimes called "primary" rocks because they crystallize from a hot original silicate melt, the liquid magma of the earth's center. Granite is an igneous rock.

Sedimentary Rock : Or "layered rock" is the accumulation of particles of rock or organic material weathered by wind or water into horizontal layers, or stratification. The characteristics of different stones are based on their mineral composition, texture, the way they were deposited, and other factors. Sandstone and limestone are sedimentary rocks.

Stylolites : Or "crows feet" are irregular, wavy seams approximately parallel to the bedding plane of the stone. They are concentrations of organic material and are lines of weakness in the stone. Although ornamental in appearance, they do not polish and will weather out of the stone rapidly.

Creep : The use of thin veneers emphasizes the tendency for marble to experience plastic deformation or creep over time. This plastic flow takes place as intergranular movement along glide planes in the rock causes the panel to bend through its unsupported midsection. The wavy patterns in certain marbles are evidence of this phenomenon.

Metamorphic Marble : The deep burial of igneous or sedimentary rock by movement of the earth's crust causes their transformation into new recrystallized rocks, or metamorphic rock. True marble is a metamorphic rock. Metamorphism is a gradual process; therefore, a clear distinction is not always possible. For example, many rocks commonly called marbles are not metamorphic rock. Metamorphism usually "improves" rock by making it more uniform, stable, harder, and less porous. Nonmetamorphic marbles should be selected with attention to their use and possible shortcomings. A general rule is that true marbles (metamorphic marbles) have cool colors and nonmetamorphic marbles have warm colors.

Laird Ueberroth, Architect, and Associates; McLean, Virginia

STYLOLITE

Marble is characterized by its color, texture, and hardness. The crystals in marble vary in size from 1/4 in. to almost invisible, and colors range from pure white to black.

The crystalline nature of marble and its hardness that allows it to be polished make it an ideal material for shaping. Marble has been carved by skilled craftsmen since the earliest times. Ornamentation on buildings is still a primary use of marble.

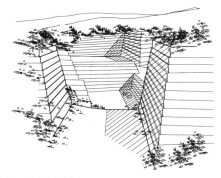

QUARRYING

Marble is cut from the earth in large blocks. The largest block ever taken weighed 94 tons. Typical architectural products are then sawn from these blocks and finished in one of several ways.

Today marble is used in a pulverized form in a variety of products. Marble dust is added to paints, concrete mixes, epoxy, and other plastic or vinyl mixes to create new materials.

Crushed marble is used in a wide variety of applications from landscaping stone, to stucco aggregate, to terrazzo chips.

WEATHERING

Marble is highly susceptible to weathering and decay caused by the increase of carbon dioxide, sulfates, and other acids present as aerosols in our atmosphere. Since the high levels of these pollutants is caused by industry and auto emissions, the rate of decay is much faster in cities. No effective method exists for protecting marble from these water-borne chemicals. A high polish, stone free from defects, and frequent cleaning are the best protections from decay.

NONMETAMORPHIC MARBLE

1. Travertine
2. Breccia
3. Onyx
4. Holston marble, Tennessee
5. Blue Belgian marble
6. Dolomite

METAMORPHIC MARBLES

1. Carrera marble
2. Vermont marble
3. Georgia marble

NONMARBLES

1. Serpentine
2. Granite
3. Gneiss
4. Schist

STANDARD MARBLE FINISHES

HONED : a satin smooth surface with little or no gloss.

POLISHED: the finest and smoothest glossy finish available.

RUBBED: a plane surface with slight scratches.

Most marble contains some pattern or veining. This lends itself to specific methods of installation. Common arrangements are illustrated below.

STANDARD MARBLE PANEL ARRANGEMENTS

BLEND PATTERN

Panels of the same variety but not necessarily from the same block arranged in a random pattern.

SIDE-SLIP END-SLIP

Panels from the same block are placed side to side or end to end to give a repetitive pattern in the horizontal or vertical.

QUARTER-MATCH END AND BOOK MATCH

Adjacent faces of panels from the same block are finished and set next to each other. End match sets adjacent panels above each other, book match sets them side by side, and quarter match creates a diamond pattern.

Perfect matches are not possible due to the unevenness of the veining in marble and to the loss of material during sawing.

PHYSICAL REQUIREMENTS OF EXTERIOR MARBLE

Physical Property	Requirement	ASTM Test
Absorbtion, max.	0.75%	C 97
Specific gravity, min.		
calcite	2.60	C 97
dolomite	2.80	C 97
serpentine	2.70	C 97
travertine	2.30	C 97
Compressive strength, min.	7500 psi	C 170
Modulus of rupture, min.	1000 psi	C 99
Abrasion resistance, min.	10.0	C 241

PROPERTIES OF MARBLE

MOHS HARDNESS Hм	SHORE HARDNESS Sн	SPECIFIC GRAVITY	POROSITY %	COMPRESSIVE STRENGTH 1000 psi	THERMAL EXPANSION C	ABRASION HARDNESS Hа
3.7 – 4.3	45 – 56	2.4 – 3.2	.6 – 2.3	10 – 35	27 – 51	7 – 42

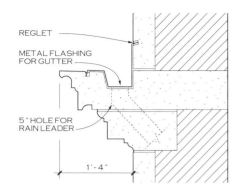

REGLET

METAL FLASHING FOR GUTTER

5" HOLE FOR RAIN LEADER

1'-4"

CORNICE WITH BUILT-IN GUTTER

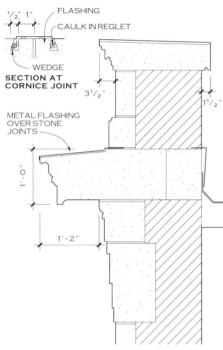

1/2" 1"

FLASHING

CAULK IN REGLET

WEDGE

SECTION AT CORNICE JOINT

3 1/2"

1 1/2"

METAL FLASHING OVER STONE JOINTS

1'-0"

1'-2"

CORNICE WITH SEPARATE PARAPET

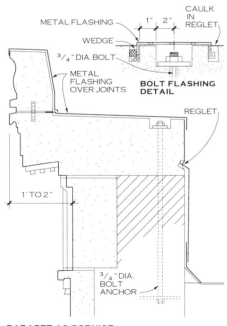

CAULK IN REGLET

METAL FLASHING

1" 2"

WEDGE

3/4" DIA. BOLT

METAL FLASHING OVER JOINTS

BOLT FLASHING DETAIL

REGLET

1' TO 2"

3/4" DIA. BOLT ANCHOR

PARAPET AS CORNICE

STONE PARAPET DETAILS

Richard J. Vitullo, Oak Leaf Studio; Crownsville, Maryland

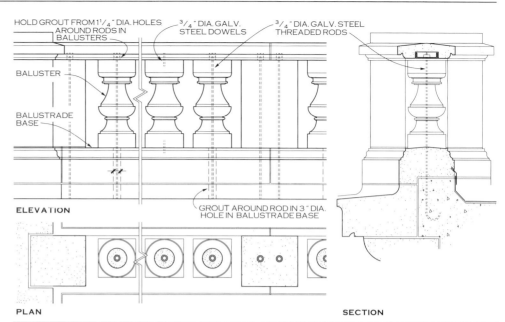

HOLD GROUT FROM 1 1/4" DIA. HOLES AROUND RODS IN BALUSTERS

3/4" DIA. GALV. STEEL DOWELS

3/4" DIA. GALV. STEEL THREADED RODS

BALUSTER

BALUSTRADE BASE

GROUT AROUND ROD IN 3" DIA. HOLE IN BALUSTRADE BASE

ELEVATION

PLAN

SECTION

STONE BALUSTRADE

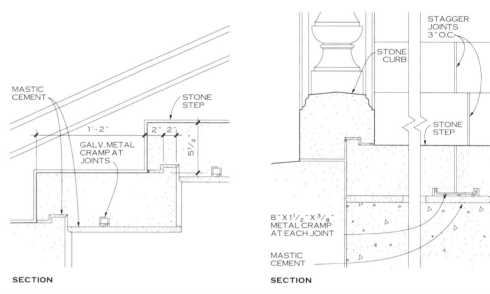

MASTIC CEMENT

STONE STEP

1'-2"

2" 2"

5 1/2"

GALV. METAL CRAMP AT JOINTS

STAGGER JOINTS 3" O.C.

STONE CURB

STONE STEP

8" X 1 1/2" X 3/8" METAL CRAMP AT EACH JOINT

MASTIC CEMENT

SECTION

SECTION

STONE STEPS AND CURBS

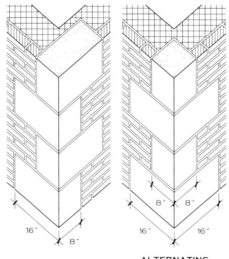

STAGGERED PATTERN

ALTERNATING PATTERN

16"

8"

8" 8"

16" 16"

STONE QUOIN IN BRICK WALL

NOTE

Dowel between stone pieces allows flat interrupted flashing. Dowel set vertically is typical for stepped flashing (min. 2 dowels per stone).

GOTHIC-TYPE STONE COPINGS, INSIDE WASH

1   10

1 1/2" MIN. CENTER DOWEL

DRIPS EACH SIDE

MOLDED COPING, INSIDE WASH

2 VERTICAL DOWELS PER STONE

STEPPED FLASHING

PLAIN COPING

STONE COPINGS

STONE

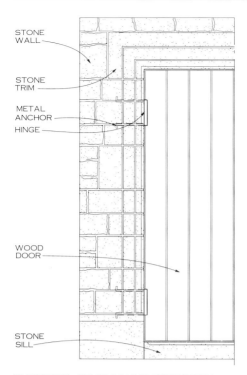

STONE WALL

STONE TRIM

METAL ANCHOR

HINGE

WOOD DOOR

STONE SILL

ELEVATION—WOOD DOOR IN STONE WALL

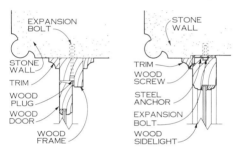

EXPANSION BOLT

STONE WALL

TRIM

WOOD PLUG

WOOD DOOR

WOOD FRAME

STONE WALL

TRIM

WOOD SCREW

STEEL ANCHOR

EXPANSION BOLT

WOOD SIDELIGHT

HEAD (AND JAMB) AT DOOR

HEAD (AND JAMB) AT SIDELIGHT

WOOD FRAME DETAILS

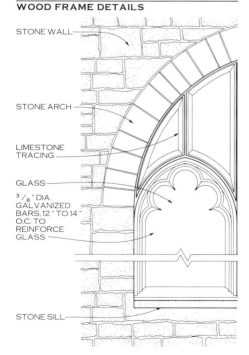

STONE WALL

STONE ARCH

LIMESTONE TRACING

GLASS

$^3/_8$" DIA. GALVANIZED BARS, 12" TO 14" O.C. TO REINFORCE GLASS

STONE SILL

ELEVATION—WINDOW IN STONE WALL

Richard J. Vitullo, Oak Leaf Studio; Crownsville, Maryland

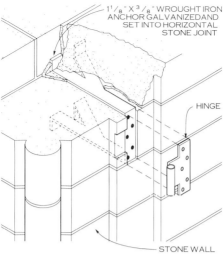

$1^1/_8$" X $^3/_8$" WROUGHT IRON ANCHOR GALVANIZED AND SET INTO HORIZONTAL STONE JOINT

HINGE

STONE WALL

HINGE DETAIL SHOWING STONE ANCHOR

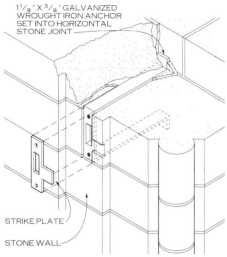

$1^1/_8$" X $^3/_8$" GALVANIZED WROUGHT IRON ANCHOR SET INTO HORIZONTAL STONE JOINT

STRIKE PLATE

STONE WALL

STRIKE DETAIL SHOWING STONE ANCHOR

CONCEALED ANCHOR DOOR DETAILS

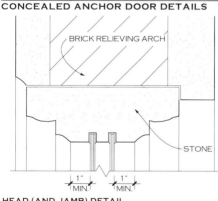

BRICK RELIEVING ARCH

STONE

1" MIN. 1" MIN.

HEAD (AND JAMB) DETAIL

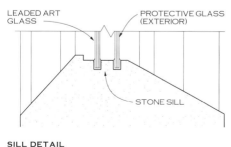

LEADED ART GLASS

PROTECTIVE GLASS (EXTERIOR)

STONE SILL

SILL DETAIL

SECTION A—WINDOW IN STONE WALL

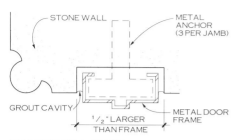

STONE WALL

METAL ANCHOR (3 PER JAMB)

GROUT CAVITY

$^1/_2$" LARGER THAN FRAME

METAL DOOR FRAME

HOLLOW METAL FRAME

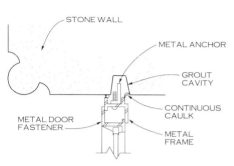

STONE WALL

METAL ANCHOR

GROUT CAVITY

CONTINUOUS CAULK

METAL DOOR FASTENER

METAL FRAME

HEAD AND JAMB DETAILS AT STONE WALL

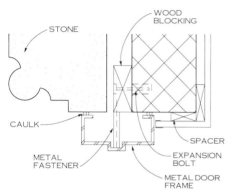

STONE

WOOD BLOCKING

CAULK

METAL FASTENER

EXPANSION BOLT

METAL DOOR FRAME

SPACER

HEAD AND JAMB DETAILS AT CAVITY WALL

ALTERNATE METAL FRAME DETAILS

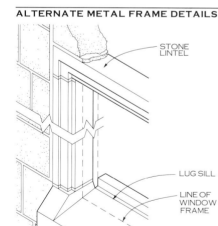

STONE LINTEL

LUG SILL

LINE OF WINDOW FRAME

STONE LUG SILL AND LINTEL DETAIL

CAULK

STONE SLIP SILL

LINE OF WINDOW FRAME

STONE SLIP SILL DETAIL

ALTERNATE STONE TRIM DETAILS

STONE

STRUCTURAL WELDING

Structural welds can be made with hundreds of different welding processes. The most common are forms of shielded metal arc and oxyfuel gas welding. These processes are designed for the specific welding conditions: type of metal, structural requirements, weld position, and joint specifications. Normally, however, the designer does not specify the process which is to be used to make a welded joint. The designer specifies the type and size of weld needed for the specific joint and leaves the details of how the joint is to be made up to the fabricator.

The two most important types of structural welds are fillet welds and groove welds. They are the most useful in structural applications. Back welds are used in conjunction with single groove welds to complete the weld penetration. Plug, slot, and flare welds are of secondary importance and are limited in application.

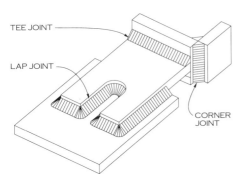

FILLET WELD JOINTS

With a triangular cross section, fillet welds join two surfaces approximately at right angles to each other in lap, tee, and corner joints. They are also used with groove welds as reinforcements in corner joints.

FILLET WELDS

Groove welds are welds made in a groove between adjacent ends, edges, or surfaces of two parts to be joined in a butt, tee, or corner joint.

The edge or ends of parts to be groove welded are usually prepared by flame cutting, arc air gouging, or edge planing to provide square, vee, bevel, U-, or J-shaped grooves that are straight and true to dimension. The preparation is done to ensure that the base metal is welded evenly completely through the joint. With thicker metal it is also done to open up the joint area for welding. Relatively thin material may be groove welded with square cut edges.

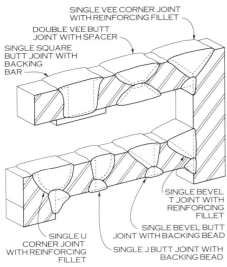

EXAMPLES OF COMPLETE PENETRATION GROOVE WELDS

The two types of groove welds are complete penetration and partial penetration. A complete penetration weld is one that achieves fusion of weld and base metal throughout the depth of the joint. It is made by welding from both sides of the joint, or, from one side to a backing bar, or back welding the first weld.

GROOVE WELDS

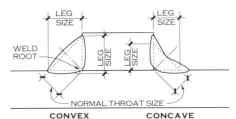

FILLET WELD NOMENCLATURE

The model cross section of a fillet weld is a right triangle with equal legs. The leg size designates the effective size of the weld. The length of a fillet weld is the distance from end-to-end of the full size fillet, measured parallel to its root line. For curved fillet welds the effective length is equal to the throat length, measured along a line bisecting the throat area.

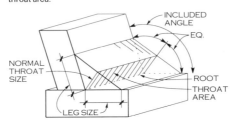

The cross section of a fillet weld may differ from the right triangle model in several ways. The included angle of the weld may vary from 60° to 135°, or unequal leg welds may be employed. When unequal leg welds are used, the use of the normal throat size as the effective size in weld strength calculations will, in most cases, be conservative. However, when the included angle of weld deposit is substantially greater than 90°, the effective throat size should be determined from the actual dimensions of the weld according to AWS specifications.

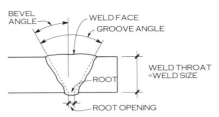

FULL PENETRATION GROOVE WELD NOMENCLATURE

Except where backing bars are employed, specifications require that the weld roots generally must be chipped or gouged to sound metal before making the second weld. For purposes of stress computation, the throat dimension of a full penetration groove weld is considered to be the full thickness of the thinner part joined, exclusive of weld reinforcement, such as backing bars.

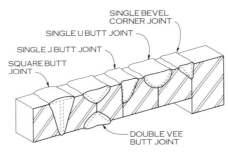

EXAMPLES OF PARTIAL PENETRATION GROOVE WELDS

Partial penetration groove welds are employed when stresses to be transferred do not require full penetration, or when welding must be done from one side of a joint only and it is not possible to use backing bars or to gouge weld roots for back welds. The application of partial penetration groove welds is governed by specifications and may limit the effective throat thickness or the thickness of the material on which they are to be used.

JOINT PREQUALIFICATION

Welded joints that conform to all American Welding Society code and specification provisions for design, material, and workmanship are prequalified joints. There are a variety of specific fillet and groove welded joints that meet most structural work requirements and are recommended for general use in buildings and bridges. Joints that are not prequalified under the AWS code are required to be qualified by tests as prescribed by the code.

For quick reference and more advanced consideration, the prequalified joints are shown in AWS "Structural Welding Code–Steel."

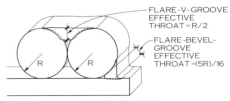

FLARE WELD NOMENCLATURE

Flare welds are special cases of groove welds in which the groove surface of one or both parts of a joint is convex. This convexity may be the result of edge preparation, but more often one or both components consists of a round rod or rounded shape. Complete penetration in a flare weld is usually difficult to achieve and the quality of the weld is difficult to control; therefore, design values should be applied conservatively and special considerations need to be taken in certain instances.

FLARE WELDS

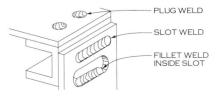

PLUG AND SLOT WELDS

Plug and slot welds are used in lap joints to transmit shear loads, prevent buckling of lapped parts, or join component parts of built-up members. Round holes or slots are punched or otherwise formed in one component of the joint before assembly. With parts in position, weld metal is deposited in the openings, which may be partially or completely filled, depending on the thickness of the punched material. AWS "Structural Welding Code–Steel" should be consulted for allowable proportion and spacing of holes and slots and the depth of welds.

It is necessary to distinguish between plug or slot welds and fillet welds placed around the inside of a hole or slot. Fillet welds in a slot are easier to make and inspect and are usually preferred over fillet welds in round holes or plug and slot welds.

PLUG AND SLOT WELDS

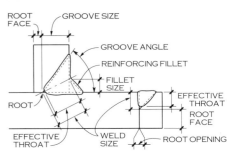

PARTIAL PENETRATION GROOVE WELD NOMENCLATURE

Edge preparation of base material for partial penetration welds is similar to that for full penetration groove welds, but it usually covers less than the full thickness. The effective throat thickness and, hence, the weld strength of partial penetration groove welds is normally limited to less than the full joint thickness.

The use of partial penetration welds is subject to AWS code and other specification provisions. These are more restrictive in bridge specifications than in building codes.

BASIC WELDING SYMBOLS

The three basic parts needed to form a welding symbol are; an arrow pointing to the joint, a reference line upon which the dimensional data is placed, and a weld device symbol indicating the weld type required. The tail of the welding symbol is only necessary to indicate additional data, such as specification, process, or detail references.

The arrow indicates the joint where the weld is to be made. The basic weld device symbol or device indicates the type of weld to be made, for example: fillet, U-groove, bevel, or plug. The position of the basic weld symbol or device indicates which side of the joint is to be welded. The bottom side of the reference line is designated as the arrow side, meaning any welding operation shown on this side of the reference line is to be performed on the same side of the joint as the arrow. When an operation is shown on the top side of the reference line it is to be performed on the joint side opposite the arrow.

The weld dimensions, size, length, pitch, etc., are placed on the reference line next to the weld device. These dimensions read from left to right regardless of which side the arrow is on.

FILLET WELDS

The dimensions needed for fillet welds are weld size and length and, for intermittent fillet welds, pitch. The weld size is equal to the weld leg size, assuming that the legs are equal. In the rare instance that the legs are not equal, the size is not given in the welding symbol but instead the weld legs are dimensioned in the drawing to avoid confusion. If there is a typical weld size for a particular drawing, the size may be noted in the notes and left off of the symbol. If the joint is to be welded on both sides, then both sides must be dimensioned, even if they are the same.

If the length of a fillet weld is omitted, it is understood to mean that the weld is to extend the full distance between abrupt changes in the part of the joint outline specified by the weld symbol arrow. If the same size fillet is required for the full length of all sides of a particular joint, regardless of abrupt changes in its direction, the weld-all-around symbol can be used to simplify the drawing.

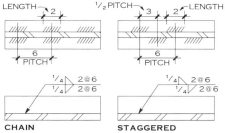

INTERMITTENT FILLET WELDS

Pitch is used with intermittent fillet welds to give the center to center dimensions between welded sections. When using pitch, length is the dimension of the individual weld sections.

COMPLETE PENETRATION GROOVE WELDS

When detailing complete penetration groove welds the dimensions usually include the weld size, root opening, the groove angle for vee, bevel, J, and U welds, and the groove radii for J and U welds. The length of groove welds is not given, because the welds are accepted to go from end to end of pieces welded. Any deviating from this requires additional detailing.

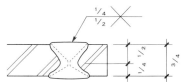

UNSYMMETRICAL GROOVE WELD CALLOUT

Normally the weld size of a complete joint penetration groove weld is understood to be the full thickness of the thinner metal connected, and its dimension need not be shown on the welding symbol. However, if the preparation of a double groove weld is not symmetrical, the size of each side of the weld must be shown.

The root opening is shown near the root of the groove device. The groove angle is to be shown within the groove

BASIC WELD DEVICE SYMBOLS

SUPPLEMENTARY WELD SYMBOLS

NOTE

For additional basic and supplementary weld symbols, see the American Welding Society A2.4-79.

STANDARD LOCATION OF ELEMENTS OF A WELDING SYMBOL

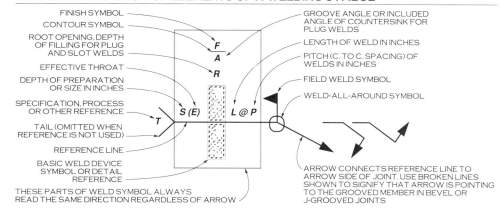

NOTES

1. Size, weld symbol, length of weld, and spacing must read in that order from left to right along the reference line. Neither orientation of reference line nor location of the arrow alters this rule.
2. The perpendicular leg of ◣ ∨ ⊢ ⏐⌒ weld symbols must be at left.
3. Arrow ond other side welds are of the same size unless otherwise shown. Dimensions of fillet welds must be shown on both the arrow side and the other side symbol.
4. The point of the field weld symbol must point toward the tail
5. Symbols apply between abrupt changes in direction of welding unless governed by the "all-around" symbol or otherwise dimensioned.
6. These symbols do not explicitly provide for the case that frequently occurs in structural work, where duplicate material (such as stiffeners) occurs on the far side of a web or gusset plate. The fabricating industry has adopted the following convention: when the billing of the detail material discloses the existence of a member on the far side as well as on the near side, the welding shown for the near side shall be duplicated on the far side.

faces of the device and above the root opening. The angle is understood to be the total, or included, angle of the groove.

There is no provision for dimensioning radii of U and J groove welds in the AWS welding symbol. This is usually covered by the fabricator's standard weld proportions, with reference to AWS prequalified joints. If not, it must be shown by note or sketch in the drawing.

PARTIAL PENETRATION GROOVE WELDS

Partial penetration groove welds require all of the same dimensions as complete penetration groove welds, plus two additional dimensions: effective throat and weld size. With

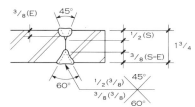

PARTIAL PENETRATION GROOVE WELD CALLOUT

partial penetration groove welds, the weld preparation usually is less than the thickness of the material being welded. Because of this the weld size must always be

given. The effective throat must also be given because it can vary from the weld size due to welding process, welding position, or the groove angle used. Depending on these factors, the depth of weld deposit, or the effective throat, can be less than the depth of the groove, or weld size.

Partial penetration groove welds can be used as intermittent welds. Consideration must be given to the transition at the beginning and end of the weld. Therefore, contact design drawings should only specify the effective weld length and the required effective throat. The shop drawings should then show the groove depth and geometry that will provide for the required effective throat.

PLUG AND SLOT WELDS

The size for plug welds specifies the diameter of the punched hole. For slot welds the size includes the width and length of the slot. Plug and slot welds will be completely filled unless the depth of the filling is shown inside the weld symbol. Slot welds are noted by detail references in the tail that refer to dimensioned sketches of the slot for clarity. The arrow and other side indicates which side of the joint is to be punched. The flush weld symbol is used if the top of the weld is to be leveled off.

CONTOUR SYMBOLS

The flush and convex symbols are used to modify the shape of the weld face. The contour symbols are placed over the weld device. Almost all of the basic weld symbols can be combined with each other and with the spacer, backing bar, back weld, and contour symbols to create many different welds.

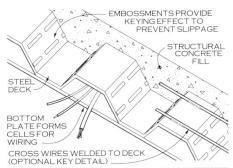

CONCRETE TOPPED STEEL DECK

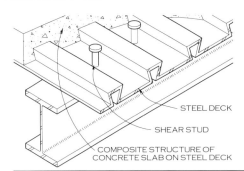

STEEL BEAM WITH STUD IN CONCRETE SLAB

STEEL-ENCASED CONCRETE COLUMNS

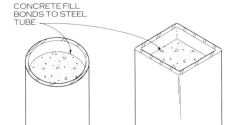

CONCRETE ENCASED STEEL COLUMNS

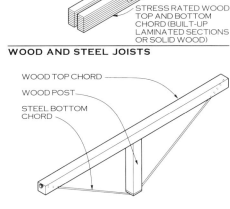

WOOD AND STEEL JOISTS

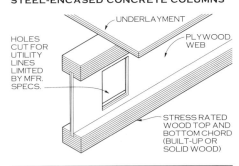

WOOD AND PLYWOOD COMPOSITE

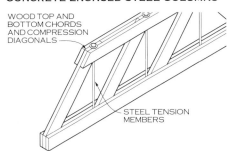

WOOD AND STEEL TRUSSES

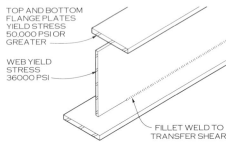

HYBRID STEEL GIRDERS USING DIFFERENT STRENGTH STEELS

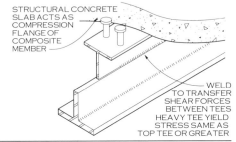

CASTELLATED BEAMS

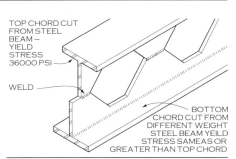

NOTES

Individual elements of the composite unit must be securely fastened to prevent slippage, especially at points where load is transferred from one element of the composite member to another. This is accomplished by the following means:

TYPES OF COMPOSITE ELEMENTS

1. Concrete topped composite steel decks.
2. Steel beams acting compositely with concrete slabs.
3. Steel columns encased by or filled with concrete.
4. Open web joists of wood and steel or joists with plywood webs and wood chords.
5. Trusses combining wood and steel.
6. Hybrid girders utilizing steels of different strengths.
7. Cast-in-place concrete slab on precast concrete joists or beams.

FLITCH BEAMS

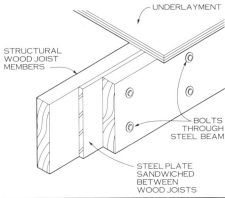

REINFORCED CONCRETE SLAB AND

Composite construction combines different materials, or different grades of a material, to form a structural member that utilizes the most desirable properties of each. Perhaps the earliest composite structural unit was the mud brick

reinforced with straw. More recently fiberglass-reinforced plastics, wire-reinforced safety glass, and glued laminated plywood and wood beams have been used.

COMPARATIVE DESIGN

A 30 ft beam with a 2.25 kip/ft uniform load carrying $2\frac{1}{2}$ in. concrete fill on a 2 in. metal deck slab uses a W24x55 in a noncomposite design and only a W18x40 with $38\frac{3}{4}$ in. steel studs in a composite design.

Richard J. Vitullo, Oak Leaf Studio; Crownsville, Maryland

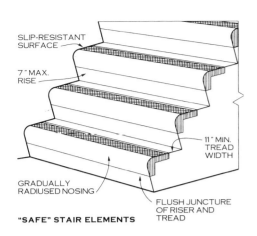

"SAFE" STAIR ELEMENTS

TREADS AND RISER SIZES

Riser and tread dimensions must be uniform for the length of the stair. ANSI specifications recommend a minimum tread dimension of 11 in. nosing-to-nosing and a riser height of 7 in. maximum. Open risers are not permitted on stairs accessible to the handicapped.

TREAD COVERING

OSHA standards require finishes to be "reasonably slip resistant" by using nosings of slip-resistant finish. Treads without nosings are acceptable provided that the tread is serrated or is of a definite slip-resistant design. Uniform color and texture are recommended for clear delineation of edges.

NOSING DESIGN

ANSI specifications recommend nosings without abrupt edges that project no more than 1 1/2 in. beyond the edge of the riser. A safe stair uses a 1/2 in. radius abrasive nosing firmly anchored to the tread, with no overhangs and a clearly visible edge.

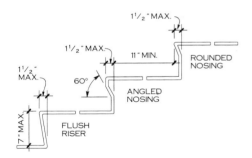

ACCEPTABLE NOSING PROFILES (ANSI 117.1-86)

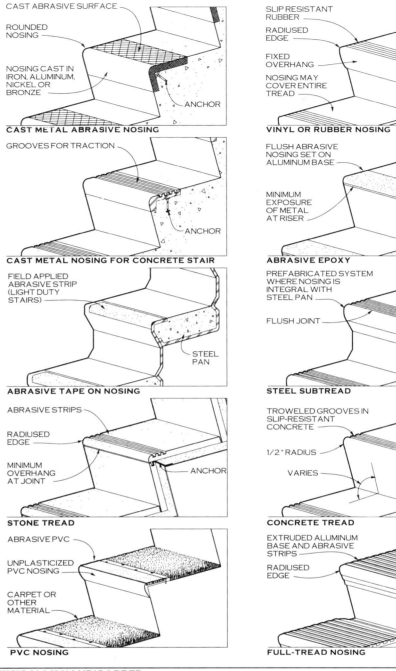

CAST METAL ABRASIVE NOSING

CAST METAL NOSING FOR CONCRETE STAIR

ABRASIVE TAPE ON NOSING

STONE TREAD

PVC NOSING

VINYL OR RUBBER NOSING

ABRASIVE EPOXY

STEEL SUBTREAD

CONCRETE TREAD

FULL-TREAD NOSING

DESIGN OF A "SAFE" STAIR USABLE BY THE PHYSICALLY HANDICAPPED

NOTE

Abrasive materials are used as treads, nosings, or inlay strips for new work and as surface-mounted replacement treads for existing work. A homogeneous epoxy abrasive is cured on an extruded aluminum base for a smoother surface, or it is used as a filler between aluminum ribs.

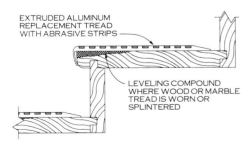

REPLACEMENT OF TREAD

Eric K. Beach, Rippeteau Architects, PC; Washington, D.C.

NOTE

Cast nosings for concrete stairs are iron, aluminum, nickel, or bronze in custom-made or stock sizes. Nosings and treads come with factory-drilled countersunk holes, with riveted strap- or wing-type anchors.

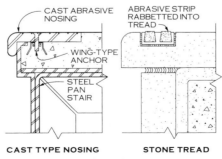

CAST TYPE NOSING   STONE TREAD

OTHER TYPICAL NOSING DETAILS

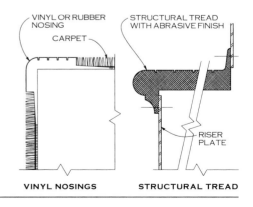

VINYL NOSINGS   STRUCTURAL TREAD

METAL FABRICATION   5

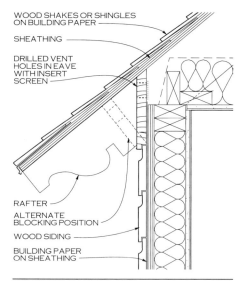

WOOD SHAKES OR SHINGLES ON BUILDING PAPER

SHEATHING

DRILLED VENT HOLES IN EAVE WITH INSERT SCREEN

RAFTER
ALTERNATE BLOCKING POSITION
WOOD SIDING
BUILDING PAPER ON SHEATHING

EXPOSED RAFTER END

NOTE

An eave is the lower edge of a sloping roof that projects past the face of the wall below. An overhang is a more general term for any projection out from a wall, sloping or flat. Both protect the wall below from precipitation by either throwing the water away from the wall (and foundation) or directing it into gutters and downspouts. Both also provide protection and shading for openings below.

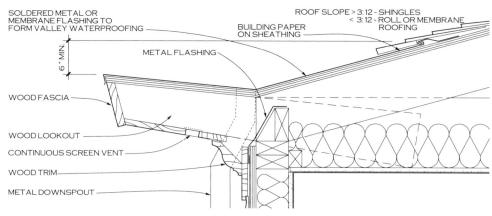

SOLDERED METAL OR MEMBRANE FLASHING TO FORM VALLEY WATERPROOFING

6" MIN.

METAL FLASHING

ROOF SLOPE > 3:12 - SHINGLES
< 3:12 - ROLL OR MEMBRANE ROOFING
BUILDING PAPER ON SHEATHING

WOOD FASCIA
WOOD LOOKOUT
CONTINUOUS SCREEN VENT
WOOD TRIM
METAL DOWNSPOUT

REVERSE SLOPE OVERHANG

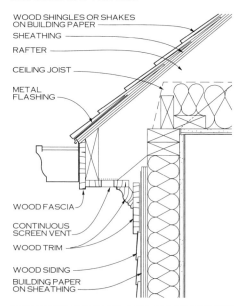

WOOD SHINGLES OR SHAKES ON BUILDING PAPER
SHEATHING
RAFTER
CEILING JOIST
METAL FLASHING

WOOD FASCIA
CONTINUOUS SCREEN VENT
WOOD TRIM
WOOD SIDING
BUILDING PAPER ON SHEATHING

EAVE AT WOOD SIDING

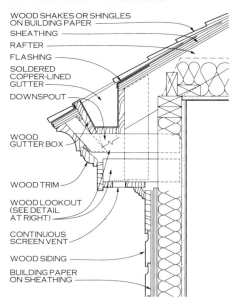

WOOD SHAKES OR SHINGLES ON BUILDING PAPER
SHEATHING
RAFTER
FLASHING
SOLDERED COPPER-LINED GUTTER
DOWNSPOUT

WOOD GUTTER BOX

WOOD TRIM
WOOD LOOKOUT (SEE DETAIL AT RIGHT)
CONTINUOUS SCREEN VENT
WOOD SIDING
BUILDING PAPER ON SHEATHING

EAVE WITH BUILT-IN GUTTER

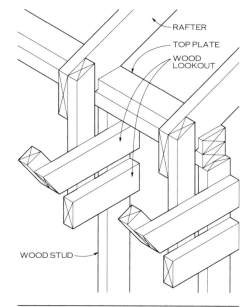

RAFTER
TOP PLATE
WOOD LOOKOUT

WOOD STUD

CORNICE SUPPORT DETAIL

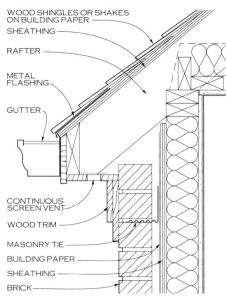

WOOD SHINGLES OR SHAKES ON BUILDING PAPER
SHEATHING
RAFTER
METAL FLASHING
GUTTER

CONTINUOUS SCREEN VENT
WOOD TRIM
MASONRY TIE
BUILDING PAPER
SHEATHING
BRICK

EAVE AT BRICK VENEER

Richard J. Vitullo, Oak Leaf Studio; Crownsville, Maryland

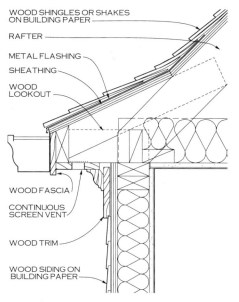

WOOD SHINGLES OR SHAKES ON BUILDING PAPER
RAFTER
METAL FLASHING
SHEATHING
WOOD LOOKOUT

WOOD FASCIA
CONTINUOUS SCREEN VENT
WOOD TRIM
WOOD SIDING ON BUILDING PAPER

PROJECTED EAVE WITH SHALLOW SLOPE

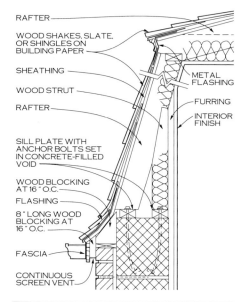

RAFTER
WOOD SHAKES, SLATE, OR SHINGLES ON BUILDING PAPER
SHEATHING
WOOD STRUT
RAFTER
METAL FLASHING
FURRING
INTERIOR FINISH
SILL PLATE WITH ANCHOR BOLTS SET IN CONCRETE-FILLED VOID
WOOD BLOCKING AT 16" O.C.
FLASHING
8" LONG WOOD BLOCKING AT 16" O.C.
FASCIA
CONTINUOUS SCREEN VENT

MANSARD ROOF

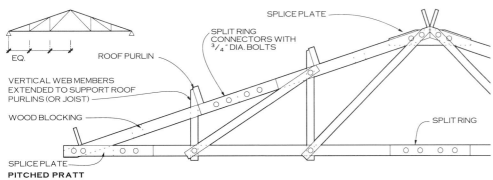

SPLICE PLATE
SPLIT RING CONNECTORS WITH ³/₄" DIA. BOLTS
ROOF PURLIN
VERTICAL WEB MEMBERS EXTENDED TO SUPPORT ROOF PURLINS (OR JOIST)
WOOD BLOCKING
SPLIT RING
SPLICE PLATE

PITCHED PRATT

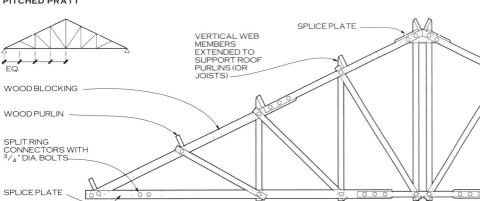

SPLICE PLATE
VERTICAL WEB MEMBERS EXTENDED TO SUPPORT ROOF PURLINS (OR JOISTS)
WOOD BLOCKING
WOOD PURLIN
SPLIT RING CONNECTORS WITH ³/₄" DIA. BOLTS
SPLICE PLATE

PITCHED HOWE

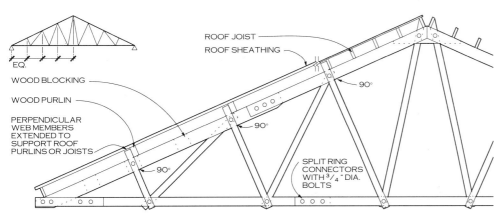

ROOF JOIST
ROOF SHEATHING
90°
WOOD BLOCKING
WOOD PURLIN
PERPENDICULAR WEB MEMBERS EXTENDED TO SUPPORT ROOF PURLINS OR JOISTS
90°
90°
SPLIT RING CONNECTORS WITH ³/₄" DIA. BOLTS

BELGIAN

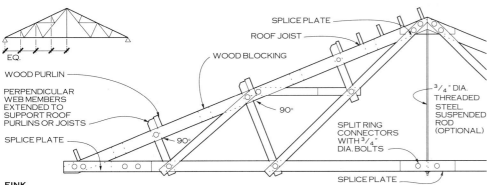

SPLICE PLATE
ROOF JOIST
WOOD BLOCKING
WOOD PURLIN
PERPENDICULAR WEB MEMBERS EXTENDED TO SUPPORT ROOF PURLINS OR JOISTS
SPLICE PLATE
90°
90°
SPLIT RING CONNECTORS WITH ³/₄" DIA. BOLTS
³/₄" DIA. THREADED STEEL. SUSPENDED ROD (OPTIONAL)
SPLICE PLATE

FINK

Pitched trusses are very economical for spans up to 70 ft (with an average spacing of 15 ft), since the member sizes are small, the joint details relatively simple, and the trusses easily fabricated.

All pitched trusses require either knee braces to columns or some other provision for lateral restraint against wind or other forces.

PITCHED TRUSSES

A typical span (l) / depth (d) ratio for the Pratt, Howe, or Belgian truss is 4 to 6, which gives a relatively normal slope of 4:12 to 6:12. Fink trusses are preferred where the slope is steep (over 7:12). Scissors trusses and other types of raised lower chord pitched roof trusses are used for special conditions where clearance or appearance requires an arched bottom chord. Consult with structural engineer to check deflection.

Richard J. Vitullo, Oak Leaf Studio; Crownsville, Maryland
TECO Products; Collier, West Virginia

GENERAL

The first wood trusses were developed for bridge design, with the kingpost truss the earliest form. It uses a primary engineering principle: a triangle will hold its shape under a load until its side members or its joints are crushed.

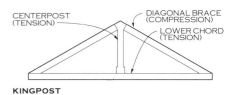

CENTERPOST (TENSION)
DIAGONAL BRACE (COMPRESSION)
LOWER CHORD (TENSION)

KINGPOST

Next came the queenpost truss, in which the peak of the kingpost was replaced by a horizontal crosspiece to allow a longer base.

QUEENPOST

Further amplifications permitted greater flexibility to overcome different spanning challenges and to integrate various combinations of inclined wood braces, wood arches, steel tension rods, etc.

NOTES

1. A built-in camber of approximately 1 in. per 40 ft span will be introduced in the top and bottom chords during fabrication.
2. When lumber is not adequately seasoned, the trusses should be inspected periodically and adjusted, if necessary, until moisture equilibrium is reached.
3. These truss designs are meant only as a guide. To develop specific designs, including bracing and anchorage, consult a structural engineer.

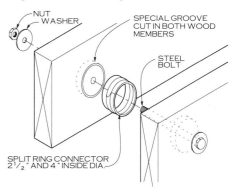

NUT
WASHER
SPECIAL GROOVE CUT IN BOTH WOOD MEMBERS
STEEL BOLT
SPLIT RING CONNECTOR 2¹/₂" AND 4" INSIDE DIA.

SPLIT RING CONNECTOR

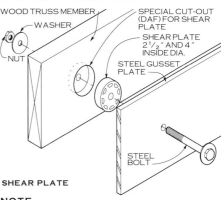

WOOD TRUSS MEMBER
WASHER
NUT
SPECIAL CUT-OUT (DAF) FOR SHEAR PLATE
SHEAR PLATE 2¹/₂" AND 4" INSIDE DIA.
STEEL GUSSET PLATE
STEEL BOLT

SHEAR PLATE

NOTE

Shear plate connectors are commonly used to connect wood truss members to steel gusset plates but may be used to connect wood to wood.

CONNECTORS

HEAVY TIMBER CONSTRUCTION ⑥

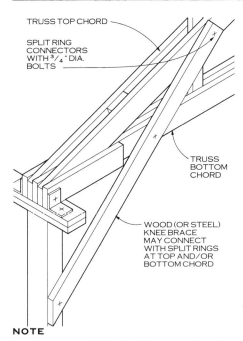

NOTE

Knee braces are useful where building supports depend on truss for stability.

DETAIL—KNEE BRACE

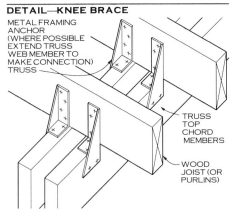

NOTE

Top chord lateral bracing is achieved by fastening roof sheathing to joists or purlins, which are securely fastened to the truss.

DETAIL—BRACE OF JOIST AND PURLIN

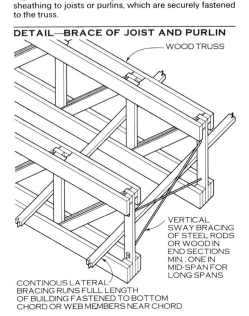

DETAIL—LATERAL AND VERTICAL

TECO Products; Collier, West Virginia
Richard J. Vitullo, Oak Leaf Studio; Crownsville, Maryland

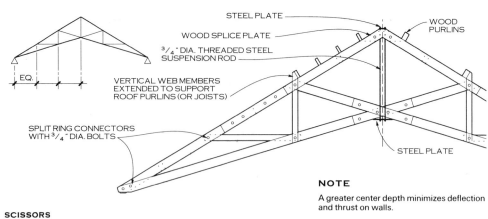

NOTE

A greater center depth minimizes deflection and thrust on walls.

SCISSORS

PITCHED TRUSSES

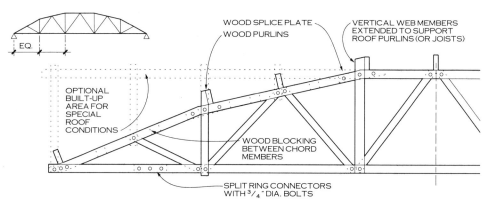

SEGMENTAL BOWSTRING

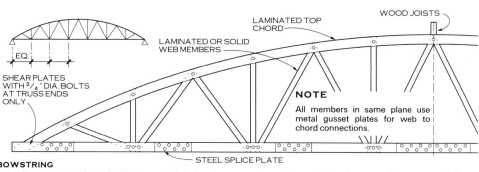

SEGMENTAL BOWSTRING

BOWSTRING

Bowstring trusses are theoretically the most efficient and economical of all wood truss types for larger spans, particularly over 80 ft, although spans up to 250 ft are obtainable. Connections are simple and designed to give minimum stresses to the web members. A typical span (1)/depth (d) ratio for bowstring trusses is 6 to 8.

Connections and knee brace requirements are similar to that of pitched trusses, since lateral load forces have a similar effect on them. The bottom chord members may also be glue laminated to eliminate splices.

BOWSTRING TRUSSES

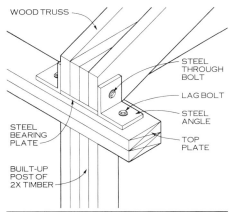

WOOD TRUSS

STEEL THROUGH BOLT

LAG BOLT

STEEL ANGLE

STEEL BEARING PLATE

TOP PLATE

BUILT-UP POST OF 2X TIMBER

DETAIL—STEEL ANGLE BRACE TO

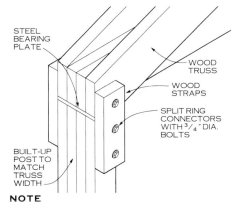

STEEL BEARING PLATE

WOOD TRUSS

WOOD STRAPS

SPLIT RING CONNECTORS WITH $3/4$" DIA. BOLTS

BUILT-UP POST TO MATCH TRUSS WIDTH

NOTE

End grain bearing of posts provides support for the truss.

DETAIL—WOOD STRAP AT WOOD

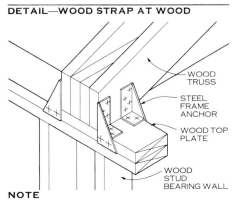

WOOD TRUSS

STEEL FRAME ANCHOR

WOOD TOP PLATE

WOOD STUD BEARING WALL

NOTE

This detail for use with light vertical and horizotal loads.

DETAIL—STEEL FRAMING ANCHOR

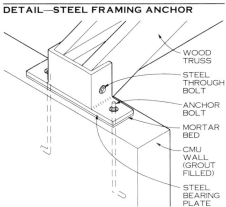

WOOD TRUSS

STEEL THROUGH BOLT

ANCHOR BOLT

MORTAR BED

CMU WALL (GROUT FILLED)

STEEL BEARING PLATE

NOTE

With scissor trusses, use slotted holes in steel to allow for thrust.

DETAIL—BEARING ON MASONRY WALL

TECO Products; Collier, West Virginia
Richard J. Vitullo, Oak Leaf Studio; Crownsville, Maryland

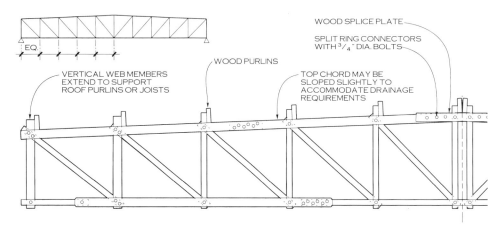

EQ.

VERTICAL WEB MEMBERS EXTEND TO SUPPORT ROOF PURLINS OR JOISTS

WOOD PURLINS

WOOD SPLICE PLATE

SPLIT RING CONNECTORS WITH $3/4$" DIA. BOLTS

TOP CHORD MAY BE SLOPED SLIGHTLY TO ACCOMMODATE DRAINAGE REQUIREMENTS

FLAT PRATT

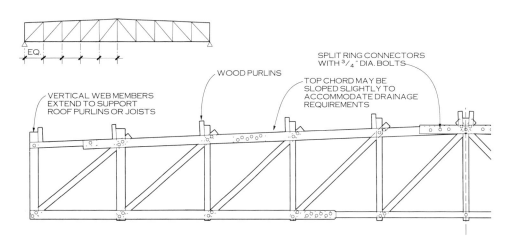

EQ.

VERTICAL WEB MEMBERS EXTEND TO SUPPORT ROOF PURLINS OR JOISTS

WOOD PURLINS

SPLIT RING CONNECTORS WITH $3/4$" DIA. BOLTS

TOP CHORD MAY BE SLOPED SLIGHTLY TO ACCOMMODATE DRAINAGE REQUIREMENTS

FLAT HOWE

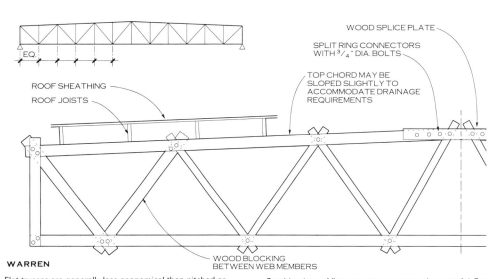

EQ.

ROOF SHEATHING

ROOF JOISTS

WOOD SPLICE PLATE

SPLIT RING CONNECTORS WITH $3/4$" DIA. BOLTS

TOP CHORD MAY BE SLOPED SLIGHTLY TO ACCOMMODATE DRAINAGE REQUIREMENTS

WOOD BLOCKING BETWEEN WEB MEMBERS

WARREN

Flat trusses are generally less economical than pitched or bowstring trusses, since connections are usually more complicated and higher side walls are required. But because of their geometry, flat trusses allow the smallest roof area versus pitched or bowstring trusses for the same span. As in pitched trusses, the maximum span for flat trusses is about 70 ft.

A typical span (1)/depth (d) ratio for all types of flat trusses is generally 8 to 10.

Combinations of flat truss types are sometimes useful. For instance, a truss may be built having one-half Pratt and one-half Howe design. Warren trusses may have ends of either Pratt or Howe designs incorporated, depending on the type of support. In general, Warren trusses are used for shorter spans.

Flat trusses do not require knee braces since the upper and lower chords take the place of a lateral brace.

FLAT TRUSSES

STRUCTURAL GLUED LAMINATED TIMBER

The term "structural glued laminated timber" refers to an engineered, stress-rated product made of wood laminations bonded with adhesives, with the grain approximately parallel lengthwise. Laminated pieces can be end-joined to form any length, or glued edge-to-edge to make wider pieces, or curved during gluing.

STANDARD DEPTHS

Dimensional lumber surfaced to 1 1/2 in. (38 mm) is used to laminate straight members and members that have a curvature within the bending radius limitations for the species. Boards surfaced to 3/4 in. (19 mm) are recommended for laminating curved members when bending radius is too short to permit the use of dimension lumber, provided that the bending radius limitations for the species are observed. Other lamination thicknesses may be used to meet special requirements.

STANDARD WIDTHS

Nom-inal width	in.	3	4	6	8	10	12	14	16
Net finished width	in.	2 1/8	3 1/8*	5 1/8*	6 3/4	8 3/4	10 3/4	12 1/4	14 1/4
	mm	57	79	130	171	222	273	311	362

* 3 in. and 5 in. for Southern pine

CAMBER

Camber is curvature (circular or parabolic) made into structural glued laminated beams opposite the anticipated deflection movement. The recommended minimum camber is one and one-half times dead load deflection. After plastic deformation has taken place, this usually will produce a near level floor or roof beam under dead load conditions. Additional camber or slope may insure adequate drainage of roof beams. On long-span roof beams and floor beams of multistory buildings, additional camber may be needed to counter the optical illusion of the beam sagging.

FIRE SAFETY

The self-insulating qualities of heavy timber cause a slow burning. Good structural details, elimination of concealed spaces, and use of vertical fire stops contribute to its fire performance. Heavy timber retains its strength under fire longer than unprotected metals.

Building codes generally classify glued laminated timber as heavy timber construction if certain minimum dimensional requirements are met.

Fire-retardant treatments do not substantially increase the fire resistance of heavy timber construction. In considering fire-retardant treatments, the reduction of strength related to type and penetration of treatment, the compatibility of treatment and adhesive, the use of special gluing procedures, the difficulty of application, and the effect on wood

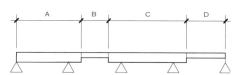

A - SINGLE CANTILEVER
B - SUSPENDED
C - DOUBLE CANTILEVER
D - SINGLE END SUSPENDED

CANTILEVERED AND CONTINUOUS SPAN

Cantilever beam systems may be composed of any of the various types and combinations of beams shown here. Cantilever systems generally permit longer spans or larger loads per size member than do simple span systems.

For economy, the negative bending moment at the support of a cantilevered beam should be equal in magnitude to the positive moment.

NOTE

More complicated shapes may be fabricated. Contact the American Institute of Timber Construction (AITC).

Richard J. Vitullo, Oak Leaf Studio; Crownsville, Maryland

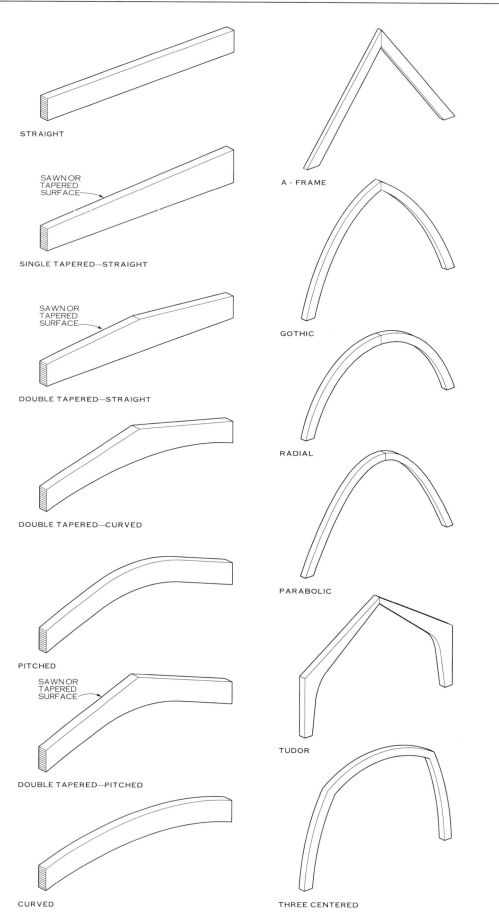

STRAIGHT

SINGLE TAPERED—STRAIGHT

DOUBLE TAPERED—STRAIGHT

DOUBLE TAPERED—CURVED

PITCHED

DOUBLE TAPERED—PITCHED

CURVED

A - FRAME

GOTHIC

RADIAL

PARABOLIC

TUDOR

THREE CENTERED

STRUCTURAL GLUED LAMINATED TIMBER SHAPES

ALLOWABLE UNIT STRESS RANGES FOR STRUCTURAL GLUED LAMINATED TIMBER – NORMAL DURATION OF LOADING

SPECIES	EXTREME FIBER IN BENDING	TENSION PARALLEL TO GRAIN	COMPRESSION PARALLEL TO GRAIN	HORIZONTAL SHEAR	COMPRESSION PERPENDICULAR TO GRAIN	MODULUS OF ELASTICITY
DRY CONDITIONS OF USE—MOISTURE CONTENT IN SERVICE LESS THAN 16%						
Douglas fir - larch	1600 TO 2400	900 TO 1600	1200 TO 2400	165	560 TO 650	1.5 TO 1.8
Hemlock fir	1600 TO 2400	800 TO 1400	975 TO 1750	155	375 TO 500	1.4 TO 1.5
Southern pine	1600 TO 2400	900 TO 1550	675 TO 2300	200	560 TO 650	1.4 TO 1.8
California redwood	1600	875 TO 1000	1350 TO 1600	125	315	1.1
WET CONDITIONS OF USE FACTORS—MOISTURE CONTENT IN SERVICE 16% OR MORE (REQUIRES WET-USE ADHESIVES)						
	0.800	0.800	0.730	0.875	0.530	0.833

NOTE

Multiply dry-condition-of-use stress ranges by the above factors for corresponding wet-conditions-of-use value.
For complete information see current American Institute of Timber Construction Publication AITC 117–Design.

LAMINATED FLOOR, ROOF BEAM, AND PURLIN DESIGN CHART
TYPICAL SINGLE-SPAN, SIMPLY SUPPORTED, GLUED LAMINATED BEAMS (MEMBER SIZES IN INCHES)

SPAN (FT)	SPACING (FT)	30 PSF	35 PSF	40 PSF	45 PSF	50 PSF	55 PSF	FLOOR BEAMS 50 PSF
		TOTAL LOAD CARRYING CAPACITY						
12	6	3 1/8 x 6	3 1/8 x 6	3 1/8 x 7 1/2	3 1/8 x 7 1/2	3 1/8 x 7 1/2	3 1/8 x 7 1/2	3 1/8 x 9
	8	3 1/8 x 6	3 1/8 x 7 1/2	3 1/8 x 9	3 1/8 x 9	3 1/8 x 9	3 1/8 x 9	3 1/8 x 10 1/2
	10	3 1/8 x 7 1/2	3 1/8 x 7 1/2	3 1/8 x 9	3 1/8 x 9	3 1/8 x 9	3 1/8 x 10 1/2	3 1/8 x 10 1/2
	12	3 1/8 x 7 1/2	3 1/8 x 9	3 1/8 x 9	3 1/8 x 9	3 1/8 x 10 1/2	3 1/8 x 10 1/2	3 1/8 x 9
16	8	3 1/8 x 9	3 1/8 x 9	3 1/8 x 10 1/2	3 1/8 x 10 1/2	3 1/8 x 12	3 1/8 x 12	3 1/8 x 13 1/2
	12	3 1/8 x 10 1/2	3 1/8 x 12	3 1/8 x 12	3 1/8 x 12	3 1/8 x 13 1/2	3 1/8 x 13 1/2	3 1/8 x 15
	14	3 1/8 x 12	3 1/8 x 12	3 1/8 x 13 1/2	3 1/8 x 13 1/2	3 1/8 x 15	3 1/8 x 15	3 1/8 x 15
	16	3 1/8 x 12	3 1/8 x 13 1/2	3 1/8 x 13 1/2	3 1/8 x 15	3 1/8 x 15	3 1/8 x 16 1/2	3 1/8 x 15
20	8	3 1/8 x 12	3 1/8 x 12	3 1/8 x 13 1/2	3 1/8 x 13 1/2	3 1/8 x 13 1/2	3 1/8 x 15	3 1/8 x 16 1/2
	12	3 1/8 x 13 1/2	3 1/8 x 13 1/2	3 1/8 x 15	3 1/8 x 16 1/2	3 1/8 x 16 1/2	5 1/8 x 13 1/2	5 1/8 x 15
	16	3 1/8 x 15	3 1/8 x 16 1/2	3 1/8 x 18	3 1/8 x 18	5 1/8 x 15	5 1/8 x 16 1/2	5 1/8 x 18
	20	3 1/8 x 16	3 1/8 x 18	5 1/8 x 15	5 1/8 x 16 1/2	5 1/8 x 16 1/2	5 1/8 x 18	5 1/8 x 18
24	8	3 1/8 x 13 1/2	3 1/8 x 15	3 1/8 x 15	3 1/8 x 16 1/2	3 1/8 x 16 1/2	3 1/8 x 18	5 1/8 x 19 1/2
	12	3 1/8 x 16 1/2	3 1/8 x 16 1/2	3 1/8 x 18	5 1/8 x 15	5 1/8 x 16 1/2	5 1/8 x 16 1/2	5 1/8 x 21
	16	3 1/8 x 18	5 1/8 x 16 1/2	5 1/8 x 16 1/2	5 1/8 x 18	5 1/8 x 18	5 1/8 x 19 1/2	5 1/8 x 24
	20	5 1/8 x 16 1/2	5 1/8 x 16 1/2	5 1/8 x 18	5 1/8 x 19 1/2	5 1/8 x 19 1/2	5 1/8 x 21	5 1/8 x 25 1/2
28	6	3 1/8 x 16 1/2	3 1/8 x 16 1/2	3 1/8 x 18	3 1/8 x 18	5 1/8 x 16 1/2	5 1/8 x 16 1/2	5 1/8 x 19 1/2
	8	3 1/8 x 18	5 1/8 x 16 1/2	5 1/8 x 18	5 1/8 x 18	5 1/8 x 18	5 1/8 x 19 1/2	5 1/8 x 21
	10	5 1/8 x 18	5 1/8 x 18	5 1/8 x 19 1/2	5 1/8 x 19 1/2	5 1/8 x 19 1/2	5 1/8 x 22 1/2	5 1/8 x 24
	12	5 1/8 x 18	5 1/8 x 19 1/2	5 1/8 x 21	5 1/8 x 22 1/2	5 1/8 x 21	5 1/8 x 25 1/2	5 1/8 x 25 1/2
32	8	3 1/8 x 18	5 1/8 x 16 1/2	5 1/8 x 18	5 1/8 x 18	5 1/8 x 18	5 1/8 x 19 1/2	5 1/8 x 21
	12	5 1/8 x 18	5 1/8 x 19 1/2	5 1/8 x 19 1/2	5 1/8 x 21	5 1/8 x 21	5 1/8 x 22 1/2	5 1/8 x 24
	16	5 1/8 x 19 1/2	5 1/8 x 21	5 1/8 x 22 1/2	5 1/8 x 22 1/2	5 1/8 x 24	5 1/8 x 25 1/2	5 1/8 x 27
	20	5 1/8 x 21	5 1/8 x 22 1/2	5 1/8 x 24	5 1/8 x 25 1/2	5 1/8 x 27	5 1/8 x 28 1/2	6 3/4 x 27
40	12	5 1/8 x 22 1/2	5 1/8 x 24	5 1/8 x 24	5 1/8 x 25 1/2	5 1/8 x 27	6 3/4 x 25 1/2	6 3/4 x 28 1/2
	16	5 1/8 x 24	5 1/8 x 25 1/2	5 1/8 x 27	5 1/8 x 28 1/2	6 3/4 x 27	6 3/4 x 28 1/2	6 3/4 x 31 1/2
	20	5 1/8 x 27	5 1/8 x 28 1/2	6 3/4 x 27	6 3/4 x 28 1/2	6 3/4 x 30	6 3/4 x 31 1/2	6 3/4 x 33
	24	5 1/8 x 28 1/2	6 3/4 x 27	6 3/4 x 28 1/2	6 3/4 x 31 1/2	6 3/4 x 33	6 3/4 x 34 1/2	6 3/4 x 36
48	12	5 1/8 x 27	5 1/8 x 28 1/2	5 1/8 x 30	5 1/8 x 30	6 3/4 x 28 1/2	6 3/4 x 30	6 3/4 x 33
	16	5 1/8 x 30	6 3/4 x 28 1/2	6 3/4 x 30	6 3/4 x 30	6 3/4 x 31 1/2	6 3/4 x 34 1/2	6 3/4 x 37 1/2
	20	6 3/4 x 28 1/2	6 3/4 x 30	6 3/4 x 31 1/2	6 3/4 x 34 1/2	6 3/4 x 36	6 3/4 x 37 1/2	8 3/4 x 36
	24	6 3/4 x 30	6 3/4 x 33	6 3/4 x 34 1/2	6 3/4 x 37 1/2	6 3/4 x 39	8 3/4 x 36	8 3/4 x 36
60	12	6 3/4 x 30	6 3/4 x 31 1/2	6 3/4 x 33	6 3/4 x 34 1/2	6 3/4 x 36	6 3/4 x 37 1/2	8 3/4 x 39
	16	6 3/4 x 33	6 3/4 x 34 1/2	6 3/4 x 36	6 3/4 x 39	8 3/4 x 36	8 3/4 x 37 1/2	8 3/4 x 42
	20	6 3/4 x 36	6 3/4 x 37 1/2	8 3/4 x 36	8 3/4 x 37 1/2	8 3/4 x 40 1/2	8 3/4 x 42	8 3/4 x 45
	24	6 3/4 x 39	8 3/4 x 36	8 3/4 x 39	8 3/4 x 42	8 3/4 x 43 1/2	8 3/4 x 45	8 3/4 x 48

APPEARANCE GRADES

Structural glued laminated timber is produced in three appearance grades that do not modify design stresses, fabrication controls, grades of lumber used, or other provisions of the applicable standards. A textured (rough sawn) surface may be called for instead of the surfacing described. In all grades, lamination will possess the natural growth characteristics of the lumber grade.

INDUSTRIAL APPEARANCE GRADE

Void filling on lamination edges is not required. The wide face of laminations exposed to view will be free of loose knots and open knot holes. Edge joints on the wide face will not be filled. Members will be surfaced on two sides only, an occasional miss being permitted.

ARCHITECTURAL APPEARANCE GRADE

On exposed surfaces, knot holes and other voids wider than 3/4 in. (19 mm) will be dressed with clear wood inserts or a wood-tone colored filler. Inserts will be selected for similarity of the grain and color to the adjacent wood. The wide face of laminations exposed to view will be free of loose knots and open knot holes; all voids greater than 1/16 in. (2 mm) wide in edge joints on this face will be filled. Exposed faces must be surface smooth. The corners on the wide face of laminations exposed to view will be eased. The current practice for eased edges is for a radius between 1/8 in. (3 mm) and 1/2 in. (13 mm).

PREMIUM APPEARANCE GRADE

Similar to architectural grade except that all knot holes and other voids on exposed surfaces will be replaced with wood inserts or a wood-tone colored filler. Remaining knots will be limited in size to 20% of the net face width of the lamination, with no more than two maximum size knots occurring in a 6 ft (1.8 m) length.

FINISHES

Glued laminated timber finishes include sealers, stains, and paints.

End sealers retard moisture transmission and minimize checking and normally are applied to the ends of all members.

Two types of surfaces protect against soiling, control grain raising, minimize checking, and serve as a moisture retardant. Penetrating sealers provide limited protection and are used when the final finish requires staining or a natural finish. Primer and sealer coats provide maximum protection by sealing the surface of the wood but should not be specified for a natural or stained final finish. Wood color is modified by any sealer application; therefore, wood sealers followed by staining will look different from stained untreated wood.

Richard J. Vitullo, Oak Leaf Studio; Crownsville, Maryland

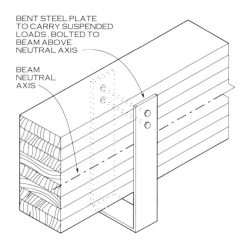

NOTE

Very light loads may be placed near bottom of beam; however; the heavier the load the higher on the beam the suspension points should be located.

SUSPENDED LOAD – BENT PLATE ATTACHED TO SIDE

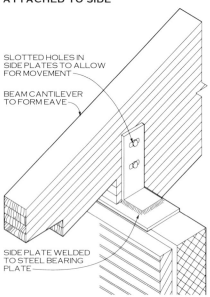

RAFTER TO BEARING WALL

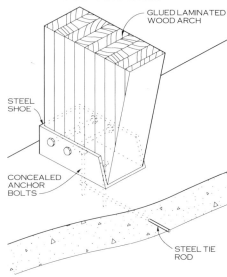

ARCH SHOE DETAIL

Richard J. Vitullo, Oak Leaf Studio; Crownsville, Maryland

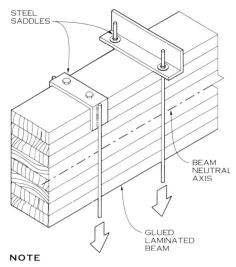

NOTE

This detail is recommended for use with heavy loads.

SUSPENDED LOAD – SADDLE CONDITION

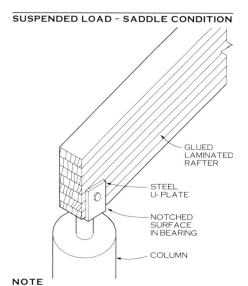

NOTE

An abrupt notch in the end of a wood member reduces the effective shear strength of the member and may permit a more rapid migration of moisture in the lower portion of the member causing potential splitting.

NOTCHED BEARING CONDITION

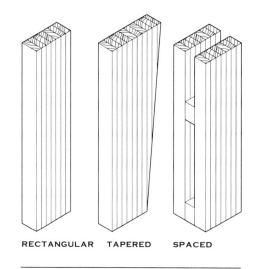

RECTANGULAR   TAPERED   SPACED

GLUED LAMINATED COLUMNS

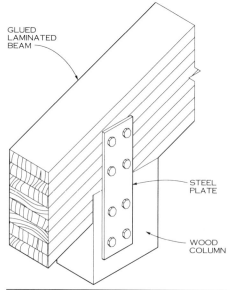

RAFTER TO COLUMN CONDITION

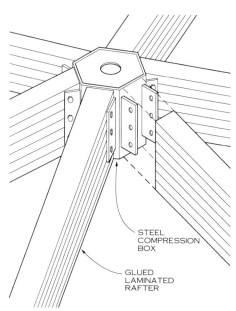

STEEL COMPRESSION BOX

CONNECTION DESIGN

The design of connections for glued laminated timber and sawn timber is similar. Glued laminated timbers and their loads, however, often are much larger than sawn lumber, so the effect of increased size should be taken into account in the design.

Used to add strength to transfer loads, connections should be designed to avoid splitting and to accommodate swelling and shrinking.

GLUED LAMINATED COLUMNS

Structural glued laminated timber columns offer higher allowable stresses, controlled appearance, and the ability to fabricate variable sections. For simple rectangular columns, the slenderness ratio (the ratio of the unsupported length between points of lateral support to the least column dimension) may not exceed 50. The least dimension for tapered columns is the sum of the smaller dimension and one-third the difference between the smaller and greater dimensions. Spaced columns consist of two or more members with longitudinal axes parallel, separated at the ends and at the midpoint by blocking, and joined at the ends by shear fastenings. The members act together to carry the total column load; because of the end fixity developed, a greater slenderness ratio than allowed for solid columns is permitted.

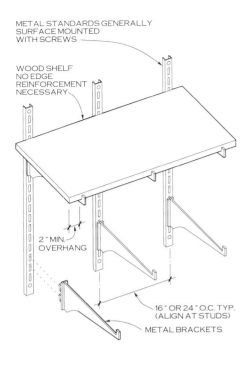

METAL STANDARDS GENERALLY
SURFACE MOUNTED
WITH SCREWS

WOOD SHELF
NO EDGE
REINFORCEMENT
NECESSARY

2 " MIN.
OVERHANG

16 " OR 24 " O.C. TYP.
(ALIGN AT STUDS)

METAL BRACKETS

STANDARDS AND BRACKETS SYSTEM

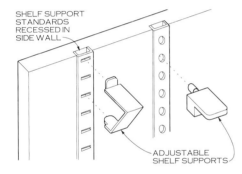

SHELF SUPPORT
STANDARDS
RECESSED IN
SIDE WALL

ADJUSTABLE
SHELF SUPPORTS

STANDARDS AND CLIP SYSTEM

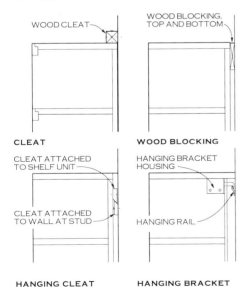

WOOD CLEAT

WOOD BLOCKING,
TOP AND BOTTOM

CLEAT

WOOD BLOCKING

CLEAT ATTACHED
TO SHELF UNIT

HANGING BRACKET
HOUSING

CLEAT ATTACHED
TO WALL AT STUD

HANGING RAIL

HANGING CLEAT

HANGING BRACKET

NOTE

All details except hanging bracket and rail must also be
floor supported.

BOOKSHELF WALL ATTACHMENT

Richard J. Vitullo, Oak Leaf Studio; Crownsville, Maryland
Helmut Guenschel, Inc. ; Baltimore, Maryland

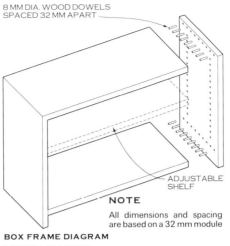

8 MM DIA. WOOD DOWELS
SPACED 32 MM APART

ADJUSTABLE
SHELF

NOTE

All dimensions and spacing
are based on a 32 mm module

BOX FRAME DIAGRAM

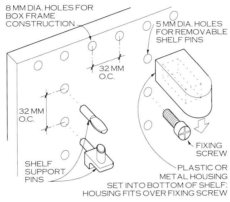

8 MM DIA. HOLES FOR
BOX FRAME
CONSTRUCTION

5 MM DIA. HOLES
FOR REMOVABLE
SHELF PINS

32 MM
O.C.

32 MM
O.C.

SHELF
SUPPORT
PINS

FIXING
SCREW

PLASTIC OR
METAL HOUSING
SET INTO BOTTOM OF SHELF;
HOUSING FITS OVER FIXING SCREW

32 MM BOX FRAME SYSTEM

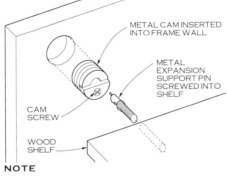

METAL CAM INSERTED
INTO FRAME WALL

METAL
EXPANSION
SUPPORT PIN
SCREWED INTO
SHELF

CAM
SCREW

WOOD
SHELF

NOTE

This system can be hand mounted or machine inserted. A
half turn of the cam screw tightens connection and prevents disassembly.

SEMI-FIXED FRAME/SHELF DETAIL

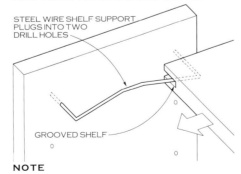

STEEL WIRE SHELF SUPPORT
PLUGS INTO TWO
DRILL HOLES

GROOVED SHELF

NOTE

This system can be used for horizontal shelf attachment or
vertical divider support.

REMOVABLE GROOVED SHELF DETAIL

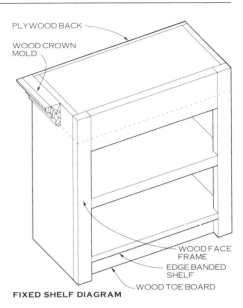

PLYWOOD BACK

WOOD CROWN
MOLD

WOOD FACE
FRAME

EDGE BANDED
SHELF

WOOD TOE BOARD

FIXED SHELF DIAGRAM

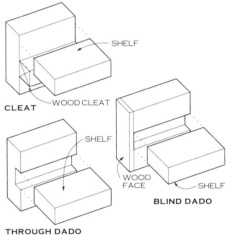

SHELF

CLEAT

WOOD CLEAT

SHELF

WOOD
FACE

SHELF

BLIND DADO

THROUGH DADO

SUPPORT DETAILS AT SIDE

FIXED SHELF SYSTEM

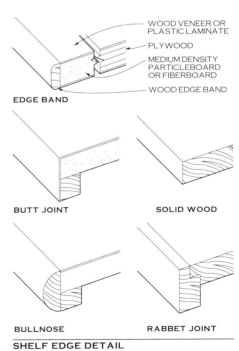

WOOD VENEER OR
PLASTIC LAMINATE

PLYWOOD

MEDIUM DENSITY
PARTICLEBOARD
OR FIBERBOARD

WOOD EDGE BAND

EDGE BAND

BUTT JOINT

SOLID WOOD

BULLNOSE

RABBET JOINT

SHELF EDGE DETAIL

CHARACTERISTICS

The European-style kitchen cabinet system is based on the ability of the whole cabinet assembly to be easily installed, adjusted, or broken down and moved like furniture.

Wall cabinets are typically hung from a metal bracket attached at each top corner and then placed on a metal support rail attached to the finished wall. Adjustment can occur in three directions for plumb and level after the cabinet is hung; the adjustment mechanism, which is actually the back of the hanging bracket, is exposed on the inside of the cabinet. Above the cabinets, either no soffit is built, allowing over-cabinet storage, or an allowance of 3/4 in. clear is needed, so the cabinet can be lifted up and set down over the metal support rail.

The base cabinets are generally not secured to the wall or floor but are set onto metal or PVC legs, four per cabinet, which are adjustable for leveling. A removable toe kick panel allows for further adjustment to the legs or for cleaning. For island installations or peninsula cabinets, the leveling leg system should be augmented with traditional wood blocking as an anchor.

The construction and features of the cabinet itself differ from a typical American-style cabinet as follows:

1. The carcass is frameless and is put together by dowels running from the side panels into the top and bottom panels.
2. Sizes are based on a 32 mm module system. Dowels are drilled 32 mm apart, center posts dividing cabinets in half are 32 mm deep, shelves and carcass parts are 16 mm (1/2 module), etc.
3. Predrilled holes in the side panels accommodate shelf supports for the adjustable shelves.
4. Concealed cup hinges allow near 180° opening of cabinet doors; some varieties are also adjustable in three directions.
5. An increased toe-kick height (6 to 9 in.) can accommodate a drawer under base cabinets.

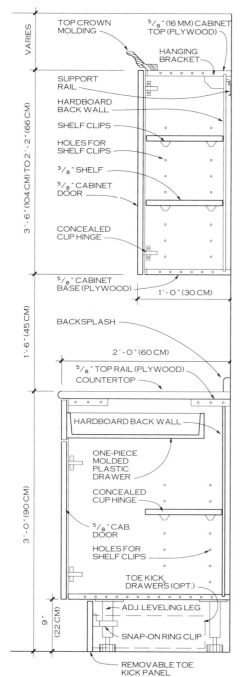

SECTION THROUGH BASE AND WALL

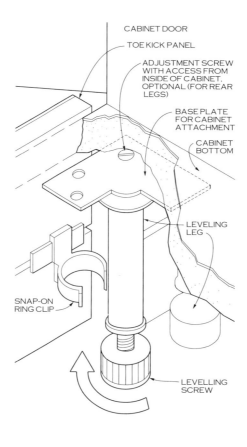

LEVELING LEG/TOE KICK PANEL DETAIL

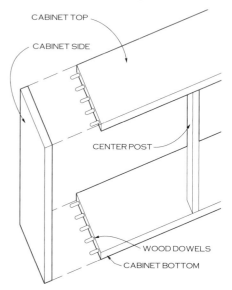

DOWELED CABINET CONSTRUCTION

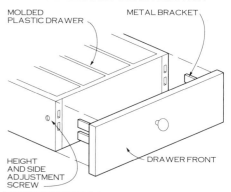

DRAWER DETAIL

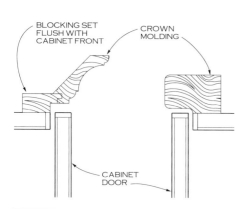

TOP CROWN MOLDING DETAILS

Richard J. Vitullo, Oak Leaf Studio; Crownsville, Maryland

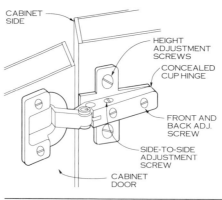

CONCEALED CUP HINGE

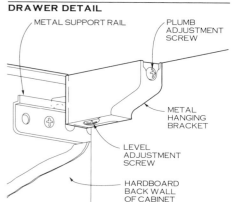

HANGING BRACKET AND RAIL DETAIL

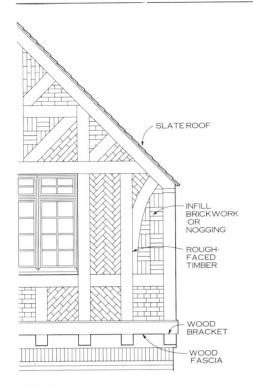

GENERAL

In the 16th and 17th centuries half timber structures were built with strong timber foundations, supports, and studs. The spaces between the framework were filled in with either stone, brick, plaster, or boarding laid horizontally. Today the primary structure is wood stud or masonry backup, and the half timber construction is attached as veneer. Half timber is an inherently leaky type of wall construction in which the timbers are subject to premature decay.

NOTE

Shown are some of many brick infill panel design types.

ELEVATION – BRICK AND TIMBER

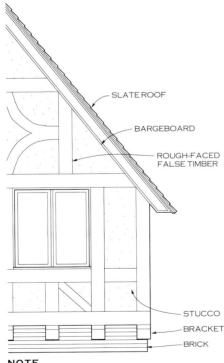

NOTE

To preserve historical character of half-timber construction a ridge vent is recommended for attic venting.

ELEVATION – STUCCO AND TIMBER

Richard J. Vitullo, Oak Leaf Studio; Crownsville, Maryland

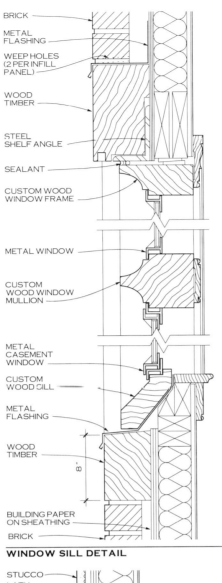

WINDOW SILL DETAIL

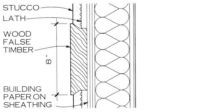

FALSE TIMBER DETAIL

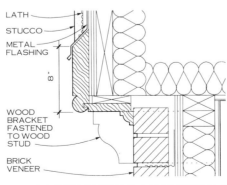

OVERHANG DETAIL

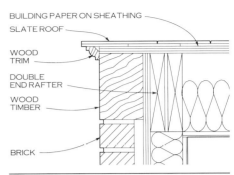

GABLE EDGE DETAIL

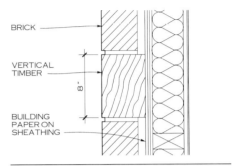

TIMBER DETAIL

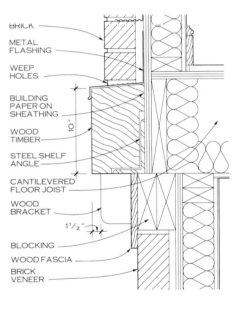

TIMBER SHELF DETAIL

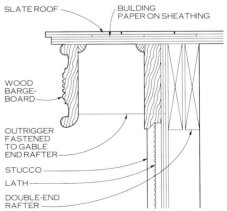

BARGEBOARD DETAIL

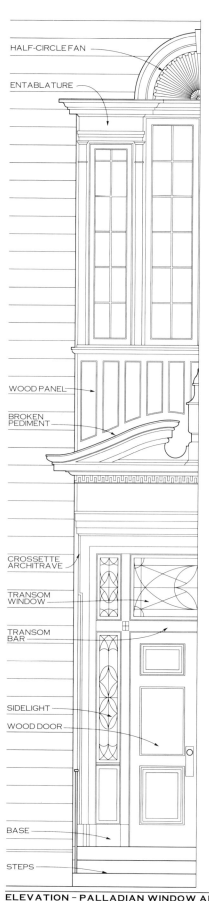

ALTERNATE ELEVATION – HALF-CIRCLE WINDOW

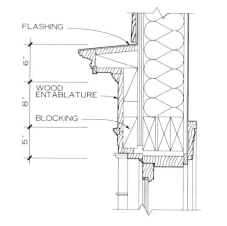

ENTABLATURE SECTION

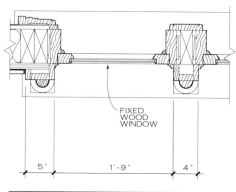

WINDOW PLAN

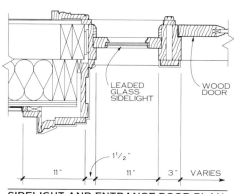

SIDELIGHT AND ENTRANCE DOOR PLAN

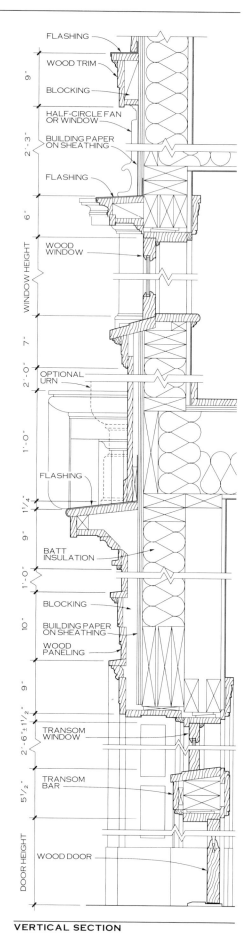

VERTICAL SECTION

ELEVATION – PALLADIAN WINDOW AND DOORWAY

Richard J. Vitullo, Oak Leaf Studio; Crownsville, Maryland

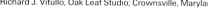

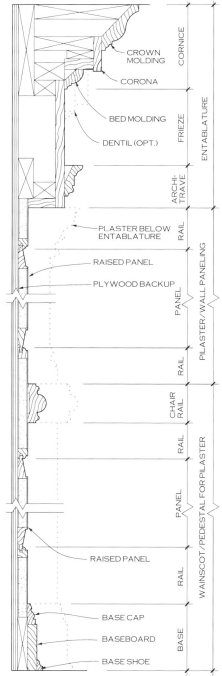

CROWN MOLDING

CORONA

BED MOLDING

DENTIL (OPT.)

PLASTER BELOW ENTABLATURE

RAISED PANEL

PLYWOOD BACKUP

RAISED PANEL

BASE CAP

BASEBOARD

BASE SHOE

CORNICE

FRIEZE

ARCHITRAVE

ENTABLATURE

RAIL

PANEL

RAIL

CHAIR RAIL

RAIL

PANEL

RAIL

BASE

PILASTER/WALL PANELING

WAINSCOT/PEDESTAL FOR PILASTER

NOTES

1. Because of its stability, plywood is preferable to solid lumber or other materials as backup.

2. To join stile to rail, mortise and tenon or dowelled joints are used. Stile to stile joints at outside corners are spline joints or lock miters; inside corners are butt jointed.

SECTION – FULL HEIGHT WALL PANEL

INTERIOR WALL PANEL DETAILS

Architectural interior paneling consists of a series of thin sheets of wood (panels) framed together by means of stouter strips of wood, vertical (stiles) and horizontal (rails), to form either a door, screen, or lining for internal walls. Paneling was first used as a wall covering in England in the 13th century. Up to the 16th century, the framing was almost as massive as half-timber construction. Then it was progressively lightened until by the middle of that century when the thickness of the framing was reduced to an inch. Today, inch thick or less panels are made from veneers over plywood or composition boards, which can be treated for fire protection. The stiles and rails are made from solid wood or veneered boards. Rim and lip moldings and other trims are almost exclusively made from solid wood.

Richard J. Vitullo, Oak Leaf Studio; Crownsville, Maryland
Architectural Woodwork Institute; Arlington, Virginia.

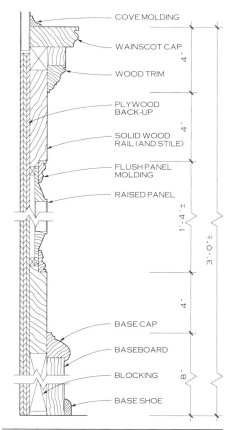

COVE MOLDING

WAINSCOT CAP

WOOD TRIM

PLYWOOD BACK-UP

SOLID WOOD RAIL (AND STILE)

FLUSH PANEL MOLDING

RAISED PANEL

BASE CAP

BASEBOARD

BLOCKING

BASE SHOE

SECTION – WAINSCOT WITH RAISED PANEL AND FLUSH MOLDING

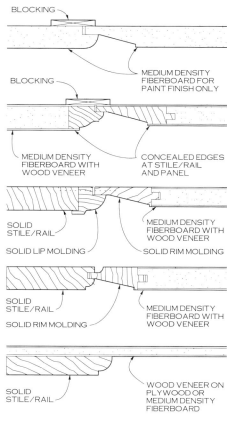

BLOCKING

BLOCKING

MEDIUM DENSITY FIBERBOARD FOR PAINT FINISH ONLY

MEDIUM DENSITY FIBERBOARD WITH WOOD VENEER

CONCEALED EDGES AT STILE/RAIL AND PANEL

SOLID STILE/RAIL

SOLID LIP MOLDING

MEDIUM DENSITY FIBERBOARD WITH WOOD VENEER

SOLID RIM MOLDING

SOLID STILE/RAIL

SOLID RIM MOLDING

MEDIUM DENSITY FIBERBOARD WITH WOOD VENEER

SOLID STILE/RAIL

WOOD VENEER ON PLYWOOD OR MEDIUM DENSITY FIBERBOARD

STILE/RAIL TO PANEL JOINERY TYPES

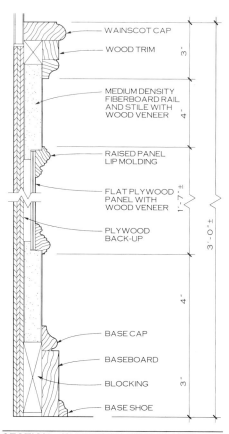

WAINSCOT CAP

WOOD TRIM

MEDIUM DENSITY FIBERBOARD RAIL AND STILE WITH WOOD VENEER

RAISED PANEL LIP MOLDING

FLAT PLYWOOD PANEL WITH WOOD VENEER

PLYWOOD BACK-UP

BASE CAP

BASEBOARD

BLOCKING

BASE SHOE

SECTION – WAINSCOT WITH FLUSH PANEL AND RAISED MOLDING

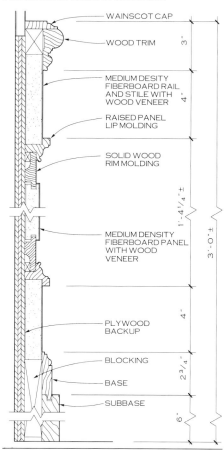

WAINSCOT CAP

WOOD TRIM

MEDIUM DESITY FIBERBOARD RAIL AND STILE WITH WOOD VENEER

RAISED PANEL LIP MOLDING

SOLID WOOD RIM MOLDING

MEDIUM DENSITY FIBERBOARD PANEL WITH WOOD VENEER

PLYWOOD BACKUP

BLOCKING

BASE

SUBBASE

SECTION – WAINSCOT WITH RAISED PANEL AND RAISED MOLDING

STRUCTURAL PLASTICS

Structural plastic is a composite of a continuous reinforcing mat embedded in a resin. Usually there is a synthetic surfacing veil over the composite. Many additives are available depending on the particular requirements of the product. The final product is usually coated with a UV inhibitor to preserve color and reduce degradation. The reinforcing mat may be made of one of the following common materials:

1. GLASS FIBERS for cost-effective applications

2. CARBON FIBERS for high strength applications

3. POLYESTER FIBERS for high bending applications

4. ARAMID FIBERS for security applications.

There are several resins used in structural plastics, with many variations and additives for specific needs. Resins are broadly categorized into two types:

1. THERMOPLASTIC, which can be reshaped

2. THERMOSET, which cannot be reshaped.

Most mass produced fiber reinforced plastic (FRP) structural shapes are thermoset. There are several common resin types:

1. ISOPTHALTIC BASED RESIN

2. VINYL ESTER RESIN

3. EPOXY RESIN.

Custom fabrication recipes are possible. Color is created by adding pigment to the recipe therefore color is throughout the shape. Other common additives are a flame retardant and an ultraviolet light inhibitor to reduce color fade and degradation.

The surfacing veil is an outer coating of resin to prevent water absorption and "fiber blooming," which is the eruption of reinforcing fibers through the surface of the shape.

Standard industry colors designate special characteristics of the structural shape. Standard colors are as follows:

1. OLIVE GREEN—no flame retardant or UV inhibitor
2. GREY—flame retardant and UV inhibitor
3. BEIGE—vinyl ester resin with flame retardant and UV inhibitor.

STRUCTURAL PLASTICS ADVANTAGES

1. LIGHT WEIGHT – 30% less than aluminum

2. CORROSION RESISTANT – will not rot; impervious to many chemicals

3. NONCONDUCTIVE – thermally and electrically a good insulator

4. NONMAGNETIC – radio frequency transparent

5. HIGH STRENGTH – stronger per pound than steel

6. DIMENSIONALLY STABLE – expands less than steel.

STRUCTURAL PLASTICS DISADVANTAGES

1. TEMPERATURE – cannot stand sustained temperatures in excess of 200° F.

2. CORROSION – susceptible to degradation by certain chemicals; will contaminate potable water.

3. WATER ABSORPTION – because it is a composite, shapes are susceptible to wicking action. Once water has been absorbed into a shape, its electrical insulation qualities are reduced.

4. STIFFNESS – more elastic than steel; deflection often requires use of larger shapes.

5. COST – substantially more than structural steel.

6. COMBUSTIBLE – if untreated.

TYPES OF STRUCTURAL PLASTICS

Fiberglass floor gratings are perhaps the most widespread structural application for plastics. The process of fabricating gratings has advanced to what is known as pultrusion, which allows for controlled placement of fiber reinforcing and shaping of the product. In pultrusion fibers are pulled through a bath of liquid resin and shaped and wrapped into specific shapes before curing.

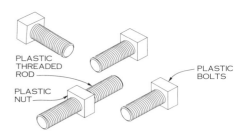

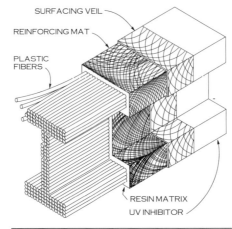

PULTRUSION PROCESS EXPLODED

Pultrusion allows fiber reinforced plastic (FRP) shapes to be fabricated similarly to steel or aluminum structural shapes.

WORKABILITY

Structural plastics can be cut and shaped much like wood. Care must be taken to seal cut ends with a compatible resin equal to that used in fabrication. Connections are made with bolts or with bolts and epoxy adhesive where disassembly is not anticipated.

USES OF STRUCTURAL PLASTICS

Water applications: where structural elements are constantly exposed to water, as in off-shore drilling rigs, waste-water treatment facilities, and cooling towers.

Severe environment applications: where corrosive chemicals, caustic fumes, or electrolysis processes are used, such as chemical plants, paper mills, and mining and plating operations.

Electrical applications: where high voltage equipment is used or the potential for lightning is high.

Lightweight applications: where weight and/or ease of erection is critical, such as in exhibits, temporary structures, mezzanines.

High-tech applications: where interference with magnetic fields or radio frequency transmissions is unacceptable.

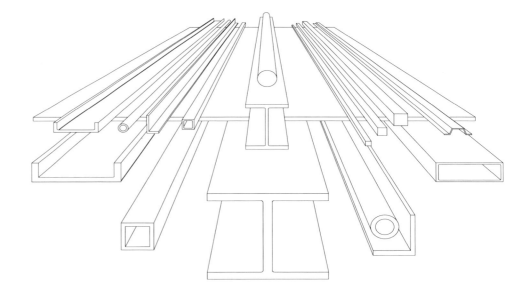

STRUCTURAL PLASTIC SHAPES

SHAPE DESIGNATION	MINIMUM SIZE		MAXIMUM SIZE	
Equal leg angles	1 x $^1/_8$	.17 lb/ft	6 x $^3/_8$	3.44 lb/ft
Channels	2 x $^9/_{16}$ x $^1/_8$	.26 lb/ft	18 x 2 x $^3/_{16}$	3.8 lb/ft
Beams	3 x 1$^1/_2$ x $^1/_4$	1.1 lb/ft	12 x 6 x $^1/_2$	9.24 lb/ft
Round tube	1 x $^1/_8$	.25 lb/ft	10 x $^3/_{16}$	4.5 lb/ft
Square tube	1 x $^1/_8$	.32 lb/ft	4 x $^1/_4$	3.08 lb/ft
Rectangular tube	4 x 2 x $^1/_8$	1.52 lb/ft	9 x 11 x $^3/_4$	23.3 lb/ft
Square bar	$^1/_2$	.22 lb/ft	1 $^1/_2$	1.91 lb/ft
Rod	$^1/_4$	.043 lb/ft	2	2.69 lb/ft
Plate	$^1/_8$	1.14 lb/sq. ft	1	9.27 lb/sq. ft

Laird Ueberroth, Architect, and Associates; McLean, Virginia

STRUCTURAL PLASTIC

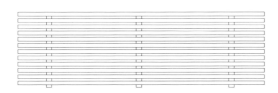

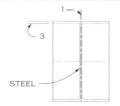
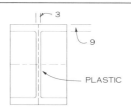

STEEL   PLASTIC

FIBERGLASS REINFORCED PLASTIC GRATINGS

Gratings and treads are one of the most common uses of structural plastics. In corrosive environments they can last up to 20 times longer than steel. Current grating designs are the fifth generation of a rapidly evolving FRP technology. Most of fiber bloom, excessive movement of components, delamination, UV degradation, and chipping problems have been solved.

Maximum panel size 60 ˝ x 240 ˝

2 INCH GRATING   1.5 INCH GRATING   1 INCH GRATING

GRATING PROFILES

BAR DEPTH (IN.)	BAR CENTERS (IN.)	NO. OF BARS PER FOOT	BAR (%) OPEN AREA	APPROX. WEIGHT (LB/SQ FT)
1	1	8	60	2.3
1.5	1	8	60	3.3
2	1	6	50	3.1

LOAD DEFLECTION TABLE

1 INCH BEARING BARS

SPAN					LOAD/DEFLECTION						MAX. LOAD
2 FT	U	200	300	500	750	1000	1250	1500	2000	2500	2,900 lb
	Δ	.05	.08	.12	.19	.25	.31	.373	.498	.622	.721 in
	C	200	300	500	750	1000	1250	1500	2000	2500	2,900 lb
	Δ	.04	.06	.10	.15	.199	.249	.298	.398	.498	.577 in
3 FT	U	67	133	200	267	333	500	667	833		1,287 lb
	Δ	.08	.15	.23	.31	.38	.58	.77	.98		1.48 in
	C	100	200	300	400	500	750	1000	1250		1,933 lb
	Δ	.06	.12	.18	.25	.30	.46	.614	.766		1.18 in
5 FT	U	40	80	120							453 lb
	Δ	.34	.68	1.0							3.9 in
	C	100	200	300							1,018 lb
	Δ	.27	.55	.82							3.1 in

1.5 INCH BEARING BARS

SPAN					LOAD/DEFLECTION						MAX. LOAD
2 FT	U	200	300	500	750	1000	1250	1500	2000	3000	4,400 lb
	Δ	.02	.03	.05	.07	.09	.114	.138	.183	.274	.402 in
	C	200	300	500	750	1000	1250	1500	2000	3000	4,400 lb
	Δ	.02	.02	.04	.06	.07	.09	.11	.146	.219	.321 in
3 FT	U	67	133	200	267	333	500	667	833	1000	1,896 lb
	Δ	.03	.06	.09	.12	.15	.22	.23	.36	.439	.826 in
	C	100	200	300	400	500	750	1000	1250	1500	2,844 lb
	Δ	.02	.05	.07	.09	.11	.17	.233	.290	.349	.661 in
5 FT	U	40	80	120	160	200	300	400			608 lb
	Δ	.13	.26	.38	.51	.64	.96	1.3			1.94 in
	C	100	200	300	400	500	750	1000			1,520 lb
	Δ	.10	.20	.30	.40	.51	.77	1.02			1.55 in

2 INCH BEARING BARS

SPAN					LOAD/DEFLECTION						MAX. LOAD
2 FT	U	200	300	500	750	1000	1250	1500	2000	3000	5,667 lb
	Δ	.01	.02	.03	.04	.054	.067	.080	.107	.161	.303 in
	C	200	300	500	750	1000	1250	1500	2000	3000	5,667 lb
	Δ	.01	.01	.02	.03	.043	.054	.064	.086	.128	.243 in
3 FT	U	67	133	200	267	333	500	667	833	100	2,519 lb
	Δ	.02	.04	.05	.07	.09	.13	.17	.22	.26	.654 in
	C	100	200	300	400	500	750	1000	1250	1500	3,778 lb
	Δ	.01	.03	.04	.06	.07	.10	.14	.17	.20	.524 in
5 FT	U	40	80	120	160	200	300	400	500		907 lb
	Δ	.08	.15	.23	.30	.38	.56	.75	.94		1.70 in
	C	100	200	300	400	500	750	1000	1250		2,267 lb
	Δ	.06	.12	.18	.24	.30	.45	.60	.75		1.36 in

U= Uniform load, C= Concentrated load, Δ= Deflection

Consult with structural engineer familiar with their unique properties before specifying structural plastics.

Laird Ueberroth, Architect and Associates, McLean, Virginia.

STEEL VS. PLASTIC STRUCTURAL SHAPES

FRP shapes have approximately one fifth the weight of steel but over one third the strength. This means an FRP shape equal in strength to a steel shape would weigh only slightly more than half the steel shape. Structural plastic shapes are generally continuously extruded (or pultruded), so length is a factor of transportability rather than fabrication. Durability is a function of the environment. Exposure to chemicals and intensity of sunlight affect the lifespan of structural plastics.

FIBERGLASS REINFORCED PLASTIC WIDE FLANGE BEAM LOAD TABLE
ALLOWABLE UNIFORM LOADS IN POUNDS PER FOOT

W SHAPE	SPAN IN FT	LATERALLY UNSUPPORTED Fʙ'	W	LATERALLY SUPPORTED DEFLECTION L/180	L/240	L/360
6 x 6 x ¹/₄	8	3761	369	303	227	152
	10	2507	158	171	128	86
	12	1823	80	105	79	52
	14	1407	45	69	51	34
8 x 8 x ³/₈	8	5074	1020	884	663	442
	10	4379	724	525	394	263
	12	3150	362	333	250	167
	14	2405	203	223	167	111
10 x 10 x ³/₈	12	3630	961	905	679	452
	16	2620	271	289	217	144
	20	1756	116	159	119	80
	24	1284	59	96	72	48
12 x 12 x ¹/₂	16	3761	739	606	454	303
	20	2507	316	342	257	171
	24	1823	159	210	157	105
	28	1407	90	137	103	69

FIBERGLASS REINFORCED PLASTIC CHANNEL LOAD TABLE
ALLOWABLE UNIFORM LOADS IN POUNDS PER FOOT

C SHAPE	SPAN IN FT	Fʙ'	LATERALLY SUPPORTED DEFLECTION L/150	L/180	L/240	L/360
4 x 1¹/₁₆ x ¹/₈	4	353	193	160	120	80
	6	191	64	54	40	27
	8	107	28	24	18	12
	10	69	15	12	9	6
6 x 1⁵/₈ x ¹/₄	6	690	376	314	235	157
	8	469	174	145	109	73
	10	300	93	78	58	39
	12	208	55	46	35	23
8 x 2³/₁₆ x ¹/₄	8	705	390	325	244	163
	10	555	216	180	135	90
	12	386	131	109	82	54
	14	283	85	70	53	35
10 x 2³/₄ x ¹/₂	8	1688	1290	1075	807	538
	10	1350	736	613	460	307
	12	1125	454	378	284	189
	14	830	298	248	186	124

Consult with structrual engineer familiar with their unique properties before specifying structural plastics

STRUCTURAL PLASTICS SPECIFICATIONS

ASTM-F 1092-87	Fiberglass Handrail Specification
ASTM-D 3917	Standard Specification for Dimensional Tolerances of Thermosetting Glass-Reinforced Plastic Pultruded Shapes
ASTM-D 3918	Standard Definition of Terms Relating to Reinforced Plastic Pultruded Products
ASTM-D 3647	Standard Practice for Classifying Reinforced Plastic Pultruded Shapes According to Composition
ASTM-D 4385	Standard Practice for Classifying Visual Defects in Thermosetting Reinforced Plastic Pultruded Products
ASTM-E 84	Flame Rating
ASTM-D 635	Self Extinguishing

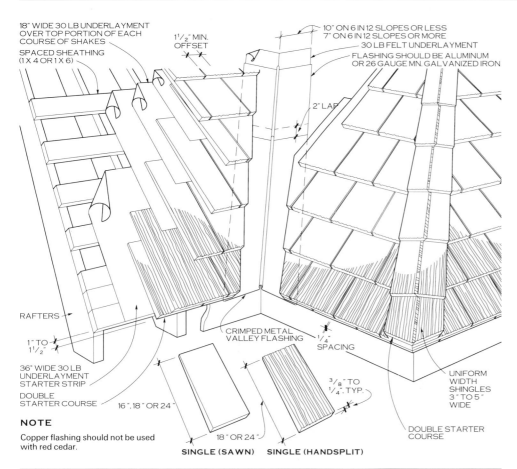

18" WIDE 30 LB UNDERLAYMENT OVER TOP PORTION OF EACH COURSE OF SHAKES

SPACED SHEATHING (1 X 4 OR 1 X 6)

1 1/2" MIN. OFFSET

10" ON 6 IN 12 SLOPES OR LESS
7" ON 6 IN 12 SLOPES OR MORE
30 LB FELT UNDERLAYMENT
FLASHING SHOULD BE ALUMINUM OR 26 GAUGE MN. GALVANIZED IRON

2" LAP

RAFTERS

1" TO 1 1/2"

36" WIDE 30 LB UNDERLAYMENT STARTER STRIP

DOUBLE STARTER COURSE

16", 18" OR 24"

CRIMPED METAL VALLEY FLASHING

1/4" SPACING

3/8" TO 1/4". TYP.

UNIFORM WIDTH SHINGLES 3" TO 5" WIDE

DOUBLE STARTER COURSE

NOTE

Copper flashing should not be used with red cedar.

18" OR 24"

SINGLE (SAWN)   SINGLE (HANDSPLIT)

RED CEDAR HANDSPLIT SHAKES

RED CEDAR HANDSPLIT SHAKES

GRADE	LENGTH AND THICKNESS	DESCRIPTION
No. 1 handsplit and resawn	15" starter-finish 18 x 1/2" medium 18 x 3/4" heavy 24 x 3/8" 24 x 1/2" medium 24 x 3/4" heavy	These shakes have split faces and sawn backs. Cedar logs are first cut into desired lengths. Blanks or boards of proper thickness are split and then run diagonally through a bandsaw to produce two tapered shakes from each blank.
No. 1 tapersplit	24 x 1/2"	Produced largely by hand, using a sharp bladed steel froe and a wooden mallet. The natural shinglelike taper is achieved by reversing the block, end-for-end, with each split.
No. 1 straight	18 x 3/8" side wall 18 x 3/8" 24 x 3/8"	Produced in the same manner as tapersplit shakes except that by splitting from the same end of the block, the shakes acquire the same thickness throughout.

RED CEDAR SHINGLES

	NO. 1 BLUE LABEL			NO. 2 RED LABEL			NO. 3 BLACK LABEL		
MAXIMUM EXPOSURE RECOMMENDED FOR ROOFS (IN.)									
ROOF PITCH	16	18	24	16	18	24	16	18	24
3 in 12 to 4 in 12	3 3/4	4 1/4	5 3/4	3 1/2	4	5 1/2	3	3 1/2	5
4 in 12 and steeper	5	5 1/2	7 1/2	4	4 1/2	6 1/2	3 1/2	4	5 1/2

UNDERLAYMENT AND SHEATHING

ROOFING TYPE	SHEATHING	UNDERLAYMENT	NORMAL SLOPE		LOW SLOPE	
Wood shakes and shingles	Solid or spaced	No. 30 asphalt saturated felt interlayment	4 in 12 and up	Underlayment starter course; interlayment over entire roof	3 in 12 to 4 in 12	Single layer underlayment over entire roof; interlayment over entire roof

Richard J. Vitullo, Oak Leaf Studio; Crownsville, Maryland

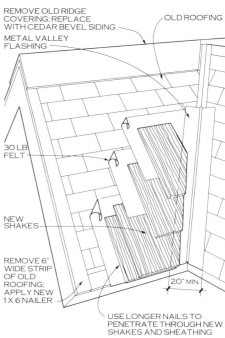

REMOVE OLD RIDGE COVERING; REPLACE WITH CEDAR BEVEL SIDING

OLD ROOFING

METAL VALLEY FLASHING

30 LB FELT

NEW SHAKES

REMOVE 6" WIDE STRIP OF OLD ROOFING; APPLY NEW 1 X 6 NAILER

20" MIN.

USE LONGER NAILS TO PENETRATE THROUGH NEW SHAKES AND SHEATHING

NOTES

Shakes can also be applied over any existing wall or roof. Brick or other masonry requires vertical frameboards and horizontal nailing strips.

Over stucco, horizontal nailing strips are attached directly to wall. Nails should penetrate shading or studs. Over wood, apply shakes directly just as if on new sheathing.

WOOD SHAKES APPLIED TO EXISTING ROOF

GENERAL NOTES

1. Wood shingles and shakes are cut from wood species that are naturally resistant to water, sunlight, rot, and hail: i.e., red cedar, redwood, and tidewater red cypress. They are typically installed in the natural state, although stains, primers, and paint may be applied.

2. Nails must be hot dipped in zinc or aluminum. Nail heads should be driven flush with the surface of the shingle or shake but never into the wood.

3. Underlayment and sheathing should be designed to augment the protection provided by the shingles or shakes, depending on roof pitch and climate. A low-pitched roof subject to wind driven snow should have solid sheathing and an additional underlayment.

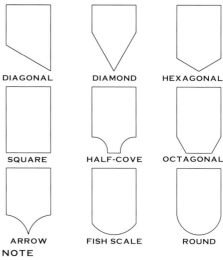

DIAGONAL   DIAMOND   HEXAGONAL

SQUARE   HALF-COVE   OCTAGONAL

ARROW   FISH SCALE   ROUND

NOTE

Fancy butt shingles are 5 in. wide and 7 1/2 in. long, custom produced to individual orders.

FANCY BUTT RED CEDAR SHINGLE SHAPES

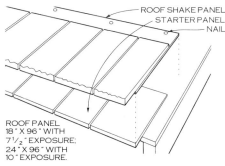

ROOF PANEL
18" X 96" WITH
7 1/2" EXPOSURE;
24" X 96" WITH
10" EXPOSURE.

ROOF PANEL SYSTEM

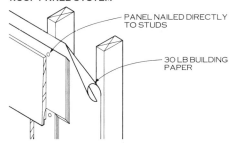

SIDEWALL PANEL APPLIED TO STUDS

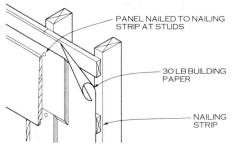

SIDEWALL PANEL APPLIED TO NAILING STRIPS

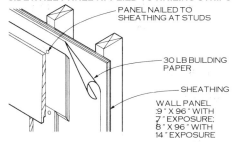

WALL PANEL
:9" X 96" WITH
7" EXPOSURE;
8" X 96" WITH
14" EXPOSURE

SIDEWALL PANEL APPLIED TO SHEATHING

NOTES

1. With the panel system, shakes and shingles plus sheathing go up in one operation: 8 ft roof panels have 16 handsplit shakes bonded to 6 x 1/2 in. plywood strip, which form a solid deck when the panels are nailed. A 4 to 12 or steeper roof pitch is recommended.

2. After application of starter panels, attach panels directly to rafters. Although designed to center on 16 in. or 24 in. spacing, they may meet between rafters. Use two 6d nails at each rafter.

3. 8 ft sidewall panels are of two-ply construction:

   a. Surface layer of individual #1 grade shingles or shakes.

   b. Backup of exterior grade plywood shakes or shingles are bonded under pressure with exterior type adhesives to plywood backup.

4. Lap building paper behind panels 3 in. vertically and horizontally. Stagger joints between panels.

5. Application types are determined by local building codes.

6. Matching factory-made corners for sidewall or roof panels are available.

PANEL SYSTEMS

Richard J. Vitullo; Oak Leaf Studio; Crownsville, Maryland

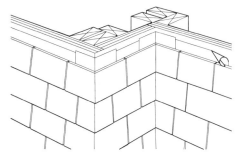

MITERED OUTSIDE AND INSIDE CORNERS (RECOMMENDED)

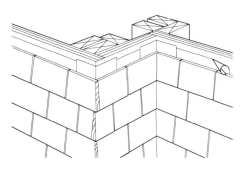

WOVEN OUTSIDE AND INSIDE CORNERS (MORE ECONOMICAL)

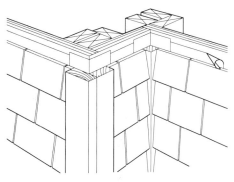

CORNER BOARDS AT OUTSIDE AND INSIDE CORNERS

WOOD SHINGLES AND SHAKES FOR SIDING

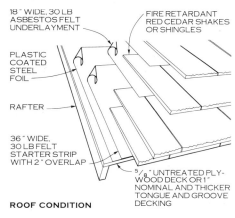

ROOF CONDITION

NOTE

In treating shakes, fire-retardant chemicals are pressure impregnated into the wood cells, and chemicals are then fixed in the wood to prevent leaching. Treatment does not alter appearance. Fire-retardant red cedar shakes are classified as Class C by UL. Class B classification by UL can be met with the addition of the deck constructed of 5/8 in. plywood with exterior glue or 1 in. nominal tongue and groove boards, overlaid with a layer of approved asbestos felt lapped 2 in. on all joints and an 18 in. wide strip of approved asbestos felt between each shake and not exposed to the weather. Decorative stains may be applied.

FIRE RATED CONSTRUCTION

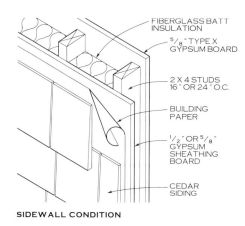

SINGLE COURSING APPLICATION   **DOUBLE COURSING APPLICATION**

EXPOSURE FOR SHINGLES AND SHAKES USED FOR SIDING (IN.)

LENGTH OF SHINGLES	EXPOSURE OF SHINGLES	
	SGL. COURSE	DBL. COURSE
16	6 to 7 1/2	8 to 12
18	6 to 8 1/2	9 to 14
24	8 to 11 1/2	12 to 20

NAILING: THICKNESS AND NAILS

16" long	5 butts = 2"	3d
18" long	5 butts = 2 1/4"	3d
24" long	4 butts = 2"	4d
25" to 27"	1 butt = 1/2"	5 or 6d
25" to 27"	1 butt = 5/8" to 1 1/4"	7 or 8d

SHEATHING NOTES

1. Sheathing may be strip type, solid 1 x 6 in., and diagonal type, in plywood, fiberboard, or gypsum board. Horizontal wood nailing strips (1 x 2 in.) should be used over fiberboard and gypsum sheathing. Space strips equal to shingle exposure.

2. Many finishes can be used on red cedar shakes and shingles: solid color or semitransparent ("weathering") stains, exterior latex paint with primer, wood preservative, and bleaches.

SIDEWALL CONDITION

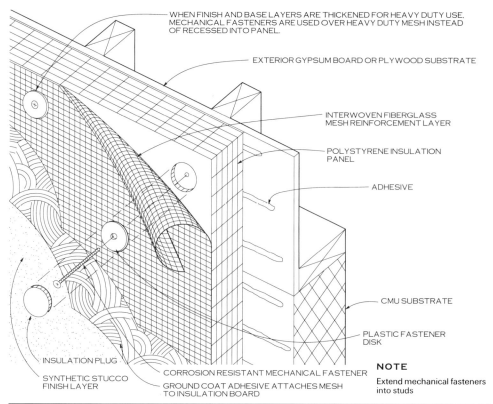

WHEN FINISH AND BASE LAYERS ARE THICKENED FOR HEAVY DUTY USE, MECHANICAL FASTENERS ARE USED OVER HEAVY DUTY MESH INSTEAD OF RECESSED INTO PANEL.

EXTERIOR GYPSUM BOARD OR PLYWOOD SUBSTRATE

INTERWOVEN FIBERGLASS MESH REINFORCEMENT LAYER

POLYSTYRENE INSULATION PANEL

ADHESIVE

CMU SUBSTRATE

PLASTIC FASTENER DISK

INSULATION PLUG

SYNTHETIC STUCCO FINISH LAYER

CORROSION RESISTANT MECHANICAL FASTENER
GROUND COAT ADHESIVE ATTACHES MESH TO INSULATION BOARD

NOTE
Extend mechanical fasteners into studs

EXTERIOR INSULATION AND FINISH SYSTEM

GENERAL

Exterior insulation and finish systems provide an uninterrupted layer of rigid insulation that is attached by adhesives or mechanical fasteners directly onto the building substrate. A continuous fiberglass mesh layer is then applied and attached by adhesives or mechanical fasteners. A finish coat covers and seals the entire system.

NOTES

1. Insulation panels are made in varying thicknesses from 1 to 4 in., depending on the wall U-factor requirements. They come in varying sizes, generally 2 x 2 ft, 2 x 4 ft, or 2 x 8 ft, depending on manufacturer or system used. Expanded polystyrene (1 to 2 lb/cu ft) is generally used above grade; extruded polystyrene (2 to 3 lb0/cu ft) is generally used below grade or in high traffic areas.

2. For areas likely to receive abuse by high impact or high traffic, a heavy duty fiberglass mesh reinforcement layer is used in addition to, or in place of, the standard mesh. Also zinc casing beads are frequently used at finish layer edges.

3. When mechanical fasteners are used they should be installed flush with, or preferably recessed into, the insulation panel to prevent "bubbles" on the surface. When recessed, some manufacturers provide an insulation plug over the fastener to leave a continuous layer of insulation at the surface before the finish is applied.

4. For walls with damaged or brittle substrates, a mechanically fastened track system is used by some manufacturers to fasten the insulation panels to the substrate.

5. The synthetic-stucco finish layer is generally weather resistant, crack resistant, and vapor permeable and is trowelled, rolled, or sprayed onto the surface over the ground coat adhesive. It is generally made from acrylic polymers with an aggregate or silica sand, quartz chips, or marble chips to give it the desired texture. Color is achieved by either tinting the finish coat with pigment or painting the surface.

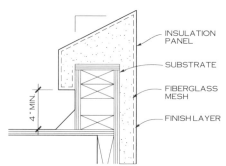

INSULATION PANEL

SUBSTRATE

FIBERGLASS MESH

FINISH LAYER

4" MIN.

PARAPET DETAIL

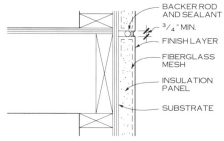

BACKER ROD AND SEALANT
3/4" MIN.
FINISH LAYER
FIBERGLASS MESH
INSULATION PANEL

SUBSTRATE

EXPANSION JOINT DETAIL AT FLOOR LEVEL

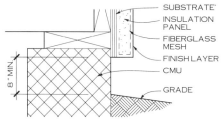

SUBSTRATE
INSULATION PANEL
FIBERGLASS MESH
FINISH LAYER
CMU
GRADE
8" MIN.

DETAIL AT GRADE

WOOD FRAME DETAILS

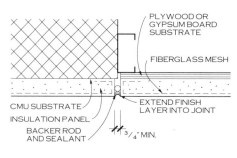

PLYWOOD OR GYPSUM BOARD SUBSTRATE

FIBERGLASS MESH

CMU SUBSTRATE
INSULATION PANEL
BACKER ROD AND SEALANT

EXTEND FINISH LAYER INTO JOINT

3/4" MIN.

EXPANSION JOINT AT DISSIMILAR SUBSTRATES

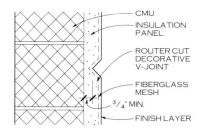

CMU
INSULATION PANEL
ROUTER CUT DECORATIVE V-JOINT
FIBERGLASS MESH
3/4" MIN.
FINISH LAYER

DECORATIVE JOINT

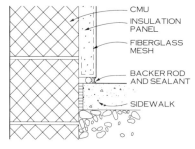

CMU
INSULATION PANEL
FIBERGLASS MESH
BACKER ROD AND SEALANT
SIDEWALK

DETAIL AT SIDEWALK

MASONRY DETAILS

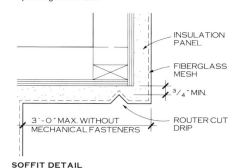

INSULATION PANEL
FIBERGLASS MESH
3/4" MIN.
3'-0" MAX. WITHOUT MECHANICAL FASTENERS
ROUTER CUT DRIP

SOFFIT DETAIL

EXPANDED POLYSTYRENE INSULATION BOARD
EXTRUDED POLYSTYRENE INSULATION BOARD
CMU
GRADE
12" MIN.
12" MIN.
4" MIN.
BRING GROUND COAT, FIBERGLASS MESH, AND FINISH LAYER DOWN ONTO WALL.

DETAIL BELOW GRADE

MISCELLANEOUS DETAILS

Richard J. Vitullo, Oak Leaf Studio; Crownsville, Maryland

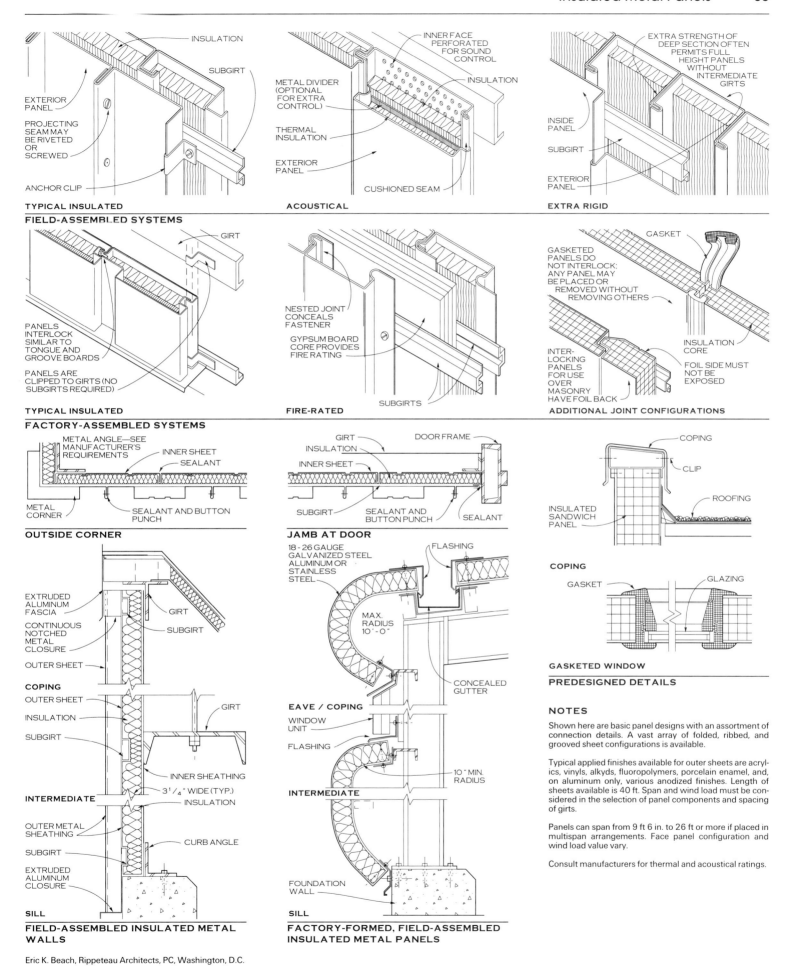

FIELD-ASSEMBLED SYSTEMS

TYPICAL INSULATED

INSULATION

SUBGIRT

EXTERIOR PANEL

PROJECTING SEAM MAY BE RIVETED OR SCREWED

ANCHOR CLIP

ACOUSTICAL

INNER FACE PERFORATED FOR SOUND CONTROL

INSULATION

METAL DIVIDER (OPTIONAL FOR EXTRA CONTROL)

THERMAL INSULATION

EXTERIOR PANEL

CUSHIONED SEAM

EXTRA RIGID

EXTRA STRENGTH OF DEEP SECTION OFTEN PERMITS FULL HEIGHT PANELS WITHOUT INTERMEDIATE GIRTS

INSIDE PANEL

SUBGIRT

EXTERIOR PANEL

FACTORY-ASSEMBLED SYSTEMS

TYPICAL INSULATED

GIRT

PANELS INTERLOCK SIMILAR TO TONGUE AND GROOVE BOARDS

PANELS ARE CLIPPED TO GIRTS (NO SUBGIRTS REQUIRED)

FIRE-RATED

NESTED JOINT CONCEALS FASTENER

GYPSUM BOARD CORE PROVIDES FIRE RATING

SUBGIRTS

ADDITIONAL JOINT CONFIGURATIONS

GASKET

GASKETED PANELS DO NOT INTERLOCK; ANY PANEL MAY BE PLACED OR REMOVED WITHOUT REMOVING OTHERS

INSULATION CORE

INTERLOCKING PANELS FOR USE OVER MASONRY HAVE FOIL BACK

FOIL SIDE MUST NOT BE EXPOSED

OUTSIDE CORNER

METAL ANGLE—SEE MANUFACTURER'S REQUIREMENTS

INNER SHEET

SEALANT

METAL CORNER

SEALANT AND BUTTON PUNCH

JAMB AT DOOR

GIRT

INSULATION

INNER SHEET

DOOR FRAME

SUBGIRT

SEALANT AND BUTTON PUNCH

SEALANT

PREDESIGNED DETAILS

COPING

CLIP

ROOFING

INSULATED SANDWICH PANEL

COPING

GASKET

GLAZING

GASKETED WINDOW

FIELD-ASSEMBLED INSULATED METAL WALLS

EXTRUDED ALUMINUM FASCIA

CONTINUOUS NOTCHED METAL CLOSURE

OUTER SHEET

GIRT

SUBGIRT

COPING

OUTER SHEET

INSULATION

SUBGIRT

GIRT

INNER SHEATHING

3¼" WIDE (TYP.)

INSULATION

INTERMEDIATE

OUTER METAL SHEATHING

SUBGIRT

EXTRUDED ALUMINUM CLOSURE

CURB ANGLE

SILL

FACTORY-FORMED, FIELD-ASSEMBLED INSULATED METAL PANELS

18 - 26 GAUGE GALVANIZED STEEL ALUMINUM OR STAINLESS STEEL

FLASHING

MAX. RADIUS 10' - 0"

CONCEALED GUTTER

EAVE / COPING

WINDOW UNIT

FLASHING

10" MIN. RADIUS

INTERMEDIATE

FOUNDATION WALL

SILL

NOTES

Shown here are basic panel designs with an assortment of connection details. A vast array of folded, ribbed, and grooved sheet configurations is available.

Typical applied finishes available for outer sheets are acrylics, vinyls, alkyds, fluoropolymers, porcelain enamel, and, on aluminum only, various anodized finishes. Length of sheets available is 40 ft. Span and wind load must be considered in the selection of panel components and spacing of girts.

Panels can span from 9 ft 6 in. to 26 ft or more if placed in multispan arrangements. Face panel configuration and wind load value vary.

Consult manufacturers for thermal and acoustical ratings.

Eric K. Beach, Rippeteau Architects, PC, Washington, D.C.

GENERAL

A watertable is a ledge or slight projection of masonry wood or other construction on the outside of a foundation wall, or just above. It protects the foundation from rain by throwing the water away from the wall. In the architectural hierarchy of a building form, the watertable forms the transitional line between the base and middle sections. A watertable is referred to as an offset when the base plane projects out from the upper plane.

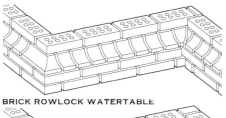

BRICK ROWLOCK WATERTABLE

BRICK STRETCHER WATERTABLE

BRICK VENEER

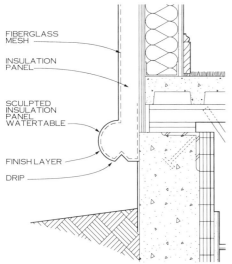

FIBERGLASS MESH

INSULATION PANEL

SCULPTED INSULATION PANEL WATERTABLE

FINISH LAYER

DRIP

EXTERIOR INSULATION AND FINISH SYSTEM

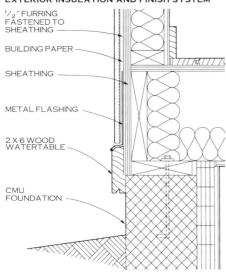

1/2" FURRING FASTENED TO SHEATHING

BUILDING PAPER

SHEATHING

METAL FLASHING

2 X 6 WOOD WATERTABLE

CMU FOUNDATION

STUCCO

TROWELED EXTERIOR VENEER

Richard J. Vitullo, Oak Leaf Studio; Crownsville, Maryland

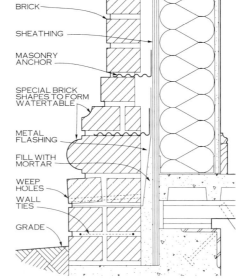

BRICK

SHEATHING

MASONRY ANCHOR

SPECIAL BRICK SHAPES TO FORM WATERTABLE

METAL FLASHING

FILL WITH MORTAR

WEEP HOLES

WALL TIES

GRADE

BRICK WATERTABLE

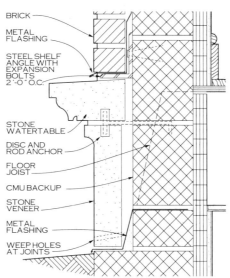

BRICK

METAL FLASHING

STEEL SHELF ANGLE WITH EXPANSION BOLTS 2'-0" O.C.

STONE WATERTABLE

DISC AND ROD ANCHOR

FLOOR JOIST

CMU BACKUP

STONE VENEER

METAL FLASHING

WEEP HOLES AT JOINTS

BRICK VENEER WITH STONE WATERTABLE

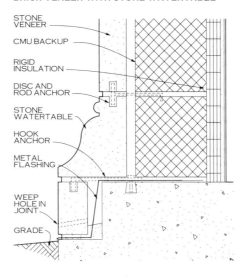

STONE VENEER

CMU BACKUP

RIGID INSULATION

DISC AND ROD ANCHOR

STONE WATERTABLE

HOOK ANCHOR

METAL FLASHING

WEEP HOLE IN JOINT

GRADE

STONE VENEER WITH STONE WATERTABLE

MASONRY VENEER

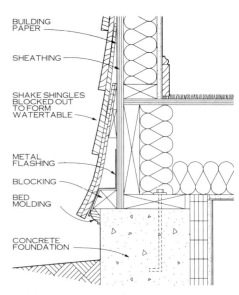

BUILDING PAPER

SHEATHING

SHAKE SHINGLES BLOCKED OUT TO FORM WATERTABLE

METAL FLASHING

BLOCKING

BED MOLDING

CONCRETE FOUNDATION

BLOCKED-OUT SHAKE SHINGLES WITH PROTRUDED FOUNDATION

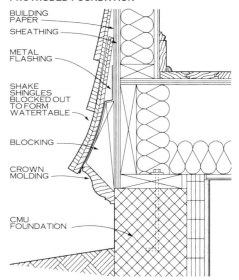

BUILDING PAPER

SHEATHING

METAL FLASHING

SHAKE SHINGLES BLOCKED OUT TO FORM WATERTABLE

BLOCKING

CROWN MOLDING

CMU FOUNDATION

BLOCKED-OUT SHAKE SHINGLES

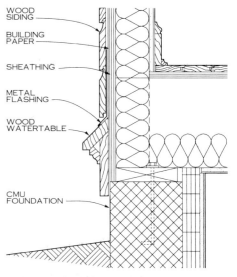

WOOD SIDING

BUILDING PAPER

SHEATHING

METAL FLASHING

WOOD WATERTABLE

CMU FOUNDATION

STRAIGHT SIDING FLUSH WITH FOUNDATION

WOOD SIDING

BACKGROUND

A successful store front or retail entrance attracts the casual passerby. In order to attract, a shopfront must:
1. Catch the eye
2. Identify the shop
3. Display the merchandise in the most appealing way
4. Entice the passerby to enter

SHOP CHARACTER

The character of a retail entrance is influenced by the following factors:
1. Neighborhood or retail development character
2. Types of products sold
3. Accessibility—on foot or by car
4. Glazed area in relation to product
5. Fascia—visibility of shop name
6. Lettering—size, color, style, use of logos
7. Illumination—intensity, color, or use of daylight
8. Color—select predominant, coordinate with interior
9. Finishes— cost , design guidelines, and durability

ENVIRONMENTAL FACTORS

The external features of a shop are influenced by the following factors:
1. Solar—shade southern exposures
2. Wind—provide protection with deep lobbies
3. Corrosive—provide protective finishes
4. Street traffic—lobbies or air locks to keep out fumes

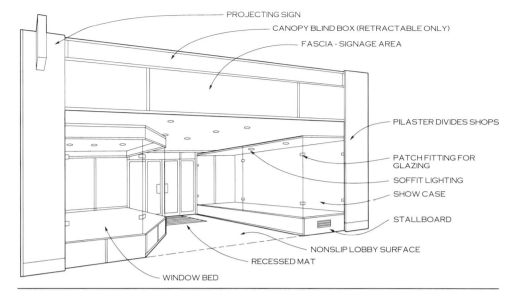

STOREFRONT INTERIOR AND EXTERIOR—COMMON ELEMENTS

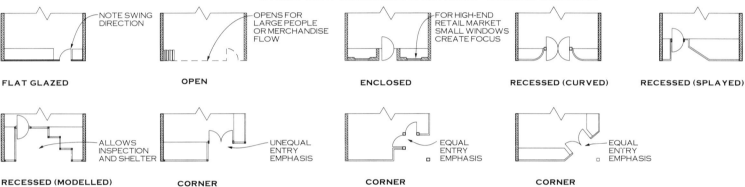

FLAT GLAZED   OPEN   ENCLOSED   RECESSED (CURVED)   RECESSED (SPLAYED)

RECESSED (MODELLED)   CORNER   CORNER   CORNER

STOREFRONT TYPES

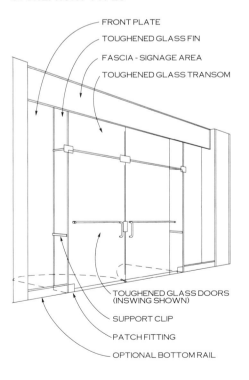

ALL-GLASS STOREFRONT

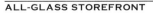

Eric K. Beach, Rippeteau Architects, PC; Washington, D.C.

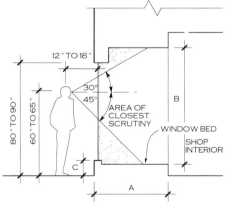

REFER TO TABLES BELOW

WINDOW DIMENSIONS

CHECK LOCAL CODES TO VERIFY REQUIREMENTS

CANOPY DIMENSIONS/SOLAR CONTROL

VIEW POINT	TYPE OF SHOP	A WINDOW DEPTH	B WINDOW HEIGHT	C SILL HEIGHT
Very close	Jewelry, eyeglass, picture, and books	18" to 36"	up to 36"	30" to 36"
Close	Toys, shoes, electronic, optical, CD's, and gifts	30" to 60"	up to 80"	18" to 30"
Medium	Clothing, china, glass sporting goods, and appliances	40" to 96"	up to 96"	12" to 18"
Distant	Furniture, floor covering, and automobiles	80" to 120"	Ceiling height	0" to 6"

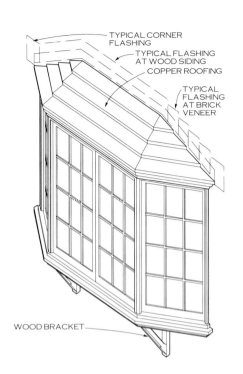

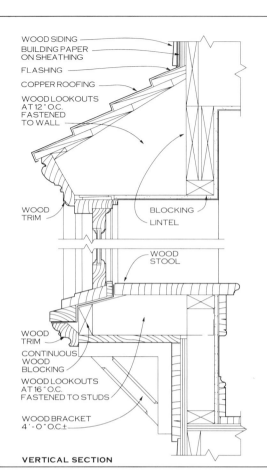

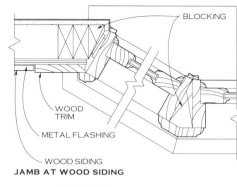

JAMB AT WOOD SIDING

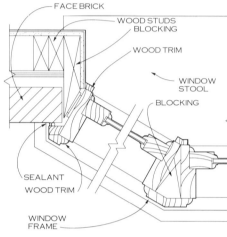

JAMB AT BRICK VENEER

VERTICAL SECTION

GENERAL

An oriel window is a window projecting from the wall face of the upper story of a building and supported on brackets, corbelling, or cantilevered. Oriels were often used in late Gothic and Tudor residential architecture.

ORIEL WINDOW

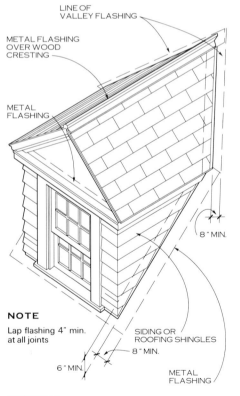

NOTE

Lap flashing 4" min. at all joints

GENERAL

A dormer is a vertical window projecting from the sloping roof of a building and having vertical sides or cheeks and a gabled or shed roof.

DORMER WINDOW

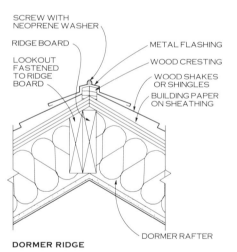

DORMER RIDGE

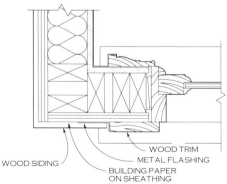

DORMER CORNER AND JAMB

VERTICAL SECTION

Richard J. Vitullo, Oak Leaf Studio; Crownsville, Maryland

SPECIAL WINDOWS

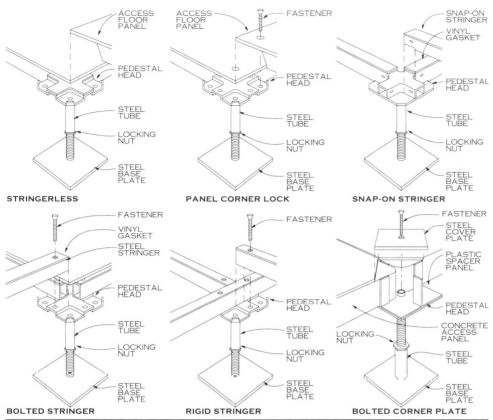

STRINGERLESS

PANEL CORNER LOCK

SNAP-ON STRINGER

BOLTED STRINGER

RIGID STRINGER

BOLTED CORNER PLATE

ACCESS FLOOR SUPPORT SYSTEMS

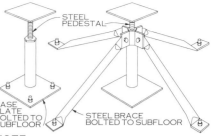

NOTE

Adhesives are commonly used to secure base plate to sub-floor; however, if lateral loads (seismic) are anticipated pedestal should be bolted to floor.

PEDESTAL ATTACHMENT DETAILS

COMPARISON TABLE FOR ACCESS FLOOR SUPPORT SYSTEMS

SUPPORT SYSTEM TYPES	RECOMMENDED USES	RECOMMENDED PANEL TYPE	EASE OF PANEL REMOVAL	LATERAL STABILITY	STATIC CONTROL (INHERENT)	PLENUM SEAL (INHERENT)
Stringerless	Computer rooms/general office	Wood core/solid steel	Excellent	Fair	Yes	No
Panel corner	General office	Wood core/solid steel	Fair	Good	Yes	No
Snap-on stringer	Computer rooms/general office	Wood core/solid steel	Excellent	Good	Yes	Yes
Bolted stringer	Computer rooms	Wood Core/solid steel	Excellent	Excellent	Yes	Yes
Rigid stringer	Heavy loading in computer rooms	Wood core/solid steel	Excellent	Excellent	Yes	Yes
Bolted corner plate	General office	Concrete	Fair	Excellent	No	No

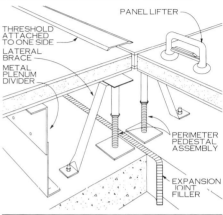

EXPANSION JOINT

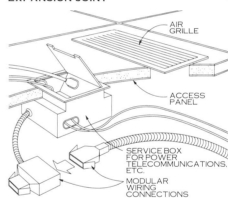

PANEL ACCESSORIES

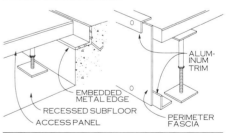

EDGE CONDITION

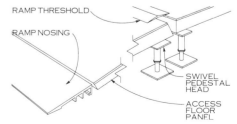

RAMP

GENERAL

Access floor systems are used in offices, hospitals, laboratories, open-area schools, television systems, computer rooms, and telephone-communication centers. They provide mechanical and electrical accessibility and flexibility in placing desks, telephone services, machines, and general office equipment. Equipment can be moved and reconnected quickly using modular wiring. Raised access floors can also be used in a recessed structural floor area. They can create a level floor over an uneven subfloor.

NOTES

1. Panel and pedestal design determine load capacity. Consult manufacturer to determine needs.
2. Floor panel types: reinforced steel, aluminum, steel- or aluminum-encased wood core, steel-encased cementitious fill or lightweight solid reinforced concrete. Basic panels are typically 24 x 24 in.
3. Since the space under the access floor can act as a plenum, special panels can be provided with perforation for maximum air distribution. Also, cable slots and sound and thermal insulation can be provided in the panels.
4. Finishes available: carpet tile (some provided with plastic edging for protection), fire-rated coverings, conductive coverings, vinyl tile, and high-pressure laminate.

Richard J. Vitullo, Oak Leaf Studio; Crownsville, Maryland

COMPUTER ROOMS

Computers place high demands on electrical, mechanical, and floor systems. The floor surface must be conductive and grounded to avoid static electricity and dust accumulation. An automatic fire detection system should be installed in below-floor plenums. Plenums may not exceed 10,000 sq ft and must be divided by noncombustible bulkheads. Computer rooms should be separated from all other occupancies within buildings by walls, floors, and ceilings with a fire-resistant rating of not less than one hour. Structural floors beneath access floors should provide for water drainage to reduce damage to computer systems. All access floor openings should be protected from debris.

Computer rooms require precision temperature and humidity control, even though heat gains are usually concentrated. Package air conditioning units suitable for computer rooms can supply air within a tolerance of ±1.5° and ±5% humidity, using the underfloor plenum with floor registers or special perforated panels. For minimum room temperature gradients, supply air distribution should match closely the load distribution. The distribution system should be flexible enough to accommodate location changes and heat gain with minimum change in the basic distribution system. Supply air systems require about 74 liters per second per kilowatt of cooling to satisfy computer room conditions.

GENERAL

Car washes are generally classified as self-service, roll-over, and tunnel.

The three types of cleaning systems in use are brush with plastic bristle brushes (seldom used today), brushless with cloth curtains and brushes (most popular), and touchless consisting of high pressure chemical jet sprays.

Water reclamation systems are increasingly important because of conservation and pollution controls. Water reclamation can run as high as 100% and require the installation of filtration systems and storage tanks. Tanks are usually buried.

Vehicular stacking and turn radius must be considered to allow straight entry into the car wash. Actual requirements and size of car wash varies according to regional preferences, land cost, climate, local codes and regulations.

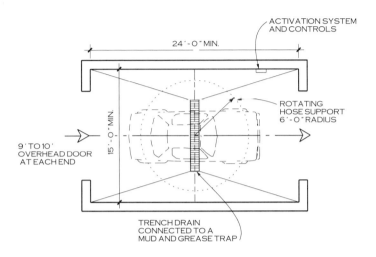

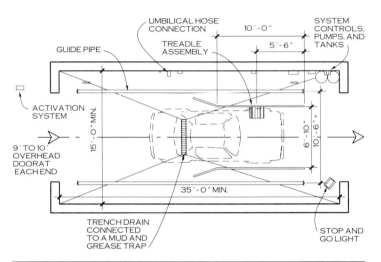

PLAN OF SELF-SERVICE CAR WASH

1. Self-service car washes consist of individual stalls for patrons to wash vehicles. Typical bays are 24 x 15 ft although 20 x 15 ft are possible in warm climates for washing only small cars and trucks. Ceiling height is 10 to 12 ft.
2. All equipment is located in an adjacent room of the same size as a stall.
3. A rotating hose is suspended from the ceiling. Patrons deposit coins for a preselected time and water pressure. Soap can be dispensed through the hose.
4. Stalls can be located back to back but are not as efficient.

PLAN OF ROLL-OVER CAR WASH

1. Roll over car washes consist of individual stalls in which patrons drive a vehicle into the stall system, which is activated to automatically clean the vehicle. Typical bays are 35 x 15 ft with a ceiling height of 12 ft.
2. The system is generally self-contained. A small mechanical room can be provided for servicing equipment and protection.
3. Brushes or jet sprays travel along track to clean, wax, and dry vehicle.
4. Stalls can be stacked side by side. Back to back is not recommended.

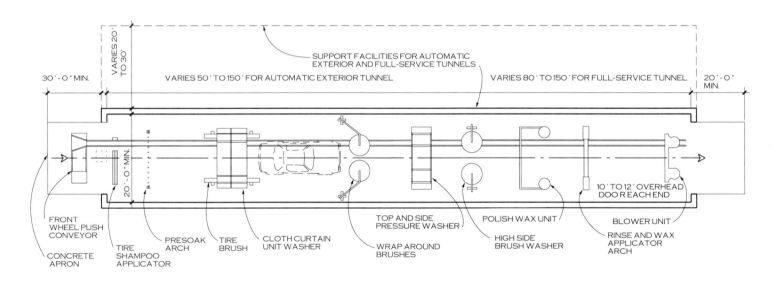

PLAN OF AUTOMATIC EXTERIOR AND FULL-SERVICE TUNNEL CAR WASH

1. Tunnel car washes consist of two types: automatic exterior and full service. The basic difference between the two is that the patron remains in the vehicle while it travels through the automatic exterior tunnel, while the vehicle is handled by an employee with the full service tunnel.

2. Automatic exterior tunnels: size varies from 20 to 30 ft width and 50 to150 ft length. Full-service tunnels: length varies from 80 to 150 ft depending on amount of traffic. Ceiling height should be a minimum of 12 ft.

3. Support facilities vary greatly, with automatic exterior

   15 x 24 ft, employee toilets, storage, and a small office. Full service tunnels require a minimum 5 ft-wide enclosed corridor for patrons, toilets, storage, employee locker room, waiting area, office area, and cashier area.

Anderson • Cooper • Georgelas; McLean, Virginia

 VEHICLE SERVICE EQUIPMENT

MOBILE FILE SYSTEM
(2 UNITS DEEP, 12 FT WIDE, FULLY LOADED)

TYPE	WEIGHT (LB)
9 Tier, legal	6200
9 Tier, letter	4850
8 Tier, legal	5550
8 Tier, letter	4350
7 Tier, legal	4900
7 Tier, letter	3850

MOBILE FILE DIMENSIONS

A	36", 42", or 48"
B	28$\frac{1}{2}$" (letter), 34$\frac{1}{2}$" (legal), 40$\frac{1}{2}$" (x-ray)
Tiers	7, 8, OR 9

PAPER WEIGHTS

FILE TYPE	POUNDS PER LINEAR INCH
Letter size	1.5
Legal size	2.0
Computer printout, hanging	1.75

MOBILE FILE SYSTEMS

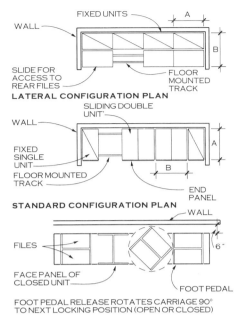

LATERAL CONFIGURATION PLAN

STANDARD CONFIGURATION PLAN

FOOT PEDAL RELEASE ROTATES CARRIAGE 90°
TO NEXT LOCKING POSITION (OPEN OR CLOSED)

ROTATING FILE SYSTEM PLAN

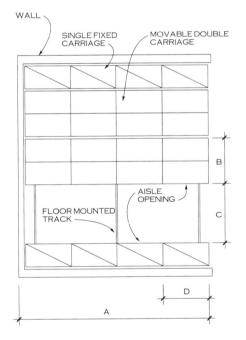

HIGH-DENSITY MOVING FILE AND STORAGE SYSTEMS

AXONOMETRIC OF CARRIAGE UNIT

STEEL SHOWN BUT WOOD SIMILAR.
DEPTH = 28$\frac{1}{2}$" WIDTH = 40$\frac{3}{4}$" TO 79$\frac{5}{16}$"
DRAWER EXTENDS 26" TO 42"

PLAN FILE SYSTEMS

HIGH DENSITY MOVING FILE

	MANUAL	MECHANICAL	ELECTRICAL
A	3' to 15'	3' to 45'	6' to 60'
B	24" (letter), 30" (legal), 36" (x-ray), up to 60" (jumbo)		
C	48" standard maximum		
D	36", 42", or 48"		
E	40$\frac{1}{4}$",64$\frac{1}{4}$", 76$\frac{1}{4}$", 88$\frac{1}{4}$", 97$\frac{1}{4}$" or 121$\frac{1}{4}$"		
F	48" to 129"		

NOTE

Minimum rated load/carriage: 30,000 lb or 1,000 lb per lineal foot.

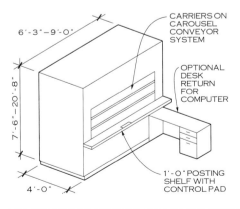

AUTOMATED VERTICAL FILE
8' - 6" WIDE UNIT

Height	8'	9'	10'	12'
Number of carriers	14	16	18	22
Filing inches per carrier	71" (hanging legal) to 88" (lateral letter)			

GENERAL

Filing systems result in significant square footage savings; however they may produce concentrated loads and require close consultation among engineer, designer and manufacturer. In areas where the designer must consider seismic shock, check with a manufacturer for equiping file units with special seismic anchors. Records that may be stored in these systems include file folders, binders, plans, books, ledgers, computer tape and print-outs, microfilm, x-ray files, drugs, supplies, parts, checks, cards, or inventory items.

AUTOMATED VERTICAL FILE SYSTEMS

O'Brien - Kilgore, Inc.; Washington, D. C.

INTRODUCTION

Developments in ventilation, glazing, and horticulture have helped achieve satisfactory plant growth in greenhouses to make the practice economical. Site selection considerations include: topography (flat is advisable), drainage, quantity and quality of water supply, air quality, direction and average wind speed, and, most important, the amount of available light. Orientation for optimal solar gain is east-west except in conditions where shadow casting obstructions outweigh the orientation rule. Once a site has been selected, development of a plan for growth (even if only one greenhouse is built at first) is essential, factoring in access, mechanical room locations, and circulation of materials and labor. Heating and cooling needs will vary with latitude, plant type, skin or glazing, and growth period.

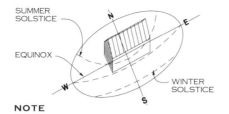

NOTE

Use of an uneven span greenhouse allows for optimal solar orientation. Slope of glass is determined by latitude.

OPTIMAL SOLAR ORIENTATION

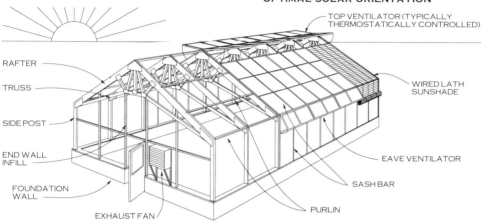

GENERIC GREENHOUSE

When properly maintained, a glass greenhouse will last 40 to 50 years. Structural design of a greenhouse is similar to curtain wall design with live loads of wind, snow, piping, and hanging basket plants.

GLASS-SHEATHED GREENHOUSE

Rigid or flexible plastic greenhouses feature economy, ease of fabrication, and flexibility of form making. Plastic's liabilities are its poor durability, reduced light transmission over time, and discoloration or brittleness.

PLASTIC-SHEATHED GREENHOUSE

HEATING SYSTEMS

Heat distribution is achieved through use of solar, hot air, or radiant pipe systems. Solar heating will usually need the augmentation of the two latter systems at the coolest or windiest part of the year.

RADIANT/HOT WATER PIPE

Systems use a boiler to heat and distribute water. Pipes located at the greenhouse perimeter are the most convenient and efficient method of achieving uniform temperature.

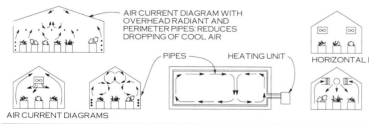

AIR CURRENT DIAGRAM WITH OVERHEAD RADIANT AND PERIMETER PIPES: REDUCES DROPPING OF COOL AIR

AIR CURRENT DIAGRAMS

HEATING SYSTEMS

Eric K. Beach, Rippeteau Architects, PC; Washington, D. C.

FRAME TYPES

MATERIAL	FEATURES
Pipe frame	Economy/simple connections
Steel frame	50′ span (installation by professionals)
Aluminum frame	No rust, deeper sections than steel
Wood frame	Pressure treated lifespan: 10-15 yrs.

PLASTIC TYPE MATERIAL

PLASTIC TYPE	MATERIAL
Flexible	Polyethylene, mylar
Rigid	PVC, acrylic, fiberglass

NOTE

The size of a plastic greenhouse is limited only by the width of a single sheet of plastic.

INSULATION

Insulation augments heating systems and helps reduce heat loss from convection and radiation. Three basic systems are most widely used: movable night curtains, plastic covering over glass, and permanent reflective insulation of north wall and roof.

HOT AIR

Systems burn various fossil fuels and distribute the warmed air with fans.

PIPES   HEATING UNIT   HORIZONTAL DISCHARGE   PLASTIC DUCT

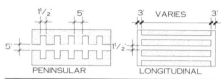

SPACING OF STRUCTURES

PENINSULAR   LONGITUDINAL

BENCHING

GENERAL

Reducing summer heat gain is achieved through shading systems, and natural and fan ventilation systems. Shading is most often achieved with the use of paint on the interior glass, lath rolled on the structure's exterior, or cloth of varying density on the structure's interior.

EVAPORATIVE COOLING

Mechanical refrigeration is generally cost prohibitive cooling with the exception of pad systems, or "swamp coolers," involving pulling air through a wet pad the length of the greenhouse wall with a fan mounted high on the opposite wall.

SWAMP COOLER

NOTE

Fan and pad water pump are hooked up to the same thermostat.

EXHAUST FANS

Fan placement depends on greenhouse orientation; optimal placement is the side opposite the normal wind direction. Fans from adjacent greenhouses should be placed opposite each other, spaced at not more than 25 ft. Stratification is desired in summer cooling, where only 15 to 60% of total air volume is moved mechanically.

STRATIFICATION

COOLING SYSTEMS

Air exchange is necessary to moderate interior temperature and humidity. High humidity promotes plant disease and inhibits soil drying. The most common means of ventilation are natural venting, tube ventilation, and fan-jet ventilation.

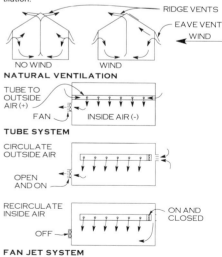

NATURAL VENTILATION

TUBE SYSTEM

FAN JET SYSTEM

VENTILATION SYSTEMS

GENERAL

All kennels for boarding dogs must provide for each animal a primary enclosure (usually indoors) for privacy, eating, and resting and a secondary enclosure (usually outdoors) for exercise.

The primary enclosure should consist of solid dividers to separate adjacent runs and provide privacy with a sloped floor to provide for drainage during cleaning. Enclosures should be large enough to allow for normal movements with minimum sizes of 3 x 4 x 4 ft for small breeds and 3 x 6 x 6 ft for larger breeds.

The secondary enclosure is for exercise and should be large enough for the dog to break into a trot with minimum sizes of 3 x 7 x 4 ft for small breeds and 3 x 11 x 6 ft for larger breeds. Separate each run with a barrier to prevent waste from flowing from one to another. Provide hose bibbs to wash down this area.

Cats are boarded in stacked cages of 2 x 3 x 3 1/2 ft with a perch at the rear. The materials can be less durable than those for dogs, since cats are not as destructive and cleaning does not require hose down. Each enclosure should contain a litter box and enough floor space for food and water and lying down. A climbing tree and removable den for hiding can be provided. Cat enclosures are usually vented individually to prevent the spread of diseases.

Cats enjoy interesting views and distractions so good lighting, cheerful colors, music, plants, outside views, caged birds, and fish tanks are recommended. Cats, however, will adapt to boarding faster if they are separated visually from one another. Community play areas are not recommended because of the possible spread of diseases.

VENTILATION

Proper ventilation is important to prevent the spread of diseases. Air should be vented to the outside, unless air cleaners are used. Recommended ventilation standards should be 10 to 15 room air changes per hour.

HEATING AND COOLING

Temperatures should be designed and maintained between 60-80°F, with humidity maintained between 30-70%. Radiant heat in the floor is highly recommended as it provides heat at the level of the animal.

DRAINAGE

The flooring of all runs should be sloped 1/4 in. per foot from the rear to the front. Drainage should be quick and complete, with the floor finish being not so smooth that it becomes slippery when wet or so rough that it is hard to clean and harms the animal. Waste materials should be collected outside the runs or cages and run to minimum 3 in. diameter floor drains.

LIGHTING

All areas should be bright and cheerful with abundant natural light for the health of the animals. Skylights and ample windows located a minimum of 6 ft off the floor are desirable. Windows should be operable and hinged at the sill to tilt inward to prevent escapes.

NOISE CONTROL

Noise control is important to decrease boarding stress and employee health problems such as hearing loss and to meet local noise ordinances. Noise reducing materials should be considered including ceiling and wall baffles.

MATERIALS

All materials used should be durable and easy to clean and maintain. Concrete block sealed or painted is the usual choice. Prefabricated and modular runs are available or chain link fencing can be used. Carpeting is not recommended as a flooring material.

NOTES

Kennels for the care and boarding of animals are typically defined as breeding, commercial, private, research, and veterinary/medical. The size, type, quantity, and layout of the equipment is related to the function of the kennel and amount and type of patronage.

The schematic drawing (right) is not meant to dictate a design standard but rather to familiarize the reader with typical characteristics of commercial kennels.

Jesse Oak, Anderson • Cooper • Georgelas; McLean, Virginia
American Boarding Kennels Association; Colorado Springs, Colorado

TYPICAL ROOMS

ROOM NAME	MINIMUM SIZES
Reception / retail sales	15 x 20
Private office	10 x 10
Customer service office	8 x 10
Pre-entry exam room	6 x 8
Grooming room	10 x 10
Bathing and drying room	8 x 8
Storage	3 x 6
Utilities	8 x 8
Exotics boarding area	8 x 10
Isolation room	6 x 6

TYPICAL ROOMS

ROOM NAME	MINIMUM SIZES
Service corridor	4 wide
Customer toilet	6 x 7
Storage	8 x 10
Kennel kitchen	10 x 15
Employee locker / lounge	8 x 10
Employee toilet / shower	6 x 8
Storage	3 x 6
Cattery	Related to number of cages
Dog kennel	Related to number of runs
Security fence	6-ft-high

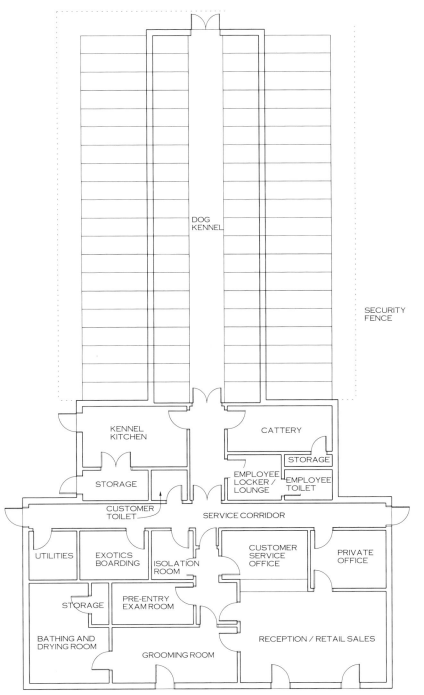

PLAN OF TYPICAL COMMERCIAL KENNEL OPERATION

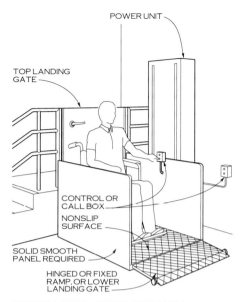

TOP LANDING GATE

POWER UNIT

CONTROL OR CALL BOX

NONSLIP SURFACE

SOLID SMOOTH PANEL REQUIRED

HINGED OR FIXED RAMP, OR LOWER LANDING GATE

OVERALL VIEW – WHEELCHAIR LIFT

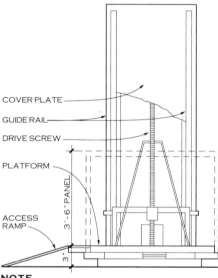

COVER PLATE

GUIDE RAIL

DRIVE SCREW

PLATFORM

3'-6" PANEL

ACCESS RAMP

3"

NOTE

Screw driven lift platform is lifted along a threaded rod, which is rotated by the power unit.

CUT-AWAY SECTION

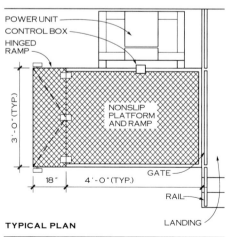

POWER UNIT

CONTROL BOX

HINGED RAMP

NONSLIP PLATFORM AND RAMP

3'-0" (TYP.)

18"   4'-0" (TYP.)

GATE

RAIL

LANDING

TYPICAL PLAN

WHEELCHAIR LIFT

Eric K. Beach, Rippeteau Architects, PC; Washington, D.C.

GENERAL

Wheelchair lifts are suitable for retrofits of buildings that are not barrier free. Bridges are available from manufacturers for installation over stairs. Recommended speed: 10 to 19 fpm. Capacity: 500 to 750 lb.

Lifts operate on standard household current and are suitable for interior or exterior applications.

WHEELCHAIR LIFT REQUIREMENTS

TYPICAL ANSI A17.1, SEC. 2000.1B	PRIVATE RESIDENCE ANSI A17.1, SEC. 2100.1
42 in. door for top and bottom landings, mechanical/electrical interlock, solid construction	36 in. door for top landing; bottom landing can have guard (other requiremenerts similar to 42 in. door)
Platform sides: 42 in. solid construction	Platform 36 in. solid construction
Grab rails	Same
Enclosure or telescoping toe guard	Obstruction switch on platform
Maximum travel 12 ft.	Maximum travel 10 ft.
	Automatic guard 6 in. at bottom landing in lieu of door
Key operation	Key operation

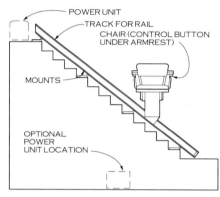

POWER UNIT

TRACK FOR RAIL

CHAIR (CONTROL BUTTON UNDER ARMREST)

MOUNTS

OPTIONAL POWER UNIT LOCATION

NOTE

Chair lift power unit may also be located in chair chassis. Chair lift's compact size may make this lift type more feasible than others for residential use.

CHAIR LIFT – SECTION

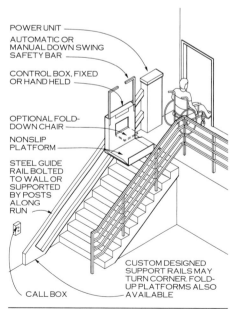

POWER UNIT

AUTOMATIC OR MANUAL DOWN SWING SAFETY BAR

CONTROL BOX, FIXED OR HAND HELD

OPTIONAL FOLD-DOWN CHAIR

NONSLIP PLATFORM

STEEL GUIDE RAIL BOLTED TO WALL OR SUPPORTED BY POSTS ALONG RUN

CUSTOM DESIGNED SUPPORT RAILS MAY TURN CORNER. FOLD-UP PLATFORMS ALSO AVAILABLE

CALL BOX

STAIR LIFT OR PLATFORM (STRAIGHT RUN)

Inclined stair lifts can be adapted to straight run and spiral stairs. Standard types run along guide rails or tubes fastened to solid wall, stairs, or floor structure. Power units may be placed at the top or bottom of the lift run or in the lift chassis, depending on the manufacturer. Some inclined lift systems fold up out of the way for daily stair use.

Where stair width necessitates a more compact lift, as in residential use, chair lifts are available for straight run or spiral stairs. However, many inclined stair lifts come with standard fold-down seats.

Recommended speed, 20 to 25 fpm on straight runs, 10 fpm on curved sections. Capacity, 500 lb. Typical platform size, 30 x 40 in. Check local code capacities.

INCLINED WHEELCHAIR LIFT REQUIREMENTS

TYPICAL RESIDENCE ANSI A17.1, SEC. 2001	PRIVATE ANSI A17.1, SEC.2100
42 in. self-closing door: solid construction, mechanical/electrical interlock, lower landing	36 in. self-closing door: solid construction mechanical/electrical interlock, upper landing
42 in. platform side guard: not used as exit, solid construction	36 in. platform side guard: not used as exit, solid construction
6 in. guard: permitted in lieu of side guard	6 in. guard: permitted in lieu of side guard
6 in. retractable guard: to prevent wheelchair rolling off platform	6 in. retractable guard: to prevent wheelchair rolling off platform
Door required at bottom landing	Underside obstruction switch bottom landing
Travel 3 floors max.	Travel 3 floors max.
Key operation; attendant operation is push button	Key operation: attendant operation is push button and requires door at bottom landing

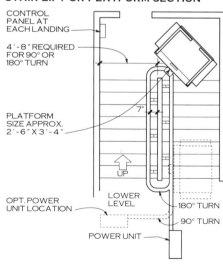

SUPPORT POST

CALL BOX

POWER UNIT

PLATFORM SET FOR ENTRY AT LEVEL 3

PASSENGER SEAT

CALL BOX

LEVEL 3

PLATFORM CONTROL

6"-8" MIN.

LEVEL 2

CALL BOX

PLATFORM

SET FOR EXIT TO LEVEL 1

LEVEL 1

STAIR LIFT OR PLATFORM SECTION

CONTROL PANEL AT EACH LANDING

4'-8" REQUIRED FOR 90° OR 180° TURN

7"

PLATFORM SIZE APPROX. 2'-6" X 3'-4"

UP

OPT. POWER UNIT LOCATION

LOWER LEVEL

180° TURN

90° TURN

POWER UNIT

STAIR LIFT CHAIR OR PLATFORM PLAN WITH TURNS

Escalators are a very efficient form of vertical transportation for very heavy traffic where the number of floors served is limited, normally a maximum of five to six floors. Escalators are not usually accepted as a required exit.

Dimensions shown are general and will vary somewhat with the manufacturer. Consult manufacturers for structural support, electrical supply, and specific dimensional requirements.

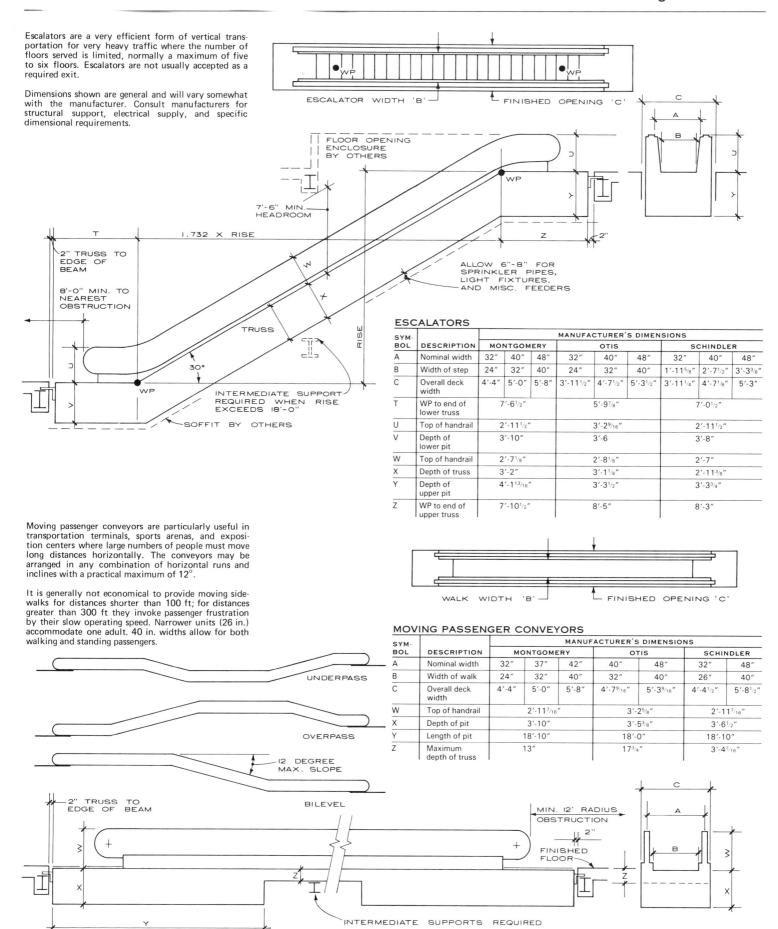

ESCALATORS

SYM-BOL	DESCRIPTION	MANUFACTURER'S DIMENSIONS								
		MONTGOMERY			OTIS			SCHINDLER		
A	Nominal width	32"	40"	48"	32"	40"	48"	32"	40"	48"
B	Width of step	24"	32"	40"	24"	32"	40"	1'-11⅝"	2'-7½"	3'-3⅜"
C	Overall deck width	4'-4"	5'-0"	5'-8"	3'-11½"	4'-7½"	5'-3½"	3'-11¼"	4'-7⅛"	5'-3"
T	WP to end of lower truss	7'-6½"			5'-9⅞"			7'-0½"		
U	Top of handrail	2'-11½"			3'-2⁹⁄₁₆"			2'-11½"		
V	Depth of lower pit	3'-10"			3'-6			3'-8"		
W	Top of handrail	2'-7⅛"			2'-8⅛"			2'-7"		
X	Depth of truss	3'-2"			3'-1⅛"			2'-11⅜"		
Y	Depth of upper pit	4'-1¹³⁄₁₆"			3'-3½"			3'-3¾"		
Z	WP to end of upper truss	7'-10½"			8'-5"			8'-3"		

Moving passenger conveyors are particularly useful in transportation terminals, sports arenas, and exposition centers where large numbers of people must move long distances horizontally. The conveyors may be arranged in any combination of horizontal runs and inclines with a practical maximum of 12°.

It is generally not economical to provide moving sidewalks for distances shorter than 100 ft; for distances greater than 300 ft they invoke passenger frustration by their slow operating speed. Narrower units (26 in.) accommodate one adult. 40 in. widths allow for both walking and standing passengers.

MOVING PASSENGER CONVEYORS

SYM-BOL	DESCRIPTION	MANUFACTURER'S DIMENSIONS							
		MONTGOMERY			OTIS		SCHINDLER	
A	Nominal width	32"	37"	42"	40"	48"	32"	48"
B	Width of walk	24"	32"	40"	32"	40"	26"	40"
C	Overall deck width	4'-4"	5'-0"	5'-8"	4'-7⁹⁄₁₆"	5'-3⁹⁄₁₆"	4'-4½"	5'-8½"
W	Top of handrail	2'-11⁷⁄₁₆"			3'-2⅝"		2'-11⁷⁄₁₆"	
X	Depth of pit	3'-10"			3'-5⅜"		3'-6½"	
Y	Length of pit	18'-10"			18'-0"		18'-10"	
Z	Maximum depth of truss	13"			17¾"		3'-4⁷⁄₁₆"	

Alan H. Rider, AIA; Daniel, Mann, Johnson & Mendenhall; Washington, D.C.

GENERAL

Waste and linen chutes should extend full diameter through the roof and be capped with a metal safety vent or glass explosion cap. Sprinklers or flushing spray are recommended at alternate floors. Bottom-hinged hopper doors are commonly used for waste and loose linen. Square side-hinged doors are used for bagged linen. "B" label doors are recommended. To prevent clogging, door size is restricted in proportion to chute diameter. Type "H" hopper discharge doors are installed when discharge is built into wall and the receptacle is a cart or bin. Type "A" direct-open discharge doors (not shown) are commonly used when discharge is into a compactor.

AVERAGE WASTE PRODUCTION/DAY

BUILDING	AMOUNT
Apartment	5 lb/apartment + 1 lb/bedroom
Dormitory	3 lb/person
Hospital	8 lb/bed
Nursing home	6 lb/person
Hotel, motel	3 lb/room
School	10 lb/room + $\frac{1}{4}$ lb/pupil

AVERAGE LINEN PRODUCTION/DAY

BUILDING	AMOUNT
Hospital	15 lb/bed
Hotel, Motel	12 lb/bed

FULL DIAMETER METAL VENT CAP OR GLASS EXPLOSION CAP

VENT STACK EQUALS DIAMETER OF CHUTE

4'-0" TYP.

FLASHING AS REQ'D FOR ROOF TYPE

ROOF

SPRINKLER AND (OPT.) FLUSHING SPRAY AT EACH INTAKE DOOR

CHUTE FACTORY ASSEMBLED WITH ONE EXPANSION JOINT PER FLOOR

SELF-CLOSING INTAKE DOOR BOTTOM, SIDE, OR TOP HINGED

2 HR. FIRE WALL AROUND ENTIRE CHUTE

OPT. FOOT OPERATOR

TYPICAL FLOOR

VARIES

FLOOR OPENING $\frac{3}{4}$" CLEAR MIN.

TYPICAL CHUTE SUPPORT

DISCHARGE DOOR OPEN EXCEPT WHEN FLUSHING

HORIZONTAL DOORS WITH FUSIBLE LINK AVAILABLE

2" DRAIN

SUPPORTING PEDESTAL OPTIONAL

TOP HINGED DISCHARGE DOOR W/ 165° FUSIBLE LINK

ADJ. WALL ANCHORS

4'-0" TYP.

WASTE OR LINEN CHUTE
NOTES

1. Fire stops may be required at underside of every slab; check local codes.
2. Chute material: #18 - #16 U.S. gauge aluminized steel or stainless steel.

NOTES

1. Chutes should be used only for first class mail. The chute dimensions should be 2 x 8 in. and extend in a vertical line from beginning point to a receiving box or mailroom. A chute must be accessible its entire length. Chutes in pairs have a divider and dual receiving boxes.
2. Receiving boxes must be placed near the building's main entrance or near the loading area for U.S. Postal Service (USPS) mail collection. Using the shortest line, receiving boxes may not be placed more than 100 ft from the entrance used by the collection person. Locations require local postmaster approval. Receiving boxes must be placed on the same floor the collection person uses to enter the building. Doors must operate freely. Door openings must be at least 12 x 20 in. and not more than 18 x 30 in.
3. Auxiliary boxes should be located near receiving box if receiving box is too small to accommodate the first class mail volume.
4. A bundle drop must accept a bundle at least $6\frac{1}{2}$ in. wide by $11\frac{1}{2}$ in. long and 4 in. high. To prevent removal of mail, the deposit opening must be fully protected by inside baffle plates. Inlet doors must be inscribed "Letters" and "Letter Mail Tied in Bundles." The bottom of the opening must be at least 61 in. above floor level.

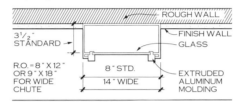

ROUGH WALL

$3\frac{1}{2}$" STANDARD

FINISH WALL

GLASS

R.O. = 8" X 12" OR 9" X 18" FOR WIDE CHUTE

8" STD.

14" WIDE

EXTRUDED ALUMINUM MOLDING

MAIL CHUTE PLAN

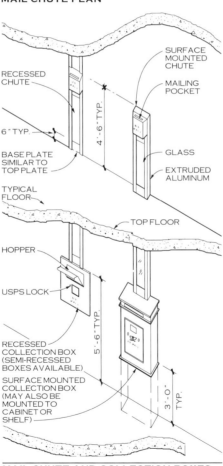

RECESSED CHUTE

SURFACE MOUNTED CHUTE

MAILING POCKET

6" TYP.

4'-6" TYP.

BASE PLATE SIMILAR TO TOP PLATE

GLASS

EXTRUDED ALUMINUM

TYPICAL FLOOR

TOP FLOOR

HOPPER

USPS LOCK

RECESSED COLLECTION BOX (SEMI-RECESSED BOXES AVAILABLE)

SURFACE MOUNTED COLLECTION BOX (MAY ALSO BE MOUNTED TO CABINET OR SHELF)

5'-6" TYP.

3'-0" TYP.

MAIL CHUTE AND COLLECTION BOXES
NOTES

1. All installations must comply with USPS requirements and are subject to inspection.
2. Floor penetrations may need fire stopping methods.
3. USPS provides listing of approved manufacturers.

CAR DOORS OPPOSITE

CAR DOORS ADJACENT

CAR DOOR FRONT

PLANS OF TYPICAL DUMBWAITER

ELEVATOR CAPACITY

CAR SIZE			
W	D	H	CAPACITY (LB)
18"	18"	24"	25-75
20"	20"	30"	100
28"	24"	36"	150-250
32"	30"	42"	300-350
36"	36"	48"	400-500

Capacity is determined by the maximum weight of the contents to be transported and the size of the dumbwaiter car. Maximum capacity is 500 lb. Normal speed is 50 ft per minute. The car platform may not exceed 9 sq. ft. Car heights cannot exceed 4 ft. Machines may be located above, below, or adjacent to the hatchway. Drum type machines have a maximum rise of 35 to 40 ft; traction type machines have unlimited travel.

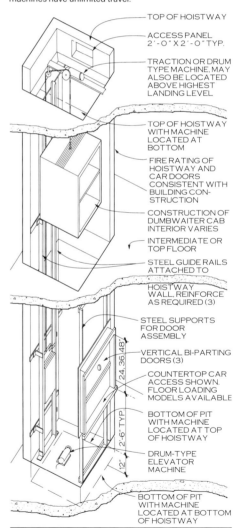

TOP OF HOISTWAY

ACCESS PANEL 2'-0" X 2'-0" TYP.

TRACTION OR DRUM TYPE MACHINE, MAY ALSO BE LOCATED ABOVE HIGHEST LANDING LEVEL

TOP OF HOISTWAY WITH MACHINE LOCATED AT BOTTOM

FIRE RATING OF HOISTWAY AND CAR DOORS CONSISTENT WITH BUILDING CONSTRUCTION

CONSTRUCTION OF DUMBWAITER CAB INTERIOR VARIES

INTERMEDIATE OR TOP FLOOR

STEEL GUIDE RAILS ATTACHED TO

HOISTWAY WALL, REINFORCE AS REQUIRED (3)

STEEL SUPPORTS FOR DOOR ASSEMBLY

VERTICAL BI-PARTING DOORS (3)

24, 36, 48"

COUNTERTOP CAR ACCESS SHOWN. FLOOR LOADING MODELS AVAILABLE

BOTTOM OF PIT WITH MACHINE LOCATED AT TOP OF HOISTWAY

DRUM-TYPE ELEVATOR MACHINE

2'-6" TYP.

12'

BOTTOM OF PIT WITH MACHINE LOCATED AT BOTTOM OF HOISTWAY

DUMBWAITERS
NOTE

Consult manufacturer's literature for specific dimensions and load capacity

Eric K. Beach, Rippeteau Architects, PC; Washington, D. C.
Wilkinson Company, Inc., Cutler Manufacturing Corporation, Atlas Elevator Company, and Sidgwick Lifts, Inc.

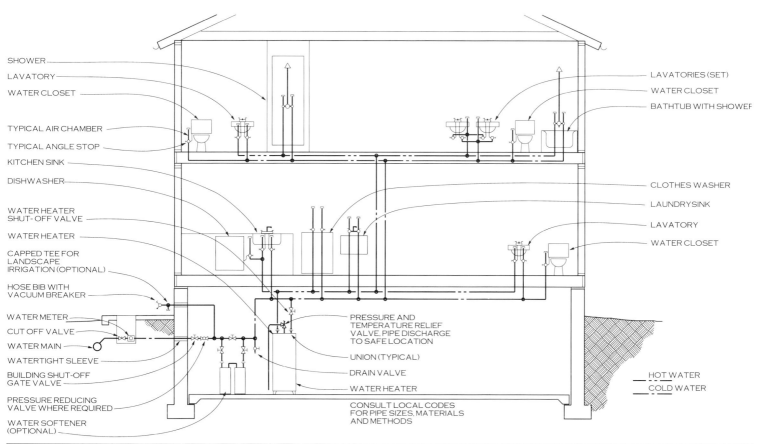

SHOWER
LAVATORY
WATER CLOSET

TYPICAL AIR CHAMBER
TYPICAL ANGLE STOP

KITCHEN SINK

DISHWASHER

WATER HEATER
SHUT-OFF VALVE

WATER HEATER

CAPPED TEE FOR
LANDSCAPE
IRRIGATION (OPTIONAL)

HOSE BIB WITH
VACUUM BREAKER

WATER METER
CUT OFF VALVE
WATER MAIN
WATERTIGHT SLEEVE
BUILDING SHUT-OFF
GATE VALVE
PRESSURE REDUCING
VALVE WHERE REQUIRED
WATER SOFTENER
(OPTIONAL)

LAVATORIES (SET)
WATER CLOSET
BATHTUB WITH SHOWER

CLOTHES WASHER
LAUNDRY SINK
LAVATORY
WATER CLOSET

PRESSURE AND
TEMPERATURE RELIEF
VALVE, PIPE DISCHARGE
TO SAFE LOCATION

UNION (TYPICAL)
DRAIN VALVE
WATER HEATER

CONSULT LOCAL CODES
FOR PIPE SIZES, MATERIALS
AND METHODS

HOT WATER
COLD WATER

WATER SUPPLY PIPING

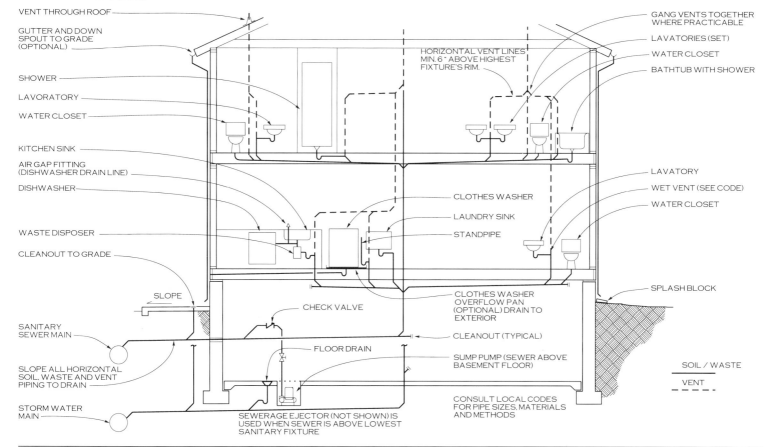

VENT THROUGH ROOF

GUTTER AND DOWN
SPOUT TO GRADE
(OPTIONAL)

SHOWER

LAVORATORY

WATER CLOSET

KITCHEN SINK

AIR GAP FITTING
(DISHWASHER DRAIN LINE)

DISHWASHER

WASTE DISPOSER

CLEANOUT TO GRADE

SLOPE

SANITARY
SEWER MAIN

SLOPE ALL HORIZONTAL
SOIL, WASTE AND VENT
PIPING TO DRAIN

STORM WATER
MAIN

GANG VENTS TOGETHER
WHERE PRACTICABLE

LAVATORIES (SET)
WATER CLOSET
BATHTUB WITH SHOWER

HORIZONTAL VENT LINES
MIN. 6" ABOVE HIGHEST
FIXTURE'S RIM.

LAVATORY
WET VENT (SEE CODE)
WATER CLOSET

CLOTHES WASHER
LAUNDRY SINK
STANDPIPE

CHECK VALVE

CLOTHES WASHER
OVERFLOW PAN
(OPTIONAL) DRAIN TO
EXTERIOR

CLEANOUT (TYPICAL)

FLOOR DRAIN

SUMP PUMP (SEWER ABOVE
BASEMENT FLOOR)

SPLASH BLOCK

CONSULT LOCAL CODES
FOR PIPE SIZES, MATERIALS
AND METHODS

SEWERAGE EJECTOR (NOT SHOWN) IS
USED WHEN SEWER IS ABOVE LOWEST
SANITARY FIXTURE

SOIL / WASTE
VENT

SOIL, WASTE AND VENT PIPING

Brent Dickens, AIA, Architecture & Planning; San Rafael, California
Drawn by David S. Penney, P.E.

PLUMBING **15**

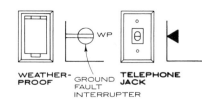

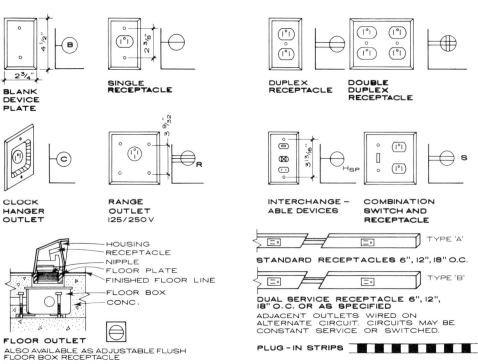

GANG	HORIZONTAL	
	HEIGHT	WIDTH
2	4 1/2"	4 9/16"
3	4 1/2"	6 3/8"
4	4 1/2"	8 3/16"
5	4 1/2"	10"
6	4 1/2"	11 13/16"

NOTE: Add 1 13/16" each added gang. Screws 1 13/16" o.c.

Plates Made in Plastic, Brass (0.04 to 0.06 inches thick), Stainless Steel & Aluminum.

NOTES

1. All devices to be Underwriters Laboratory approved.
2. All devices to comply with requirements of National Electric Code.
3. All devices to be of NEMA configuration.
4. Ground fault interrupter receptacles or circuits are required in bathrooms, garages, unfinished basements, outdoors at grade level, and within 6 ft of kitchen sinks.

RECEPTACLES, OUTLET TYPES AND SIZES

SWITCHES

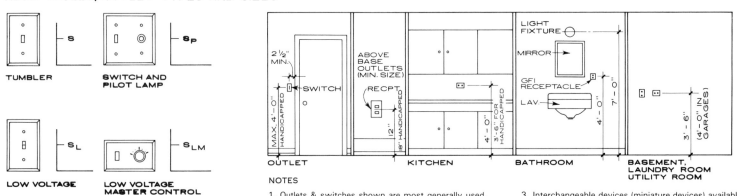

NOTES

1. Outlets & switches shown are most generally used. Number of gangs behind one wall plate depends on types of devices used.
2. Symbols used are ASA standard. See page on "Electric Symbols."
3. Interchangeable devices (miniature devices) available in various combinations using any 1, 2, or 3 of the following: switch, convenience outlet, radio outlet, pilot light, bell, button, in one gang. Combined gangs made.

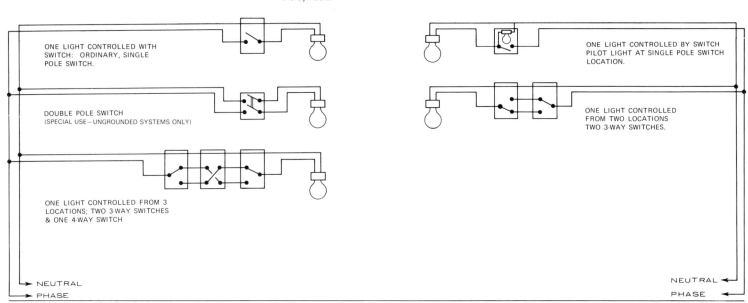

SWITCH WIRING DIAGRAMS

B. J. Baldwin; Giffels & Rossetti, Inc.; Detroit, Michigan

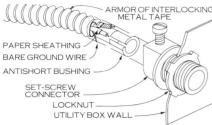

NOTE

Manufactured with 2, 3 and 4 conductor insulated wire in the following sizes: 14, 8, 6, 4, 2, 1. Also contains internal bonds that help the armor itself serve as a grounding conductor for the circle.

ARMORED CABLE (BX)

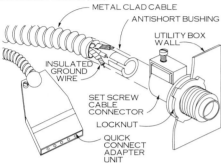

NOTE

Manufactured to similar specifications and sizes as armored cable but with a separated insulated ground conductor. Metal clad cable may be clad in aluminum or steel, corrugated, smooth, or with metal interlocking tape. May be factory assembled with quick connect adapter units for access floor or ceiling wiring systems. Consult with electrical engineer before installation.

METAL CLAD CABLE (MC)

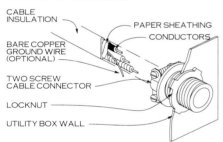

NOTE

Manufactured in 2 and 3 conductor PVC insulated wire in the following sizes: 14, 12, 10, 8, 6, and 4 with or without ground wire.

NONMETALLIC SHEATHED CABLE (NM, ROMEX)

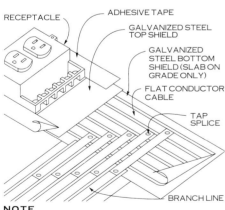

NOTE

Manufactured with combinations of 3, 4, and 5 conductors in cable for easy access under carpet squares. Consult manufacturers before installation.

FLAT CONDUCTOR CABLE

CABLES

Robert F. Faass, Electrical Engineer; Seabrook, Maryland
Richard J. Vitullo, Oak Leaf Studio; Crownsville, Maryland

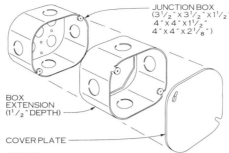

NOTE

Commonly used for ceiling fixtures

OCTAGONAL BOX

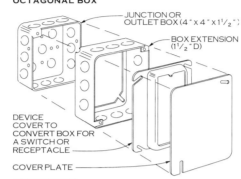

SQUARE BOX

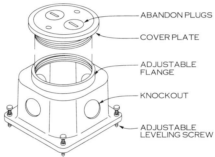

NOTE

Boxes are mounted to wood floor structure (nonadjustable) or for cast-in-place concrete with leveling screws. Concrete box materials include cast-in-place stamped steel or nonmetallic.

FLUSH FLOOR BOX

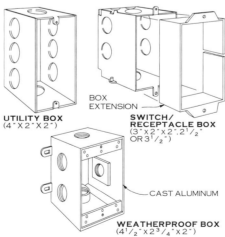

UTILITY BOX (4" X 2" X 2")

SWITCH/ RECEPTACLE BOX (3" x 2" x 2", 2½" OR 3½")

WEATHERPROOF BOX (4½" X 2¾" X 2")

NOTE

These boxes are manufactured in metallic and nonmetallic versions. Knockout locations vary. Utility and exterior boxes are not gangable; switch and masonry boxes may be gangable. Flush mounting in concrete requires a concrete tight box and rigid conduit; in CMU conduit is threaded through the cavities of block.

ELECTRICAL BOXES

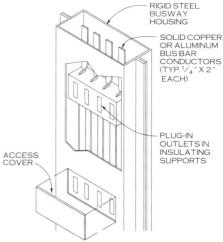

NOTE

Busways carry current from 100 to 4000 amps and voltages up to 5 kv. They are utilized when large blocks of low voltage power (600V) must be transmitted over long distances or where taps must be made at various points, as in vertical risers in office building. Consult electrical engineer before using this system. Busway housing may be hung from overhead support, mounted to wall, or braced to structure in vertical riser installation.

BUSWAY SYSTEM

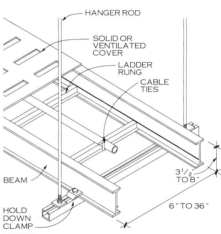

NOTE

Cable trays allow large numbers of insulated conduit and/ or cables to be protected and carried in a limited space. For more protection or where heat build-up is not a problem, perforated or solid bottoms and top covers are available. Many fittings, bends, and tees (horizontal and vertical) are available. Consult manufacturers for materials other than aluminum or steel.

CABLE TRAY SYSTEM

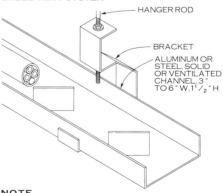

NOTE

Used as branch cable tray to carry single large cable or conduit or several small ones.

CABLE CHANNEL

CONDUIT AND CABLE SUPPORTING DEVICES

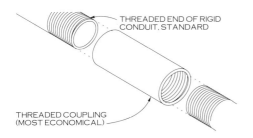

THREADED COUPLING

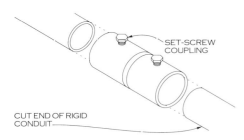

THREADLESS SET-SCREW COUPLING

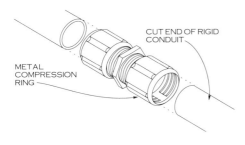

THREADLESS COMPRESSION COUPLING

NOTES

1. Manufactured in 10 ft lengths in diameters from 1/2 to 6 in. Consult manufacturers.
2. Rigid steel conduit provides heavy-duty protection of wiring from mechanical injury and corrosion and protects surroundings against fire-hazard from overheating or arcing of enclosed conductors.

RIGID STEEL CONDUIT

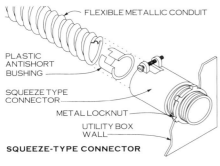

SQUEEZE-TYPE CONNECTOR

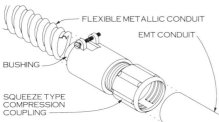

FLEXIBLE TO EMT COUPLING

NOTE

Manufactured in diameters from 5/16 to 4 in.

FLEXIBLE METALLIC CONDUIIT

Robert F. Faass, Electrical Engineer; Seabrook, Maryland
Richard J. Vitullo, Oak Leaf Studio; Crownsville, Maryland

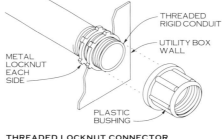

THREADED LOCKNUT CONNECTOR

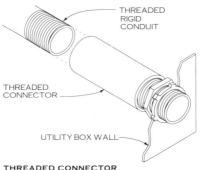

THREADED CONNECTOR

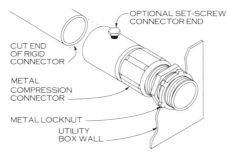

THREADLESS CONNECTORS

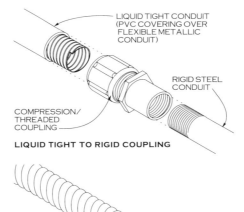

LIQUID TIGHT TO RIGID COUPLING

NONMETALLIC LIQUID TIGHT CONDUIT

NOTES

1. Manufactured in various grades according to temperature, range, and resistance factors (moisture, corrosion, and chemicals) in 1/4 to 6 in. diameters.
2. Frequently used as conduit underground or outside. Consult electrical engineer.

FLEXIBLE LIQUID TIGHT CONDUIT

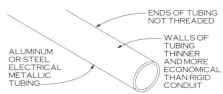

NOTES

1. Manufactured in 10 ft lengths and 1/2 to 4 in. diameters. Consult manufacturers.
2. Uses similar types of threadless couplings and connections as rigid steel conduit.

ELECTRICAL METALLIC TUBING (EMT)

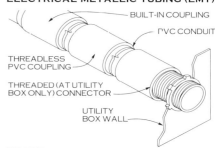

NOTES

1. All threadless connections are joined by means of solvent cement.
2. Commonly used for underground installation or cast into concrete.
3. Manufactured in heavy wall and light wall construction, in 10 ft lengths and 1/2 to 6 in. diameters.
4. Ground wire required for power cables.

RIGID NONMETALLIC CONDUIT

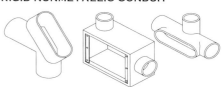

NOTES

1. Conduit outlet bodies are installed as pull outlets for conductors.
2. Fittings are manufactured for rigid steel, EMT, and nonmetallic conduit. Many shapes are available. Consult manufacturers.

CONDUIT OUTLET BODIES

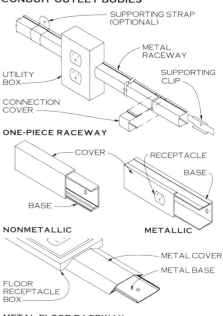

ONE-PIECE RACEWAY

METAL FLOOR RACEWAY

RACEWAY SYSTEMS

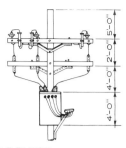

SINGLE OR 3 PHASE

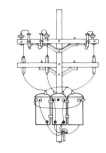

3 PHASE

OVERHEAD TRANSFORMER

OVERHEAD TRANSFORMER: Three-phase transformers are available up to 500 kVA in a single unit. Three single-phase units can total to 1500 kVA with adequate platform support. Service lateral to building can be either overhead or underground.

Typical dimensions for 15 and 25 kV. See the National Electrical Safety Code (ANSI C2) for required clearances;

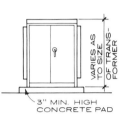

VARIES AS TO SIZE OF TRANSFORMER

3" MIN. HIGH CONCRETE PAD

7'-0" x 6" DIA. CONCRETE FILLED STEEL POST SET IN CONCRETE 4'-0" ABOVE GRADE WHERE EXPOSED TO VEHICULAR TRAFFIC. MIN. CLEARANCE OF 1'-0" FOR FRONT AND SIDE OF PAD

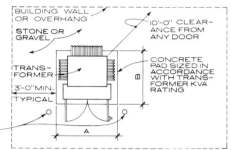

BUILDING WALL OR OVERHANG
STONE OR GRAVEL
TRANS-FORMER
3'-0"MIN. TYPICAL
10'-0" CLEARANCE FROM ANY DOOR
CONCRETE PAD SIZED IN ACCORDANCE WITH TRANSFORMER KVA RATING
A
B

PAD MOUNTED TRANSFORMER

PAD MOUNTED TRANSFORMER: Pad mounted transformers with weatherproof tamperproof enclosure permit installation at ground level without danger from exposed live parts. Three phase units up to 1500 kVA are available and are normally used with underground primary and secondary feeders. Customer's grounding grids or grounding electrical conductors should not be connected at pad mounted transformer locations.

	A	B
Typical pad sizes: 150- 300 KVA	75 in.	80 in.
500-1500 KVA	84 in.	84 in.

High voltage compartment requires 10 ft clearance for on–off operation of the insulated stick located on the transformer (known as ''hot stick'' operation).

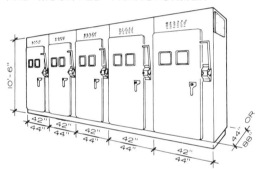

42" 44"   42" 44"   42" 44"   42" 44"   42" 44"   44" OR 88"

PRIMARY SWITCHGEAR

PRIMARY SWITCHGEAR: Where the owner's buildings cover a large area such as a college campus or medical center, the application usually requires the use of medium voltages of 5 kV to 34 kV for distribution feeders. Therefore, the utility company will terminate their primary feeders on the owner's metal clad or metal enclosed switchgear. This switchgear may be interior or exterior weatherproof construction. Code clearance in front and back of board must be provided in accordance with the National Electric Code.

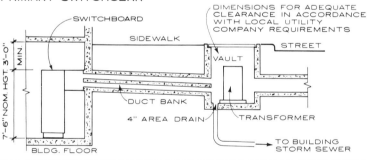

SWITCHBOARD
7'-6"NOM. HGT. 3'-0" MIN.
BLDG. FLOOR
SIDEWALK
DUCT BANK
4" AREA DRAIN
DIMENSIONS FOR ADEQUATE CLEARANCE IN ACCORDANCE WITH LOCAL UTILITY COMPANY REQUIREMENTS
STREET
VAULT
TRANSFORMER
TO BUILDING STORM SEWER

UNDERGROUND VAULT

UNDERGROUND VAULT: Underground vaults are generally used for utility company transformers where all distribution feeders are underground. These systems usually constitute a network or spot network. Vaults often are located below the sidewalks and have grating tops. Transformer is usually liquid filled.

NOTE

If oil-filled transformer is used, oil interceptor is recommended before discharge to building storm sewer.

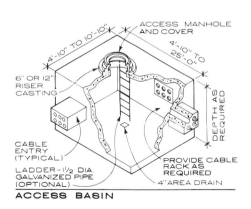

ACCESS MANHOLE AND COVER
4'-10" TO 10'-10"
4'-10" TO 25'-0"
6" OR 12" RISER CASTING
DEPTH AS REQUIRED
CABLE ENTRY (TYPICAL)
LADDER-1½ DIA. GALVANIZED PIPE (OPTIONAL)
PROVIDE CABLE RACK AS REQUIRED
4" AREA DRAIN

ACCESS BASIN

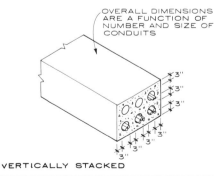

OVERALL DIMENSIONS ARE A FUNCTION OF NUMBER AND SIZE OF CONDUITS
3"
3"
3"
3"
3"
VERTICALLY STACKED

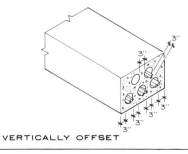

3"
3"
3"
3"
3"
VERTICALLY OFFSET

UNDERGROUND DUCT BANK

William Tao & Associates, Inc., Consulting Engineers; St. Louis, Missouri
Dennis W. Wolbert; Everett I. Brown Company; Indianapolis, Indiana

NOTES

Flooring should be level, slightly resilient, and not of non-skid material. Walls should be uniformly dark nongloss background to provide enough contrast to help players follow the ball. Lighting often varies for different standards of play, but 150-500 lumens at table height is the acceptable range. This should not be fluorescent or natural lighting, but preferably tungsten halogen. Sectional tables are stored upright when not in use.

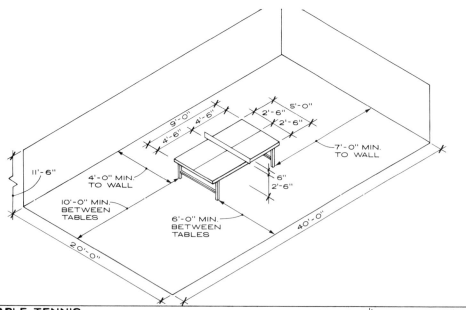

TABLE TENNIS

The flooring must be level permanently and be able to withstand point loads. Traditionally designed billiard tables weigh about 1.5 tons spread over eight legs. Lighting must not produce harsh shadows, but some modeling of the balls is desirable. Direct or reflected glare should be avoided, and true color rendering is important in snooker. An overall bright light is needed for each table; natural lighting is not essential. Lighting at the table surface should be approximately 375 lumens, which can be achieved by three 150-watt tungsten filament lamps suspended in a lighting trough. Fluorescent lamps are unacceptable. Some sound insulation is required to prevent distractions from noise outside the playing area.

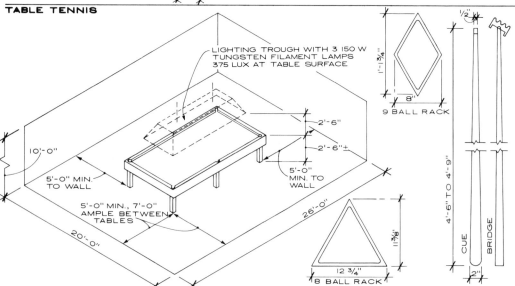

TYPE OF TABLE	PLAYING SURFACE		TABLE SIZE	
	W.	L.	W.	L.
ENGLISH (SNOOKER)	7'-2"	14'-4"	8'-2"	15'-4"
STANDARD 9'-0"	4'-2"	8'-4"	5'-2"	9'-4"
STANDARD 8'-0"	3'-8"	7'-4"	4'-8"	8'-4"
STANDARD 7'-0" *	3'-2"	6'-4"	4'-2"	7'-4"
OVERSIZED 8'-0"	3'-10"	7'-8"	4'-10"	8'-8"

TABLE HEIGHT 2'-6" ±
*Typical coin-operated table

BILLIARDS / POCKET BILLIARDS / SNOOKER

A dart board in a hanging box needs no additional storage. Lighting can be artificial, natural, or both. An adjustable spotlight is advisable. For safety reasons, the playing area should be placed away from doorways and traffic ways. Walls around the board should be surfaced with a material that will not be defaced by the darts.

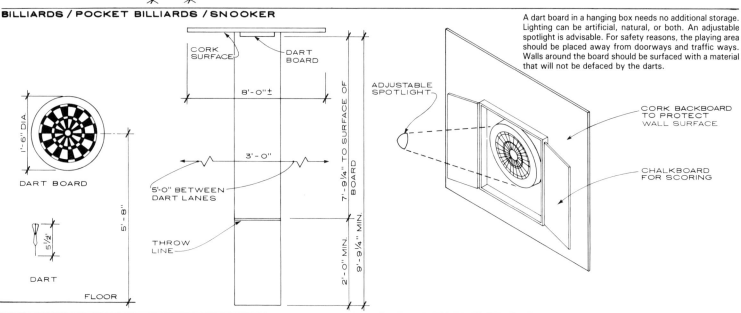

DARTS

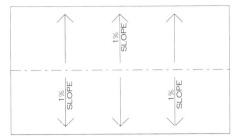

PREFERRED GRADING

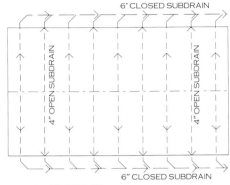

SUBSOIL DRAINAGE

RECTANGULAR SPORTS FIELDS

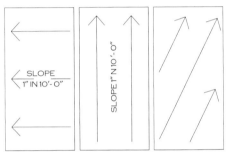

DRAINAGE DIAGRAMS

SPORTS COURTS

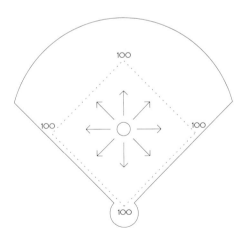

BASEBALL AND SOFTBALL DIAMONDS

NOTES

It is preferable that the base lines be level. If the diamond must pitch, the average slope shall be 2% from first base to third base or vice versa.

The minimum slope for drainage on turf areas outside the skinned area is 1% when adequate subsoil drainage is provided. The maximum is 2.5%.

Richard J. Vitullo, Oak Leaf Studio; Crownsville, Maryland

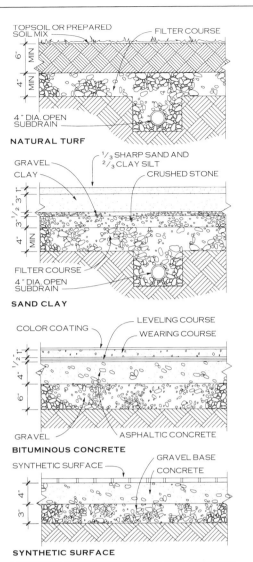

NATURAL TURF

SAND CLAY

BITUMINOUS CONCRETE

SYNTHETIC SURFACE

PLAYING SURFACES

TYPICAL GRADING AND DRAINAGE DETAILS COURT SURFACES

Paved playing surfaces should be in one plane and pitched from side to side, end to end, or corner to corner diagonally, instead of two planes pitched to or from the net. Minimum slope should be 1 in. to every 10 ft. Subgrade should slope in the same direction as the surface. Perimeter drains may be provided for paved areas. Underdrains are not recommended beneath paved areas.

PLAYING FIELDS

Preferred grading for rectangular field is a longitudinal crown with 1% slope from center to each side.

Grading may be from side to side or corner to corner diagonally, if conditions do not permit the preferred grading.

Subsoil drainage should slope in the same direction as the surface. Subdrains and filter course are to be used only when subsoil conditions require. Where subsoil drainage is necessary, the spacing of subdrains is dependent on local soil conditions and rainfall.

Subdrains are to have a minimum gradient of 0.15%.

Baseball and softball fields should be graded so that the bases are level.

LINE PAINTING

All line markings should be acrylic water-base paint only. Oil-base or traffic paints crack, craze, or peel. Spray painting usually is used. High quality courts should be hand painted. Accuracy of track layouts should be verified by registered land surveyor.

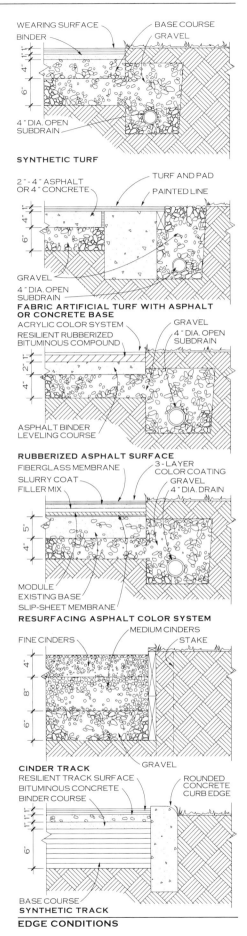

SYNTHETIC TURF

FABRIC ARTIFICIAL TURF WITH ASPHALT OR CONCRETE BASE

RUBBERIZED ASPHALT SURFACE

RESURFACING ASPHALT COLOR SYSTEM

CINDER TRACK

SYNTHETIC TRACK

EDGE CONDITIONS

REGULATION COURSES

Among the types of golf courses – regulation, executive, and par-3 courses – the regulation course is the most popular and truest of form, having originated from early Scottish courses. In 18 holes, the course should play to a par of 72 and be at least 6,000 yards from middle tees with 6,500 yards a good median. A 6,500 course, complete with clubhouse, parking, practice, and related facilities will require 160 to 180 acres.

Beginning and ending at the clubhouse, a par 72 course should contain a combination of:

10 par-4 holes   4 par-3 holes   4 par-5 holes = 18 holes
or
5 par-4 holes   2 par-3 holes   2 par-5 holes = 9 holes

A par-70 or 71 is acceptable if the size of the property or nature of terrain prevents the layout of four good par-5 holes. Then replace one or two par-5s with par-4 holes.

GOLF COURSE CONFIGURATIONS

The typical golf course configurations are:

1. Core
2. Core with fingers
3. Double-fairway loop
4. Single-fairway loop
5. Loop with returning nines
6. Loop without returning nines

To gain lot frontage for housing developments, finger or loop configurations should be used. Disadvantages include greater distances between hole and next tee; overall maintenance cost may be higher; and golf balls will be hit off the property.

COURSE LAYOUT

Lay out holes according to their centerline of play, which should run from the center of the tee to the center of the green. On par-4 and par-5 holes the centerline should run on a straight line from the tee to a dogleg point 225 yards down the fairway. On par-5 holes a second dogleg point should be set at 425 yards.

TYPICAL PAR FOUR LAYOUT

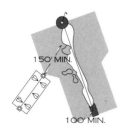

The centerline of a golf hole should be located a minimum of 150 feet from any road, right-of-way, boundary, clubhouse, or maintenance building, except a minimum of 100 feet at the tee. At a distance of 100 to 120 yards from the tee, the width should be 150 feet. On double-fairway loop courses, a minimum width of 500 feet is required.

SAFTEY ZONE

FACILITIES

Clubhouse facilities occupy 6 to 12 acres.

PARKING

Space may be needed for as many as 300 cars:

18 holes x 3 foursomes = 216 cars
25 percent course overlap = 54 cars
Employee/customer parking = 30 cars

PRACTICE FACILITIES

Ideal range is 300 yards long and 100 yards wide. At a 12-to-20 feet per practice station, a 600 feet wide facility should serve 30 to 50 golfers.

PLANNING PROCESS

Ease of utility connections is essential for clubhouse, maintenance area, and the irrigation system. Excessive front-end costs can be avoided by locating near existing infrastructure. Potable water may be from wells or the existing water supply. Irrigation water is usually contained in ponds dug on the golf course.

For an 18-hole golf course, 160 acres is an optimal size. If land is rugged, 175 to 180 acres may be needed. An area less than 150 acres is possible, although this may involve risk of injury to players.

The two most important natural factors in site selection are drainage and soil condition. Many prefer a gently rolling land with positive surface drainage. Fine old trees standing alone in open areas should be noted for use as design features. Developer may want to reserve wooded areas for housing.

VIEWS, NOISE, SUN, AND WIND ORIENTATION

Prevailing wind direction in both summer and winter should be noted. Thin or plant trees according to needs. Study sun orientation to avoid unpleasant views into the setting sun. Generally most favorable location for a clubhouse is at the "high noon" position. Any dramatic views should be noted, although screening or elimination of unpleasant views is more often necessary.

DESIGN DETAILS
GREENS

1. Backdrop of trees or natural slope needed.
2. Should vary in size and shape according to the shot being played..
3. Subdivide greens if desired.
4. Should have six pin placement areas on each green.
5. Slopes on putting surface should range from 2 to 4 percent.
6. Back usually should be raised two-to-three feet above the front.
7. Blend contours into natural environments.
8. Sides should slope 4:1, 5:1, 6:1, or 7:1, unless contour changes dramatically.

TEES

1. Provide separate tees for different caliber of golfers.
2. Single block tee should be 100 yards to accommodate four sets of tee markers.
3. Need not be rectangular boxes.
4. Tees should be distinct and integrated into the site.
5. For every 1,000 rounds per year requires 100 to 200 sq ft.
6. Tees for first and 10th holes and par-3 holes should be larger than others.

HAZARDS

1. Hazards give a golf course its character and flavor and provide challenge to the golfer.
2. Use sand where there are no natural features to provide a desired golfing challenge.
3. Sand can be used to provide depth perception, to define a target area, to frame and accentuate a green, and to divide and buffer parallel fairways.
4. Don't over or under use certain types of sand traps.
5. Use water because of the need to store large amounts for source irrigation, the desire to create strategic and heroic holes, the relative ease to construct ponds and lakes, and to emphasize its esthetic value.
6. Water can be placed across the line of play or parallel to the fairway.
7. There should be water on each classification of hole– par-3, par-4, and par-5.
8. The rough defines the fairways and generally is used as a supplemental hazard.
9. Trees typically line inland courses and serve as hazards but also as physical separators between golf holes. Trees also provide shade and add to esthetics.
10. Planting and clearing of trees should provide a variety of wide and narrow fairways, open and wooded holes, woods, and individual stands.
11. Subtle mounding and contouring of greens and aprons can define fairway limits, separating parallel fairways where there are no existing trees, providing protection for dangerous, tightly spaced areas on a golf course, create a feeling of spatial enclosure, and provide for raised spectator areas at tournaments.
12. Prevailing wind affects the routing of a course.
13. Poor drainage results in weak turf and delays the opening of a course after rain. Therefore, every square foot of a golf course should have positive surface flow to a pond or sewer pipe, either by the natural contour or installed drainage system.

Consultation with a golf course architect is recommended.

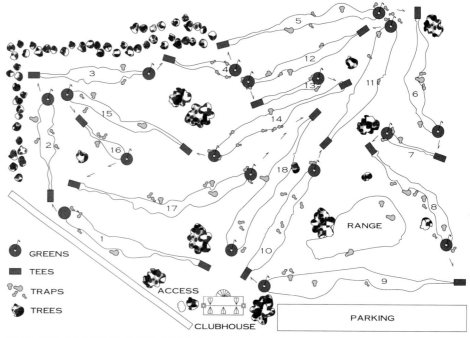

GREENS
TEES
TRAPS
TREES

RANGE

ACCESS

CLUBHOUSE   PARKING

DOUBLE FAIRWAY LOOP

GENERAL

Successful design of building envelopes for cold regions requires that all air-vapor retarders, wind barriers, and insulation be continuous. Air-vapor retarders prevent warm, moist indoor air from entering and condensing in portions of the envelope. Wind barriers prevent cold outdoor air from entering the insulation. Seal the wind barrier and air-vapor retarder at all joints and penetrations in the envelope to prevent air leakage and moisture problems. Metal or concrete bridging across the insulated layer can cause thermal short circuits. Minimize thermal short circuits with with continuous insulation; this saves energy and reduces condensation mold. Adequate slopes and continuity at flashing prevent problems due to snow and ice on roofs.

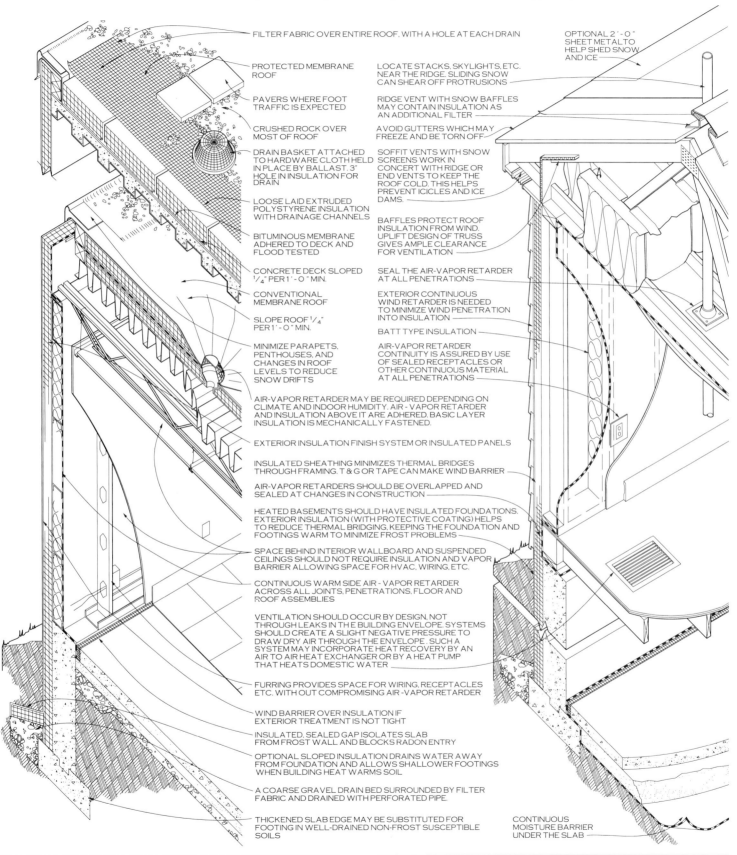

FILTER FABRIC OVER ENTIRE ROOF, WITH A HOLE AT EACH DRAIN

PROTECTED MEMBRANE ROOF

PAVERS WHERE FOOT TRAFFIC IS EXPECTED

CRUSHED ROCK OVER MOST OF ROOF

DRAIN BASKET ATTACHED TO HARDWARE CLOTH HELD IN PLACE BY BALLAST. 3" HOLE IN INSULATION FOR DRAIN

LOOSE LAID EXTRUDED POLYSTYRENE INSULATION WITH DRAINAGE CHANNELS

BITUMINOUS MEMBRANE ADHERED TO DECK AND FLOOD TESTED

CONCRETE DECK SLOPED 1/4" PER 1'-0" MIN.

CONVENTIONAL MEMBRANE ROOF

SLOPE ROOF 1/4" PER 1'-0" MIN.

MINIMIZE PARAPETS, PENTHOUSES, AND CHANGES IN ROOF LEVELS TO REDUCE SNOW DRIFTS

AIR-VAPOR RETARDER MAY BE REQUIRED DEPENDING ON CLIMATE AND INDOOR HUMIDITY. AIR-VAPOR RETARDER AND INSULATION ABOVE IT ARE ADHERED. BASIC LAYER INSULATION IS MECHANICALLY FASTENED.

EXTERIOR INSULATION FINISH SYSTEM OR INSULATED PANELS

INSULATED SHEATHING MINIMIZES THERMAL BRIDGES THROUGH FRAMING. T & G OR TAPE CAN MAKE WIND BARRIER

AIR-VAPOR RETARDERS SHOULD BE OVERLAPPED AND SEALED AT CHANGES IN CONSTRUCTION

HEATED BASEMENTS SHOULD HAVE INSULATED FOUNDATIONS. EXTERIOR INSULATION (WITH PROTECTIVE COATING) HELPS TO REDUCE THERMAL BRIDGING, KEEPING THE FOUNDATION AND FOOTINGS WARM TO MINIMIZE FROST PROBLEMS

SPACE BEHIND INTERIOR WALLBOARD AND SUSPENDED CEILINGS SHOULD NOT REQUIRE INSULATION AND VAPOR BARRIER ALLOWING SPACE FOR HVAC, WIRING, ETC.

CONTINUOUS WARM SIDE AIR-VAPOR RETARDER ACROSS ALL JOINTS, PENETRATIONS, FLOOR AND ROOF ASSEMBLIES

VENTILATION SHOULD OCCUR BY DESIGN, NOT THROUGH LEAKS IN THE BUILDING ENVELOPE. SYSTEMS SHOULD CREATE A SLIGHT NEGATIVE PRESSURE TO DRAW DRY AIR THROUGH THE ENVELOPE. SUCH A SYSTEM MAY INCORPORATE HEAT RECOVERY BY AN AIR TO AIR HEAT EXCHANGER OR BY A HEAT PUMP THAT HEATS DOMESTIC WATER

FURRING PROVIDES SPACE FOR WIRING, RECEPTACLES ETC. WITHOUT COMPROMISING AIR-VAPOR RETARDER

WIND BARRIER OVER INSULATION IF EXTERIOR TREATMENT IS NOT TIGHT

INSULATED, SEALED GAP ISOLATES SLAB FROM FROST WALL AND BLOCKS RADON ENTRY

OPTIONAL SLOPED INSULATION DRAINS WATER AWAY FROM FOUNDATION AND ALLOWS SHALLOWER FOOTINGS WHEN BUILDING HEAT WARMS SOIL

A COARSE GRAVEL DRAIN BED SURROUNDED BY FILTER FABRIC AND DRAINED WITH PERFORATED PIPE.

THICKENED SLAB EDGE MAY BE SUBSTITUTED FOR FOOTING IN WELL-DRAINED NON-FROST SUSCEPTIBLE SOILS

LOCATE STACKS, SKYLIGHTS, ETC. NEAR THE RIDGE. SLIDING SNOW CAN SHEAR OFF PROTRUSIONS

RIDGE VENT WITH SNOW BAFFLES MAY CONTAIN INSULATION AS AN ADDITIONAL FILTER

AVOID GUTTERS WHICH MAY FREEZE AND BE TORN OFF

SOFFIT VENTS WITH SNOW SCREENS WORK IN CONCERT WITH RIDGE OR END VENTS TO KEEP THE ROOF COLD. THIS HELPS PREVENT ICICLES AND ICE DAMS.

BAFFLES PROTECT ROOF INSULATION FROM WIND. UPLIFT DESIGN OF TRUSS GIVES AMPLE CLEARANCE FOR VENTILATION

SEAL THE AIR-VAPOR RETARDER AT ALL PENETRATIONS

EXTERIOR CONTINUOUS WIND RETARDER IS NEEDED TO MINIMIZE WIND PENETRATION INTO INSULATION

BATT TYPE INSULATION

AIR-VAPOR RETARDER CONTINUITY IS ASSURED BY USE OF SEALED RECEPTACLES OR OTHER CONTINUOUS MATERIAL AT ALL PENETRATIONS

OPTIONAL 2'-0" SHEET METAL TO HELP SHED SNOW AND ICE

CONTINUOUS MOISTURE BARRIER UNDER THE SLAB

CONCRETE OR STEEL CONSTRUCTION WITH MEMBRANE ROOF

FRAME CONSTRUCTION WITH A COLD ROOF

Eric K. Beach, Rippeteau Architects, PC; Washington, D.C.
Cold Regions Research and Engineering Laboratory, U.S. Army Corps of Engineers

THERMAL TRANSMISSION 18

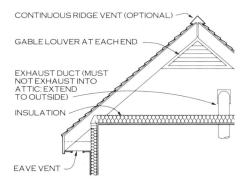

GABLE ROOF WITH UNOCCUPIED ATTIC

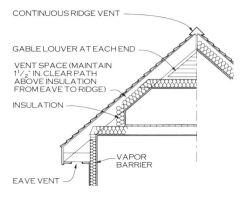

GABLE WITH OCCUPIED SPACE UNDER ROOF

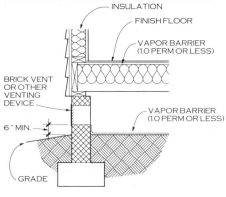

CRAWL SPACE

VENTILATION REQUIREMENTS TO PREVENT CONDENSATION

SPACE	DESCRIPTION		TOTAL NET AREA OF VENTILATION (A)	REMARKS
Joist/rafter (Finish ceiling attached to underside of joists.	Flat		A = 1/300. Uniformly distributed vents at eaves.	Vent each joist space at both ends. Maintain 1 1/2" min. clear path above insulation for ventilation.
	Sloped		A = 1/300. Uniformly distributed vents at eaves with a continuous ridge vent.	
Attic (unheated)	Gable		A = 1/300. At least two louvers on opposite sides near ridge or one continuous ridge vent. Uniformly distributed vents at eaves.	Any combination of gable/hip louvers and/or ridge vents may be used to achieve required ventilation.
	Hip			
Crawl space/basement			a = 2L/100 + A/300 Where L = crawl space/basement perimeter (linear feet) A = crawl space/basement area (square feet)	Provide at least one opening per side, as high as possible in wall.

Total net area of ventilation = 1/300 of building area at eave. With insect screens increase net area as follows: 1.0 sq ft for 1/4 in. screen; 1.25 square feet for #8 screen; 2.0 sq ft for #16 screen.

VENTILATION APPLICATIONS
GENERAL

Building attics, crawl spaces, and basements must be ventilated to remove moisture and water vapor resulting from human activity within the building. Moisture in basements and crawl spaces can be caused from water in the surrounding soil; these spaces require a high rate of ventilation. The quantity of water vapor depends on building type (e.g., residence, school, hospital), activity (e.g., kitchen, bathroom, laundry), and therefore, air temperature and relative humidity. Proper ventilation and insulation must be combined so that the temperature of the ventilated space does not fall below the dew point; this is especially critical with low outdoor temperatures and high inside humidity. Inadequate ventilation will cause condensation and eventual deterioration of framing, insulation, and interior finishes.

The vent types shown allow natural ventilation of roofs and crawl spaces. Mechanical methods (e.g., power attic ventilators, whole house fans) can combine living space and attic ventilation, but openings for natural roof ventilation must still be provided. Protect all vents against insects and vermin with metal or fiberglass screen cloth. Increase net vent areas as noted in table (above).

Vapor barriers minimize moisture migration to attics and crawl spaces; their use is required for all conditions. Always locate vapor barriers on the warm (room) side of insulation. Provide ventilation on the cold side to permit cold/hot weather ventilation while minimizing heat gain/loss.

Eric K. Beach, Rippeteau Architects, PC; Washington, D.C.

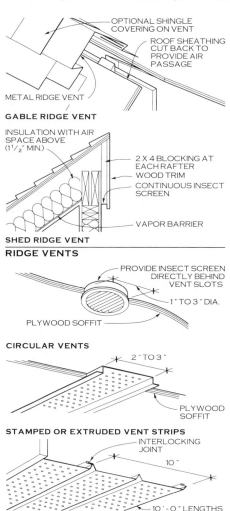

GABLE RIDGE VENT

SHED RIDGE VENT

RIDGE VENTS

CIRCULAR VENTS

STAMPED OR EXTRUDED VENT STRIPS

PERFORATED SOFFIT PANELS

EAVE VENTILATION MATERIALS

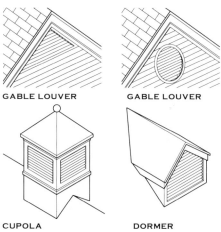

GABLE LOUVER   GABLE LOUVER

CUPOLA   DORMER

ROOF LOUVER TYPES

BRICK VENT

HOLLOW TILE

NOTE

Insect screen must be added to back of tile.

LOUVER

NOTE

Most vents for crawl spaces are set into unit masonry (and are sized accordingly) or concrete. Consult manufacturers. Metal louvers and vents have integral insect screens.

CRAWL SPACE VENTILATION MATERIALS

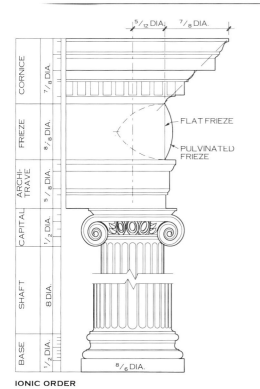

IONIC ORDER

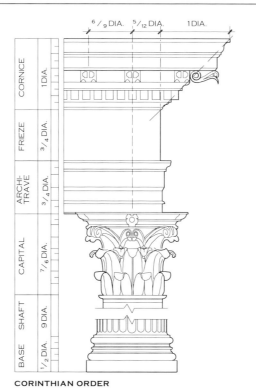

CORINTHIAN ORDER

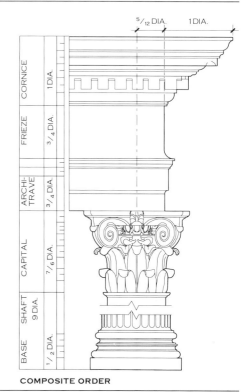

COMPOSITE ORDER

COLUMNS

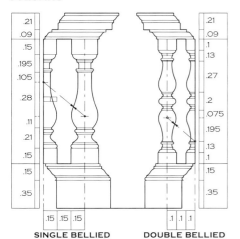

SINGLE BELLIED   **DOUBLE BELLIED**

CORINTHIAN

TUSCAN

BALUSTRADE LAYOUT TECHNIQUE

The Ionic Order single belly balustrade is an example.

1. From the baseline (presumably the top of the cornice or some similarly determinate location), draw in the horizontals representing handrails and pedestal, leaving a band for the balusters themselves.

2. Determine the length of the balustrade between dies. Each baluster is 0.3 and the space between is 0.15. The rank of balusters is usually terminated by a half baluster against the die. Set the length of the rank at a dimension divisable by 0.45. Divide the length by 0.15; each third line is then an axis of a baluster.

3. Set the baluster abacus and plinth, to the full width of 0.3 and each 0.135 in height.

4. Establish the centers A and B, for the convex and concave parts of the baluster curve, 0.87 and 1.15 above the baseline. At center A construct the convex arc with a radius 0.15, cutting diagonal AB at C.

5. At center B construct radius BC to form the concave arc, cutting the horizontal BB at D. BD is the radius of the upper cylindrical part of the baluster.

6. Construct the horizontals of base and capital moldings empirically. The base of the baluster curve is located at E.

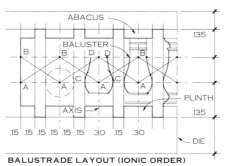

BALUSTRADE LAYOUT (IONIC ORDER)

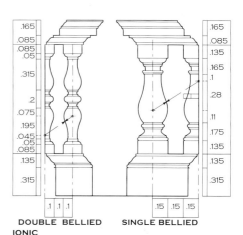

DOUBLE BELLIED   **SINGLE BELLIED**

IONIC

DOUBLE BELLIED   **SINGLE BELLIED**

DORIC

NOTES

Balustrades are often used purely ornamentally to infill arched openings or as a termination above an order. For this use, a height of about four-fifths of the entablature gives the correct proportion in terms of the cohesion of the order. However, it is perhaps unwise to depart too far from the practical dimension of 3 ft - 0 in because doing so imparts a false impression of the size of the order. In such cases it is better to find another type of ornament.

The modular form of the proportions is 1.4 Tuscan, 1.6 Doric, 1.8 Ionic, and 2.0 for Corinthian. The rest of the dimensions above are also in modular form.

Doric, Ionic, and Corinthian orders are normally turned, whereas the Tuscan order works as both turned and square balusters. Square balusters, generally, should be narrower than their turned counterparts. Otherwise they tend to look too bulky when viewed across diagonals.

BALUSTRADES

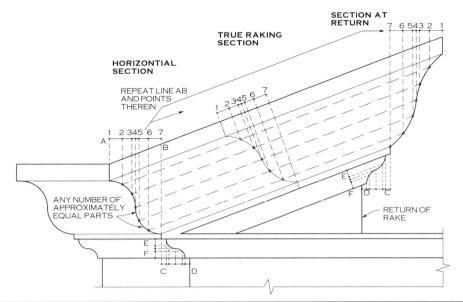

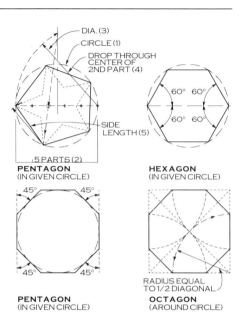

DIA. (3)
CIRCLE (1)
DROP THROUGH CENTER OF 2ND PART (4)
SIDE LENGTH (5)
5 PARTS (2)

PENTAGON (IN GIVEN CIRCLE)

60° 60°
60° 60°

HEXAGON (IN GIVEN CIRCLE)

45° 45°

45° 45°

PENTAGON (IN GIVEN CIRCLE)

RADIUS EQUAL TO 1/2 DIAGONAL

OCTAGON (AROUND CIRCLE)

RAKING MOLDINGS

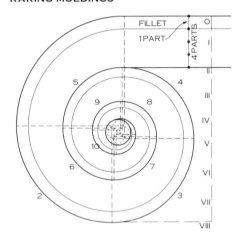

Below the centerline of the volute, draw a circle with a diameter of $1/8$ the height of the volute. Inscribe a rotated, quartered square within this circle or "eye." The sixth points of the centerline of this square give the centers for a series of diminishing arcs. From center 1 draw arc 1, from center 2, arc 2, etc. Successive arcs meet at a line defined by their centers. The inner line of the fillet is gained by repeating the process using the secondary centers shown below.

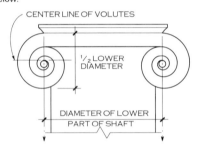

CENTER LINE OF VOLUTES

$1/2$ LOWER DIAMETER

DIAMETER OF LOWER PART OF SHAFT

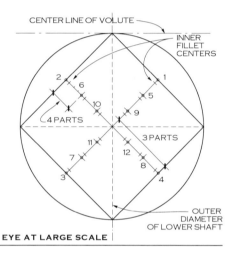

CENTER LINE OF VOLUTE

INNER FILLET CENTERS

4 PARTS

3 PARTS

OUTER DIAMETER OF LOWER SHAFT

EYE AT LARGE SCALE

METHOD OF DRAWING A VOLUTE

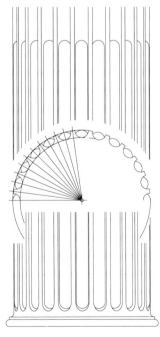

GENERAL

Most fluting follows the renaissance example where the flute is generally semicircular in section. The individual flutes are connected by a fillet which proportionally is 2:6 in relation to the flute size.

The number of flutes varies, but commonly Ionic, Corinthian, and composite shafts have as few as 20. Tuscan shafts are normally not fluted.

Fluting may extend for the entire shaft or only the diminishing part. The flutes can be empty or they may have the lower part filled with cabling. This can be either smooth or enriched in the form of rope or ribbon.

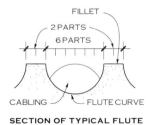

FILLET
2 PARTS
6 PARTS

CABLING   FLUTE CURVE

SECTION OF TYPICAL FLUTE

LAYOUT PROCEDURE FOR TYPICAL ENTASIS

Lay out column height, centerline, and upper and lower diameters at $1/3$ point on column, draw $1/2$ circle equal to lower diameter. Drop a line from the upper diameter to the semicircle (1). Divide the resulting minor arc and upper $2/3$ of shaft into an equal number of equal parts. Draw vertical lines from the arc divisions to the horizontal shaft divisions (2). The resulting points define the curved profile of the column shaft (3).

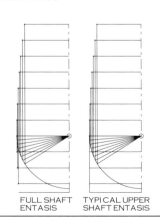

FULL SHAFT ENTASIS

TYPICAL UPPER SHAFT ENTASIS

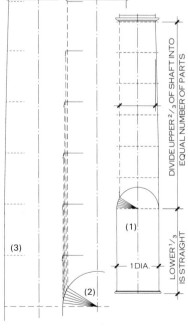

(3)

(1)

(2)

1 DIA.

DIVIDE UPPER $2/3$ OF SHAFT INTO EQUAL NUMBER OF PARTS

LOWER $1/3$ IS STRAIGHT

FLUTING

ENTASIS

PROJECT PROGRAM

A powerful tool in office design is the project program. Speculative offices by definition have a far simpler program than client occupied offices, which must locate and support every individual and piece of equipment that will occupy the finished building.

There are many approaches to programming, but all successful programs are highly interactive and require the involvement and commitment of all key participants. All programs involve the following:

1. Data collection
2. Data analysis
3. Data organization
4. Data development
5. Conceptual communication
6. Evaluation of concepts.

Design programs have become very complex and may take longer to develop than the design of the building. The program seeks to measure the influence of every element affecting the proposed project. These range from the effects of the sun and wind to the interrelationships of various organizational groupings to the most beneficial levels of light, temperature, and sound for individuals and equipment. Not all program communication is verbal. Many graphic techniques exist to aid in the analysis and communication of data and concept. The most important, but not only, product of the program is the facilities plan. Other important products are a clearly defined chain of communications, a command structure for decision making in a timely manner, a project schedule with milestones clearly defined, and a project budget. Other less objective goals are an energy conservation policy and image projection.

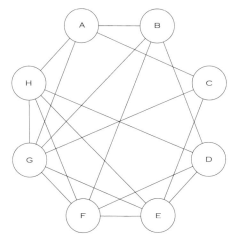

INTERACTION NET

An interaction net illustrates the number of interactions each function or space has with its peers. The items being analyzed are shown as nodes on the perimeter of a net. Each interaction is shown as a line between the relating item.

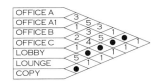

MATRIX

A matrix of relationships shows a variety of relationships within a large group. It does this by dividing the large group into several obvious classifications. A series of yes/no questions are then asked of each group and subsequent subgroup. The elements with a positive response form a subgroup, and the negative responses form a companion subgroup.

Laird Ueberroth, Architect, and Associates; McLean, Virginia

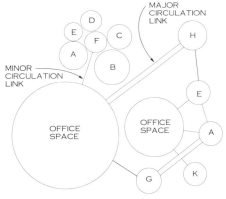

BUBBLE DIAGRAM

The bubble diagram is one of the first attempts to place spaces in their proper relationship. Bubble diagrams approximate space sizes and show strong and weak relationships by proximity of represented spaces. A loose circulation or "flow" path between spaces is generated.

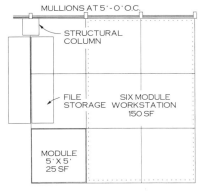

5 FT MODULE

Large modules do not necessarily create larger workstations as illustrated here. The module is a device for coordinating different building systems. Large modules reduce spacing options

MODULES

Offices can be broadly grouped into two categories: speculative and client occupied. Nearly all speculative office projects are designed using the open plan concept. The flexibility in defining tenant spaces and the reduced cost of this system are overwhelming advantages to the developer. Client occupied office designs have increasingly moved from conventional plan to the open plan concept by utilizing more developed concepts like office landscaping and cellular plans.

CONVENTIONAL PLAN

The conventional office plan is used primarily today in corporate executive offices. Conventional office plans are characterized by shallow bays and long narrow footprints with central cores that maximize window space. Conventional plans define space by creating offices with floor-to-ceiling partitions opening onto enclosed corridors. Bearing walls and interior columns are easier to accommodate in conventional plans than other types.

MODULES

MODULE

One of the first tasks of the design process is the selection of a building module. The module affects all future design decisions from furniture systems to mullion spacing and structural system. The module must successfully integrate all these systems. Once selected, the module aids in dimensionally locating the structural frame, the core, the utility risers and distribution closets and has an impact on almost every component of the building.

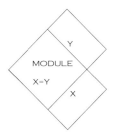

Modules range from 4 ft x 4 ft (16 sq ft) to 6 ft x 6 ft (24 sq ft) and are adjustable in 4 or 6 in. increments. Structural bay sizes are established as multiples of module dimensions.

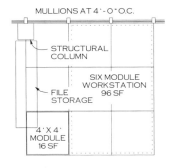

4 FT MODULE

Small modules promote flexibility and complexity.

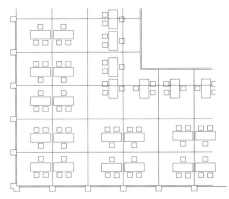

OPEN PLAN

Open plans are characterized by deep open bays with few internal columns. Privacy, acoustics, and territoriality issues are handled with integrated furniture systems incorporating privacy/acoustic panels. Delivery of power and communication to point of use has inspired the creation of several new delivery technologies: raised flooring, flatwire, and furniture systems with integrated cable raceways are examples.

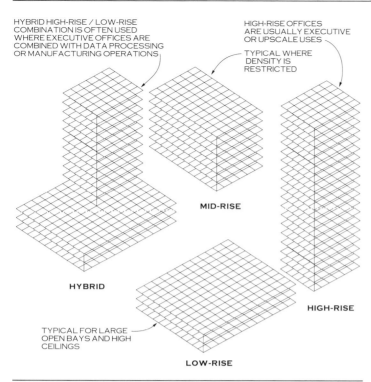

HYBRID HIGH-RISE / LOW-RISE COMBINATION IS OFTEN USED WHERE EXECUTIVE OFFICES ARE COMBINED WITH DATA PROCESSING OR MANUFACTURING OPERATIONS

HIGH-RISE OFFICES ARE USUALLY EXECUTIVE OR UPSCALE USES

TYPICAL WHERE DENSITY IS RESTRICTED

MID-RISE

HYBRID

HIGH-RISE

TYPICAL FOR LARGE OPEN BAYS AND HIGH CEILINGS

LOW-RISE

OFFICE ENVELOPE CONFIGURATIONS

FACILITIES PLAN

The program statement sets down in detail the relationships and space allocations of the components of the project. The Facilities Plan takes the information presented in the Program Statement and applies it to the Proposed building envelope as determined by Zoning, Code, and site restrictions to establish building form and orientation. All rooms/areas are laid out with spaces provided for all employees and functions.

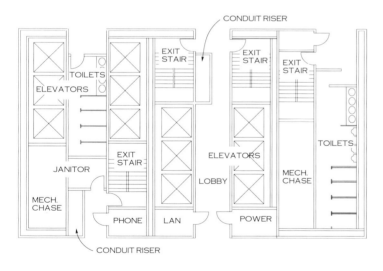

CONDUIT RISER

EXIT STAIR — EXIT STAIR — EXIT STAIR

TOILETS

ELEVATORS

EXIT STAIR

JANITOR

ELEVATORS

LOBBY

TOILETS

MECH. CHASE

MECH. CHASE

PHONE LAN POWER

CONDUIT RISER

TYPICAL HIGH-RISE OFFICE BUILDING CORE CONFIGURATION

CONCEPTUAL CORE COMPONENT GUIDELINES

Power, communication, and signal cables	2% net area
Toilet rooms	1 sq ft of toilet room per 150 sq ft net area
Elevators maximum Travel distance to elevator	200 ft
Maximum wait for elevator	30 seconds
Stair towers	2 minimum, 300 sq ft each

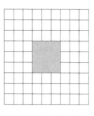
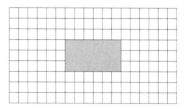

SYMMETRICAL CENTRAL CORE

ELONGATED CENTRAL CORE

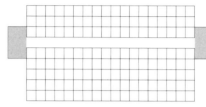

SPLIT PERIMETER CORE

PERIMETER CORE

CORE CONFIGURATIONS

The core is the consolidated placement of the major service and support structures. Because the core links the entire building together, its components are enclosed within fireproof cells. The integrity of these enclosures is critical, because once a fire or smoke enters the core it can quickly spread to all other floors. Typical cores include stair towers (2), elevators, toilets, HVAC risers, power and communication distribution closets, modularity.

Many broad core placement categories exist with many more variations. Factors that influence the placement of the core are:
1. the planning concept selected
2. site characteristics which affect the building footprint
3. structural/seismic considerations
4. the type and number of end users
5. the degree of flexibility required.

Split cores and cores located on the building perimeter increase flexibility and open planning options. Central and elongated cores lend themselves to more conventional rigid plans, although the depth of the bay can have a great influence on flexibility.

Once the core has been established, protected and unprotected circulation corridors are mapped onto individual floors in conjunction with the facilities plan. The location of the core and circulation plan must work in relation with the module developed. Careful consideration must be given to the present and possible future uses of the proposed spaces, because the distances established by the building shape and the core/circulation locations will determine what type of planning concepts can be accommodated efficiently.

OFFICE SUPPORT SYSTEMS

The trend for the foreseeable future is toward increasing the power and flexibility available in the modern office building. To accomplish this, greater demands are being made to deliver worker support—like voice and data integration, video services, security, energy, and environmental management—to more points in the building and to do so in a way that does not restrict redesign of workstation layouts or hinder free travel between stations. Thought must be given to how these systems will be accommodated within the building structure. In areas where raised floors are not provided, the structural system should be designed to place minimal restriction on poke-through accessibility of power and communication cables and easy access for rewiring large areas. In addition to flexible distribution, these systems require more support space. Computer supported voice/data switching services will require increased dedicated space in new office buildings. Local Area Networks (LAN) with distributed processing features will require increased cabling areas. Uninterrupted power supply (UPS) is another new requirement of many office buildings. UPS systems require an electric power generator, fuel storage, a monitor room, and a large battery storage room. The increased power requirements of automated workstations and computers in office buildings require increased power distribution. The increased power requirement and the need to dedicate larger amounts of power for specific uses mean an increase in the amount of space set aside for electric power panel closets and conduit risers.

ACCESS FLOOR: High first cost, but relocation is inexpensive. Floor plenum can accommodate HVAC as well as cable. Outlets are flush with floor, and relocations are easy.

POKE-THROUGH: Least expensive first cost, uses traditional distribution methods in ceiling plenum. One outlet per 65 sq ft maximum is drilled through floor above and fitted with a fireproof assembly. Outlets sit 4 in. above floor. Relocations require interference with floor below.

PLUG-IN DUCT: Power poles bring cables from ceiling space to floor or prewired furniture systems. Very flexible system but aesthetically questionable.

FLAT WIRE: Flat copper conductors are taped to the floor under carpet. Wires cannot be crossed and the system does not handle lighting, but it is flexible and accessible. Transitions from flat to round cables make the system expensive.

CELLULAR FLOOR: A metal tray is poured integral with a composite concrete floor slab. Trays are laid out on a modular grid with outlets set on the module. Inexpensive, but does not handle lighting, and difficult to adjust out of the module.

Laird Ueberroth, Architect, and Associates; McLean, Virginia

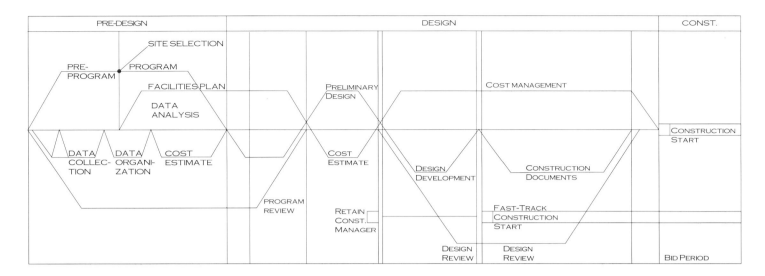

DESIGN SCHEDULE

Time and cost control has become an important part of office building design. A well thought-out schedule has become an essential management tool for tracking and controlling project progress. Many different scheduling techniques exist: CPM, Gantt Chart, and PERT are a few common examples. Most project scheduling today is automated and managed by popular computer software packages.

Office building schedules can be broken down into several broad categories; preprogram, program, design, construction, and postconstruction. The preprogram involves all work related to preparing for the project. Site selection and raw data collection are examples of this phase. In the program phase project specific information is collected, organized, and analyzed, and concepts are developed and presented for review. The program culminates in the facilities plan. The design phase selects all building components and systems and dimensionally locates and sizes them. This phase is further broken down into design development and construction documents. Construction may start in the construction documents stage of the design, depending on the type of delivery approach selected.

DELIVERY APPROACHES

Design and construction have evolved as separate disciplines. The separation of these two essential components of a building project has many logical and time tested advantages. Increased competition and the importance of time have generated several new delivery approaches which are gaining popularity in office building. Delivery approaches differ in two fundamental ways: whether the design and construction are seen as integrated or separated responsibilities, and whether construction begins before or after construction documents are fully developed.

CONSTRUCTION

The importance of time in the creation of office buildings has generated many new construction approaches. Design/build and fast track are increasingly popular new construction options. Their acceptance has spurred the wider use of construction managers and overlapped design and construction techniques. These techniques tend to limit the fluidity of the design and places greater emphasis on locking in decisions during the predesign and early design phases.

FAST TRACK

As its name implies, the primary advantage of this approach is speed. It saves time by overlapping design and construction. Architects and contractors are in their traditional roles in fast track projects. With added demands of construction coordination and cost and time control, fast tracking has stimulated the emergence of the construction manager (CM). With the advantage of reduced delivery time comes the disadvantage of reduced cost control. There are two approaches to this problem. One is to proceed with construction without a fixed overall price. This requires a cost-management strategy to establish contingencies and alternates for all subcontracts. The other approach is to contract the work based on partially developed documents. Guaranteed maximum price contracts are popular with owners. It is impossible to avoid risk when an overall price is set on the basis of partially completed documents.

DESIGN BUILD

Design/build unifies the design and construction responsibilities under one contract. The advantages of this approach are: the owner has only one point of responsibility for the project, the unproductive adversarial relationship between architect and contractor is eliminated, the builder becomes a member of the decision team lending his expertise in cost control and constructability to the process, thereby fixing costs at an early stage. The primary disadvantage of this approach is that the owner loses the professional advice of an agent working for his interests. Since the owner is purchasing a complete package he gives up many opportunities to choose the best products for his purposes. Often an administrative architect is used to try and reestablish the role of an agent for the owner's interest in this process.

DESIGN-AWARD-BUILD

In this traditional approach to building, the owner writes at least two prime contracts: one with the architect and one with the contractor. The architect provides a professional service to the owner and acts as his agent, lending his expertise to the design and selection of a contractor. Traditionally a contractor is selected when the design is complete; construction is started only when the total construction cost is known. Variations of this approach allow for the writing of several prime contracts and overlapping design and construction. The construction manager is often hired by the owner when these options are used.

FAST TRACK

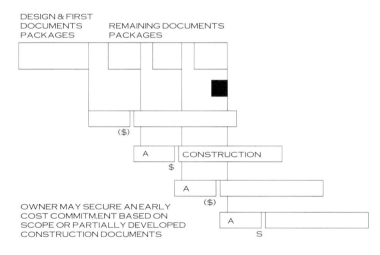

OWNER MAY SECURE AN EARLY COST COMMITM,ENT BASED ON SCOPE OR PARTIALLY DEVELOPED CONSTRUCTION DOCUMENTS

DESIGN /BUILD

DESIGN /AWARD /BUILD

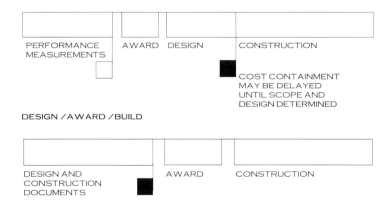

Laird Ueberroth, Architect, and Associates; McLean, Virginia

GENERAL

Most elements of a building are composed of many identical components assembled in a pattern or grid to form the "whole." Examples include the structural frames, glazing panels, , distribution closets for Power and communication, lighting, etc. Modularity is the attempt to bring all these patterns or grids into harmony. The advantage in this is a more efficient use of space and systems by eliminating "gaps" of unusable or unserviceable space. Harmony is established by defining a lowest common denominator or module and using it as a basis for all elemental grids. The most basic relationship from a planning standpoint is between the depth of bays (established by the structural frame) and the work station. The goal, which is more important in shallow bays, is to maximize the flexibility of workstation, corridor, and file space, within the bay without creating any "gaps" of unused space.

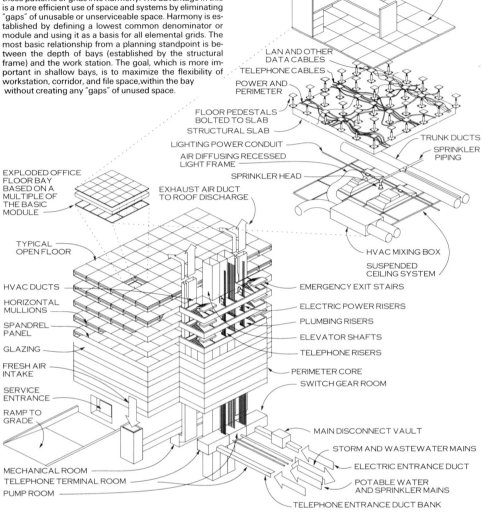

AVERAGE ILLUMINATION LEVEL FOR TYPICAL AREAS (IN FOOTCANDLES)

General offices	50
Drafting rooms	75
Conference rooms	50
Computer rooms	50
Corridors/stairs	20
Lobbies	20
Reception desks	50
Cafeterias	30

AVERAGE ELECTRICAL LOAD FOR TYPICAL SPACES (WATTS/SQ FT)

General offices	3
Copier rooms	15
Conference rooms	1
Word processing	4
Computer room	40

MINIMUM LIVE LOAD FOR TYPICAL OFFICE AREAS (LB/SQ FT)

General office	50
Equipment rooms	100
Corridors	80
Telephone exchange	150
Transformer rooms	200
File storage rooms	80

ARCHITECTURAL GRAPHIC STANDARDS REFERENCE CHART FOR EIGHTH EDITION

OFFICE SPACE ALLOWANCE GUIDE (SF)

Top executive	400–600
Managers	150–200
Assistant managers	100–125
Supervisors	80–100
Operator (60 inch desk)	50–60
Operator (55 inch desk)	50–55
Operator (50 Inch Desk)	45
Standard letter file	6
Standard legal file	7
Letter lateral file	6.5
Legal lateral file	7.5
Video studio	900
Meeting room (over 200 people)	2000

OFFICE BUILDING AUXILIARY SPACES

Office buildings serve a wide variety of users, with a diverse set of requirements. No single office building type or configuration could satisfy all of the potential requirements. As new buildings are constructed to meet the needs of individual users, new services are continuously being incorporated into their designs. Listed below are many of the auxilliary spaces found in office buildings today. Some are almost universal and some are quite rare.

1. Fire control room
2. Facilities maintenance and storage
3. Building control center
4. Video conference room
5. Shipping / receiving dock
6. Cafeteria
7. Secure storage/vault room
8. Copy / graphics room
9. UPS battery room and generator room
10. PBX frame room
11. Telephone terminal room
12. Electric power switch room
13. Record storage
14. Library

Laird Ueberroth, Architect, and Associates; McLean, Virginia

OVERVIEW OF CONDOC

ConDoc is a production methodology developed to improve the quality and usefulness of construction documents while greatly simplifying the process of creating them. ConDoc provides a means to organize and format drawings and to directly link information shown on drawings to that contained in the specifications.

A major feature of ConDoc is the use of a unique keynote system that links drawings and specifications while reducing substantially the text needed on drawings without any loss of information shown on the drawings.

BASIC PRECEPTS OF THE CONDOC METHODOLOGY

1. Will not restrict the creativity or individuality of the user.
2. Works with projects of any size or type.
3. Does not restrict the extent of information to be placed in the documents.
4. Works for all disciplines, but it is not necessary that it be used by all disciplines on a project.
5. Provides conventions for formatting the composition of individual drawings, based upon a modular sheet arrangement.
6. Uses a keynote system which directly interfaces with the specification numbering system.
7. Provides a means for standardizing procedures in the preparation of construction documents.
8. Enhances quality control, coordination, and review of documents.

THE DRAWING FORMAT

Consistency of drawing arrangement is achieved through the use of a modular subdivision of spaces with provisions for a keynote system and legend. The ConDoc modular drawing format relates to standard sheet sizes, although special sizes may be accommodated.

The use of ConDoc organizes and standardizes the arrangement of graphic information within modules (or group of modules). It establishes a standard size and location on for titles and symbols, a standard for placement of information including dimensioning, and simplifies the means to incorporate standard details and schedules.

LINKING DRAWING AND SPECIFICATIONS VIA KEYNOTES

Great advances and benefits have been realized in the preparation of specifications as a result of the development and evolution of the 16-division format and 5-digit code that identifies each of the sections used in the specifications. This same 5-digit code is used throughout the construction industry to categorize technical data and, when used as a keynote, provides immediate recognition as to which specification sections relate to information shown on the drawing.

The use of keynotes and materials legend dramatically reduces the extent of lettering on drawings, without sacrifice in the amount of information shown. The ConDoc methodology removes extraneous information, simplifies and expedites the placement of information, minimizes the time needed to compose drawings, and avoids unnecessary duplication of information.

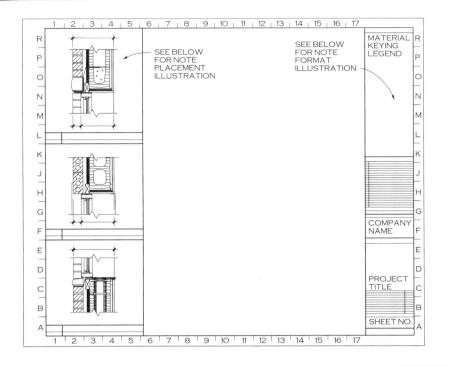

MODULAR TITLE SHEET FOR GRID IDENTIFICATION SYSTEM

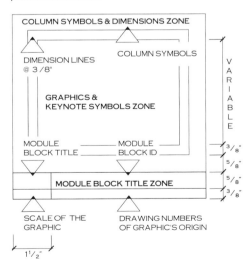

STANDARD CONDOC MODULE BLOCK

James M. Duda; Herndon, Virginia
Onkal K. Guzey and James N. Freehof; Washington, D.C.
Terry Graves, McCarty Architects; Tupelo, Mississippi

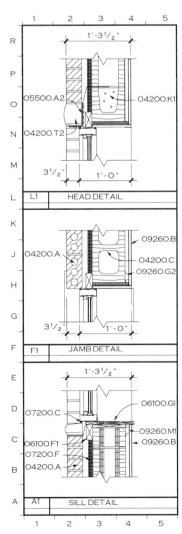

TYPICAL CONDOC DETAIL AND KEYING LEGEND

MATERIAL KEYING LEGEND

DIV. 4 MASONRY

04200.A	FACE BRICK
04200.B	SOLDIER COURSE
04200.C	8" CONCRETE BLOCK
04200.K1	CMU LINTEL - SEE STRUCTURAL
04200.N	WEEP HOLES
04200.Q	MEMBRANE FLASHING
04200.R	BLOCK INSULATION
04200.T2	CAST STONE LINTEL
04200.T3	CAST STONE SILL

DIV. 5 METALS

05500.A2	$3^1/_2$" X 5" X $^5/_{16}$" ANGLE

DIV. 6 WOOD AND PLASTICS

06100.A4	2 X 4 STUDS AT 16" O.C.
06100.F1	WOOD BLOCKING AS REQUIRED
06100.F6	TREATED 1 X 8
06100.F7	TREATED BLOCKING
06100.G6	$^3/_4$" EXTERIOR GRADE PLYWOOD
06100.GI	CULTURED MARBLE SILL

DIV. 7 THERMAL AND MOISTURE PROTECTION

07200.F	1" BOARD INSULATION
07200.A	SILICONE SEALANT
07200.C	CAULK
07200.D	BACKER ROD

DIV. 8 DOORS AND WINDOWS

08110.A	HOLLOW METAL FRAME
08110.B	HOLLOW METAL DOOR
08110.C	"B" LABEL HOLLOW METAL FRAME
08110.D	JAMB ANCHOR
08110.E	GROUT - FILL HOLLOW METAL FRAME
08211.A	SOLID CORE WOOD DOOR
08360.B	DOOR TRACK
08410.A	ALUMINUM FRAMING - SEE SCHEDULE

DIV. 9 FINISHES

09260.B	$^5/_8$" GYP. BD.
09260.F1	$^5/_8$" TYPE "X" GYP. BD.
09260.G2	METAL CORNER BEAD (TYP.)
09260.M1	$^7/_8$" FURRING CHANNEL

GRAPHIC METHODS

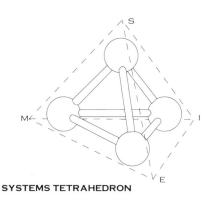

SYSTEMS TETRAHEDRON

FIGURE

BUILDING SYSTEMS INTEGRATION

Integration is rarely a conscious act. The criteria that govern building design are themselves integrative; therefore, the designs that result are always integrated. Drawing distinctions that help to articulate an activity usually cause a heightened level of performance within the activity itself. By using such distinctions to create a model of integration, a designer can hold a mirror up to the design process.

Conscious integration is an activity that involves the study of relationships through the use of questionnaires, matrices, and diagrams. Questionnaires employ mostly words. Matrices often result in numbers. Diagrams are pictorial. To fully enhance the integrative process, the optimal approach usually results in translating back and forth among the three tools.

Displayed on these pages are a series of diagrams and matrices. Coupled with the questionnaire that follows, it is possible to model the process of integration. One may evaluate any list of questions, matrix, or diagram for its own sake, but to understand these pages as an integrated whole, one must be able to appreciate the relationships among the different figures shown.

WHAT ARE THE SYSTEMS?
All buildings are composed of four basic systems: structure, envelope, mechanical, and interior. The fact that they all occur in the same building can be expressed diagrammatically by placing the systems at the points of a tetrahedron. (See figure 1)

HOW ARE SYSTEMS RELATED?
The relationship between systems is rarely as simple as would be implied by the tetrahedron. Systems are often intertwined. We define the ways that they relate to each other as remote, touching, connected, meshed, and unified. They are the LEVELS OF INTEGRATION. The systems start out completely independent and as they approach each other, like bubbles, they can touch, then connect, and finally become one. The meshed state is defined as two systems that occupy the same space, like ducts snaking through bar joists. (See figure two)

HOW DO THE SYSTEMS RELATE TO THE LEVELS OF INTEGRATION?
The Building Systems Integration Matrix shows that the possible parts of systems are not equally likely to combine at all levels of integration. Most buildings normally use only the 17 different combinations depicted by the cross points on the BSIH Matrix.

HOW DO SPECIFIC SYSTEMS RELATE TO EACH OTHER WITHIN THE SECTION OF A BUILDING?
The "E" shaped bubble diagram, shown to the right, uses the levels of integration defined above to describe the relationships between the key building systems shown in the building cross section. Each system is replaced by a bubble, and the relationship between systems is depicted by the diagram. (See figures 3 and 4)

WHAT ARE THE PERFORMANCE CRITERIA OF A BUILDING?
The basic design criteria are defined as building performance mandates. These mandates are outlined as shown: spatial performance, thermal performance, air quality, acoustical performance, visual performance, and building integrity.

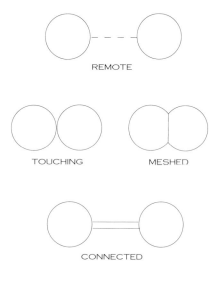

REMOTE

TOUCHING   MESHED

CONNECTED

UNIFIED

LEVELS OF INTEGRATION

FIGURE 2

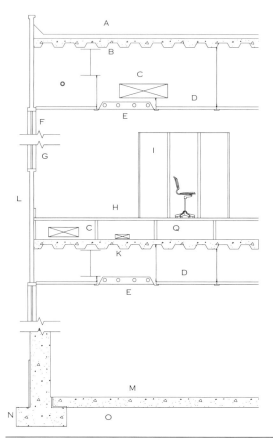

FIGURE 3

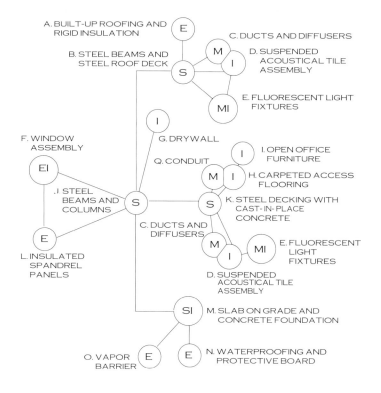

A. BUILT-UP ROOFING AND RIGID INSULATION
B. STEEL BEAMS AND STEEL ROOF DECK
C. DUCTS AND DIFFUSERS
D. SUSPENDED ACOUSTICAL TILE ASSEMBLY
E. FLUORESCENT LIGHT FIXTURES
F. WINDOW ASSEMBLY
G. DRYWALL
Q. CONDUIT
I. OPEN OFFICE FURNITURE
H. CARPETED ACCESS FLOORING
J. STEEL BEAMS AND COLUMNS
K. STEEL DECKING WITH CAST-IN-PLACE CONCRETE
C. DUCTS AND DIFFUSERS
E. FLUORESCENT LIGHT FIXTURES
D. SUSPENDED ACOUSTICAL TILE ASSEMBLY
L. INSULATED SPANDREL PANELS
M. SLAB ON GRADE AND CONCRETE FOUNDATION
N. WATERPROOFING AND PROTECTIVE BOARD
O. VAPOR BARRIER

FIGURE 4

Richard D. Rush, AIA, Integration Technology; Amesbury, Massachusetts

BUILDING SYSTEMS

BUILDING FUNCTION RELATIONSHIPS

The MATRIX OF BUILDING FUNCTION expresses the inter-relationship between all of the concepts and definitions discussed. Systems, pairs of systems, the 17 Building Systems Integration Matrix points, and performance criteria are all listed in the matrix. The cells on the lattice symbolize relationships that can be evaluated, prioritized, and assigned a numerical value. If it were possible to be exact with the numbers, a formula would result that could precisely represent the building.

All of the diagrams, words, and matrices on these pages are now integrated. One can start with a specific building system and trace through the lattice work of the matrix to specific built conditions. One can also begin with a performance mandate and trace its effect on each system or pair of systems used in the building.

Each cross point on the MATRIX OF BUILDING FUNCTION could be replaced by a question from a questionnaire: "what is the relationship between the column and the row." The same cross points could be expressed by a number evaluating the relationship. Still further, graphic symbols can replace words and numbers where size or length represents value. Each building is a specific collection of relationships. It is the integration, the relationship of the relationships, which expresses its function.

BUILDING PERFORMANCE MANDATES
I. SPATIAL PERFORMANCE
  a. Individual Space Layout: size, furniture (surface, storage, and seating); ergonomics
  b. Aggregate Space Layout: adjacencies, usable space, circulation/accessibility/wayfinding/signage, indoor-outdoor relationships, compartmentalization
  c. Conveniences and Services: sanitary, electrical, security, telecommunications, circulation/transportation
  d. Amenities
  e. Occupancy Factors and Controls
II. THERMAL PERFORMANCE
  a. Air Temperature
  b. Radiant Temperature
  c. Humidity
  d. Air Speed
  e. Occupancy Factors and Controls
III. INDOOR AIR QUALITY
  a. Fresh Air
  b. Fresh Air Movement and Distribution
  c. Mass Pollutants
  d. Energy Pollutants
  e. Occupancy Factors and Controls

IV. ACOUSTICAL PERFORMANCE
  a. Sound Source
  b. Sound Path
  c. Sound Receiver
V. VISUAL PERFORMANCE
  a. Ambient and Task Levels: Artificial light, daylight
  b. Contrast and Brightness Ratios (glare)
  c. Color Renditions
  d. View/Visual Information
  e. Occupancy Factors and Controls
VI. BUILDING INTEGRITY (versus visual, mechanical, and physical degradation of the structure, envelope servicing, and interior systems)
  a. Loads: dead loads, live loads, impact, abuse, vandalism, vibration, creep
  b. Moisture: rain, snow, ice, and vapor resulting in corrosion, penetration, migration, and condensation
  c. Temperature: thermal gradient (insulation effectiveness), thermal bridging, freeze-thaw cycle, differential thermal expansion and contraction
  d. Air Movement: corrosion, abrasion, tearing, air infiltration, exfiltration; pressure differential
  e. Radiation and Light: environmental radiation, electromagnetic long wave (solar radiation), visible light spectrum
  f. Chemical Attack
  g. Biological Attack
  h. Fire
  i. Natural Disaster: earthquake, flood, hurricane, tidal waves, volcanic eruptions, etc.
  j. Man-made Disaster

BUILDING SYSTEMS INTEGRATION MATRIX

	REMOTE	TOUCHING	CONNECTED	MESHED	UNIFIED
S + E		●	●		●
S + M		●		●	
S + I		●	●		●
E + M		●		●	
E + I	●		●		●
M + I		●	●	●	●

MATRIX OF BUILDING FUNCTION

	SPATIAL PERFORMANCE	THERMAL PERFORMANCE	AIR QUALITY	ACOUSTICAL PERFORMANCE	VISUAL PERFORMANCE	BUILDING INTEGRITY
Spatial Performance						
Thermal Performance						
Air Quality						
Acoustical Performance						
Visual Performance						
Building Integrity						
Structure						
Envelope						
Mechanical						
Interior						
Structure + Envelope						
Structure + Mechanical						
Structure + Interior						
Envelope + Mechanical						
Envelope + Interior						
Mechanical + Interior						
Envelope + Interior (Remote)						
Structure + Envelope (Touching)						
Structure + Interior (Touching)						
Mechanical + Interior (Touching)						
Structure + Envelope (Connected)						
Structure + Mechanical (Connected)						
Structure + Interior (Connected)						
Envelope + Mechanical (Connected)						
Envelope + Interior (Connected)						
Mechanical + Interior (Connected)						
Structure + Mechanical (Meshed)						
Envelope + Mechanical (Meshed)						
Mechanical + Interior (Meshed)						
Structure + Envelope (Unified)						
Structure + Interior (Unified)						
Envelope + Interior (Unified)						
Mechanical + Interior (Unified)						

NOTE

This table includes all of the relationships discussed. As a tool, it provides the map for evaluating building performance.

Richard D. Rush, AIA, Integration Technology; Amesbury, Massachusetts

BUILDING SYSTEMS

BASIC ORGANIZATION

The titles and numbers in MASTERFORMAT are grouped under the headings:

Bidding Requirements

Contract Forms

Conditions of the Contract

Specifications Divisions 1 Through 16

Documents under the first three headings are not specifications and should not be initiated or changed without specific coordination with the owner and the owner's legal and insurance counselors. However, MASTERFORMAT assigns standard locations and numbers for these documents for filing purposes and for coordination with the remainder of MASTERFORMAT.

The titles under the fourth heading are for specification sections. Specifications are the documents that define the quality of the products, materials, and workmanship upon which the construction contract is based.

DIVISIONS

The specification titles and numbers in MASTERFORMAT are organized into 16 basic groupings of related construction information called "divisions." Each division is identified by a fixed number and title. The divisions are the basic framework of MASTERFORMAT, and they indicate the location of the subordinate elements of the system. The numbers and titles of the divisions are:

DIVISION 1   GENERAL REQUIREMENTS

DIVISION 2   SITE WORK

DIVISION 3   CONCRETE

DIVISION 4   MASONRY

DIVISION 5   METALS

DIVISION 6   WOODS AND PLASTICS

DIVISION 7   THERMAL AND MOISTURE PROTECTION

DIVISION 8   DOORS AND WINDOWS

DIVISION 9   FINISHES

DIVISION 10   SPECIALTIES

DIVISION 11   EQUIPMENT

DIVISION 12   FURNISHINGS

DIVISION 13   SPECIAL CONSTRUCTION

DIVISION 14   CONVEYING SYSTEMS

DIVISION 15   MECHANICAL

DIVISION 16   ELECTRICAL

SECTIONS

Within each division specifications are written in numbered "sections," each of which covers one portion of the total work or requirements. MASTERFORMAT provides a standard system for numbering and titling these sections. The first two digits of the section number are the same as the division number.

BROADSCOPE, MEDIUMSCOPE, NARROWSCOPE

MASTERFORMAT identifies three levels of detail for a specification section—broadscope, mediumscope, and narrowscope.

Broadscope titles are for broad categories of work and provide the widest latitude in describing a unit of work.

Mediumscope titles cover units of work of more limited scope.

Narrowscope titles are for use in covering extremely limited and very specific elements of work.

The Construction Specifications Institute; Alexandria, Virginia
Construction Specifications Canada

In MASTERFORMAT the broadscope section titles are shown in boldface capital letters with five digit numbers. The hyphenated three digit numbers with indented upper and lower case titles are recommended mediumscope sections. Unnumbered, indented titles, which in most cases follow a mediumscope title, are narrowscope section titles. These, when taken together with the mediumscope titles under a broadscope heading, describe the coverage of that broadscope section. For example:

02100 SITE PREPARATION

-110 Site Clearing
        Clearing and Grubbing
        Large Tract Tree Clearing

-115 Selective Clearing
        Sod Stripping
        Tree and Shrub Removal
        Tree Pruning

-120 Structure Moving

MASTERFORMAT provides five digit number only for the broadscope and mediumscope section titles. Unused numbers are available between mediumscope numbers to permit assignment of numbers to selected narrowscope titles needed to accommodate individual project requirements. A block of numbers has also been left unassigned at the beginning of each division to be used for filing general data and cost information applicable to the entire division.

BROADSCOPE SECTION EXPLANATIONS

A general description of the coverage of each broadscope section is provided opposite the listing of titles. The broadscope explanation together with the list of associated mediumscope and narrowscope titles provide an understanding of the scope of the broadscope section. Under the headings "Related Requirements and Sections," "Related Requirements," and "Related Sections" are lists of other documents and sections in MASTERFORMAT that contain elements of work related to the broadscope section. The listings include items about which there might be confusion as to proper location and items which might require coordination with the subject broadscope.

The "Notes" under the broadscope explanations provide additional information on the relationships to other documents and sections and options available for the location of information.

KEY WORD INDEX

An alphabetical index is included to help locate particular products, materials, systems, units of work, and requirements. Each entry references one or more broadscope number. Only broadscope numbers are referenced; however, the specific item may appear as a mediumscope or narrowscope listing under the referenced broadscope number and title.

BIDDING REQUIREMENTS, CONTRACT FORMS, AND CONDITIONS OF THE CONTRACT

00010   PRE-BID INFORMATION

00100   INSTRUCTIONS TO BIDDERS

00200   INFORMATION AVAILABLE TO BIDDERS

00300   BID FORMS

00400   SUPPLEMENTS TO BID FORMS

00500   AGREEMENT FORMS

00600   BONDS AND CERTIFICATES

00700   GENERAL CONDITIONS

00800   SUPPLEMENTARY CONDITIONS

00900   ADDENDA

NOTE

The items listed above are not specification sections and are referred to as "Documents" rather than "Sections" in the "Master List of Section Titles, Numbers, and Broadscope Section Explanations."

SPECIFICATIONS

The following is a list of the broadscope section numbers and titles from MASTERFORMAT.

DIVISION 1—GENERAL REQUIREMENTS

01010   SUMMARY OF WORK
01020   ALLOWANCES
01025   MEASUREMENT AND PAYMENT
01030   ALTERNATES/ALTERNATIVES
01035   MODIFICATION PROCEDURES
01040   COORDINATION
01050   FIELD ENGINEERING
01060   REGULATORY REQUIREMENTS
01070   IDENTIFICATION SYSTEMS
01090   REFERENCES
01100   SPECIAL PROJECT PROCEDURES
01200   PROJECT MEETINGS
01300   SUBMITTALS
01400   QUALITY CONTROL
01500   CONSTRUCTION FACILITIES AND TEMPORARY CONTROLS
01600   MATERIAL AND EQUIPMENT
01650   FACILITY STARTUP/COMMISSIONING
01700   CONTRACT CLOSEOUT
01800   MAINTENANCE

DIVISION 2—SITEWORK

02010   SUBSURFACE INVESTIGATION
02050   DEMOLITION
02100   SITE PREPARATION
02140   DEWATERING
02150   SHORING AND UNDERPINNING
02160   EXCAVATION SUPPORT SYSTEMS
02170   COFFERDAMS
02200   EARTHWORK
02300   TUNNELING
02350   PILES AND CAISSONS
02450   RAILROAD WORK
02480   MARINE WORK
02500   PAVING AND SURFACING
02600   UTILITY PIPING MATERIALS
02660   WATER DISTRIBUTION
02680   FUEL AND STEAM DISTRIBUTION
02700   SEWERAGE AND DRAINAGE
02760   RESTORATION OF UNDERGROUND PIPE
02770   PONDS AND RESERVOIRS
02780   POWER AND COMMUNICATIONS
02800   SITE IMPROVEMENTS
02900   LANDSCAPING

DIVISION 3—CONCRETE

03100   CONCRETE FORMWORK
03200   CONCRETE REINFORCEMENT
03250   CONCRETE ACCESSORIES
03300   CAST-IN-PLACE CONCRETE
03370   CONCRETE CURING
03400   PRECAST CONCRETE
03500   CEMENTITIOUS DECKS AND TOPPINGS
03600   GROUT
03700   CONCRETE RESTORATION AND CLEANING
03800   MASS CONCRETE

DIVISION 4—MASONRY

04100   MORTAR AND MASONRY GROUT
04150   MASONRY ACCESSORIES
04200   UNIT MASONRY
04400   STONE
04500   MASONRY RESTORATION AND CLEANING
04550   REFRACTORIES
04600   CORROSION RESISTANT MASONRY
04700   SIMULATED MASONRY

DIVISION 5—METALS

05010   METAL MATERIALS
05030   METAL COATINGS
05050   METAL FASTENING
05100   STRUCTURAL METAL FRAMING
05200   METAL JOISTS
05300   METAL DECKING
05400   COLD-FORMED METAL FRAMING
05500   METAL FABRICATIONS
05580   SHEET METAL FABRICATIONS
05700   ORNAMENTAL METAL
05800   EXPANSION CONTROL

MASTERFORMAT

DIVISION 6—WOOD AND PLASTICS

06050 FASTENERS AND ADHESIVES
06100 ROUGH CARPENTRY
06130 HEAVY TIMBER CONSTRUCTION
06150 WOOD AND METAL SYSTEMS
06170 PREFABRICATED STRUCTURAL WOOD
06200 FINISH CARPENTRY
06300 WOOD TREATMENT
06400 ARCHITECTURAL WOODWORK
06500 STRUCTURAL PLASTICS
06600 PLASTIC FABRICATIONS
06650 SOLID POLYMER FABRICATIONS

DIVISION 7—THERMAL AND MOISTURE PROTECTION

07100 WATERPROOFING
07150 DAMPPROOFING
07180 WATER REPELLENTS
07190 VAPOR RETARDERS
07195 AIR BARRIERS
07200 INSULATION
07240 EXTERIOR INSULATION AND FINISH SYSTEMS
07250 FIREPROOFING
07270 FIRESTOPPING
07300 SHINGLES AND ROOFING TILES
07400 MANUFACTURED ROOFING AND SIDING
07480 EXTERIOR WALL ASSEMBLIES
07500 MEMBRANE ROOFING
07570 TRAFFIC COATINGS
07600 FLASHING AND SHEET METAL
07700 ROOF SPECIALTIES AND ACCESSORIES
07800 SKYLIGHTS
07900 JOINT SEALERS

DIVISION 8—DOORS AND WINDOWS

08100 METAL DOORS AND FRAMES
08200 WOOD AND PLASTIC DOORS
08250 DOOR OPENING ASSEMBLIES
08300 SPECIAL DOORS
08400 ENTRANCES AND STOREFRONTS
08500 METAL WINDOWS
08600 WOOD AND PLASTIC WINDOWS
08650 SPECIAL WINDOWS
08700 HARDWARE
08800 GLAZING
08900 GLAZED CURTAIN WALLS

DIVISION 9—FINISHES

09100 METAL SUPPORT SYSTEMS
09200 LATH AND PLASTER
09250 GYPSUM BOARD
09300 TILE
09400 TERRAZZO
09450 STONE FACING
09500 ACOUSTICAL TREATMENT
09540 SPECIAL WALL SURFACES
09545 SPECIAL CEILING SURFACES
09550 WOOD FLOORING
09600 STONE FLOORING
09630 UNIT MASONRY FLOORING
09650 RESILIENT FLOORING
09680 CARPET
09700 SPECIAL FLOORING
09780 FLOOR TREATMENT
09800 SPECIAL COATINGS
09900 PAINTING
09950 WALL COVERINGS

DIVISION 10—SPECIALTIES

10100 VISUAL DISPLAY BOARDS
10150 COMPARTMENTS AND CUBICLES
10200 LOUVERS AND VENTS
10240 GRILLES AND SCREENS
10250 SERVICE WALL SYSTEMS
10260 WALL AND CORNER GUARDS
10270 ACCESS FLOORING
10290 PEST CONTROL
10300 FIREPLACES AND STOVES
10340 MANUFACTURED EXTERIOR SPECIALTIES
10350 FLAGPOLES
10400 IDENTIFYING DEVICES
10450 PEDESTRIAN CONTROL DEVICES
10500 LOCKERS
10520 FIRE PROTECTION SPECIALTIES
10530 PROTECTIVE COVERS
10550 POSTAL SPECIALTIES
10600 PARTITIONS
10650 OPERABLE PARTITIONS
10670 STORAGE SHELVING
10700 EXTERIOR PROTECTION DEVICES FOR OPENINGS
10750 TELEPHONE SPECIALTIES
10800 TOILET AND BATH ACCESSORIES
10880 SCALES
10900 WARDROBE AND CLOSED SPECIALTIES

The Construction Specifications Institute; Alexandria, Virginia
Construction Specifications Canada

DIVISION 11—EQUIPMENT

11010 MAINTENANCE EQUIPMENT
11020 SECURITY AND VAULT EQUIPMENT
11030 TELLER AND SERVICE EQUIPMENT
11040 ECCLESIASTICAL EQUIPMENT
11050 LIBRARY EQUIPMENT
11060 THEATER AND STAGE EQUIPMENT
11070 INSTRUMENTAL EQUIPMENT
11080 REGISTRATION EQUIPMENT
11090 CHECKROOM EQUIPMENT
11100 MERCANTILE EQUIPMENT
11110 COMMERCIAL LAUNDRY AND DRY CLEANING EQUIPMENT
11120 VENDING EQUIPMENT
11130 AUDIO-VISUAL EQUIPMENT
11140 VEHICLE SERVICE EQUIPMENT
11150 PARKING CONTROL EQUIPMENT
11160 LOADING DOCK EQUIPMENT
11170 SOLID WASTE HANDLING EQUIPMENT
11190 DETENTION EQUIPMENT
11200 WATER SUPPLY AND TREATMENT EQUIPMENT
11280 HYDRAULIC GATES AND VALVES
11300 FLUID WASTE TREATMENT AND DISPOSAL EQUIPMENT
11400 FOOD SERVICE EQUIPMENT
11450 RESIDENTIAL EQUIPMENT
11460 UNIT KITCHENS
11470 DARKROOM EQUIPMENT
11480 ATHLETIC, RECREATIONAL, AND THERAPEUTIC EQUIPMENT
11500 INDUSTRIAL AND PROCESS EQUIPMENT
11600 LABORATORY EQUIPMENT
11650 PLANETARIUM EQUIPMENT
11660 OBSERVATORY EQUIPMENT
11680 OFFICE EQUIPMENT
11700 MEDICAL EQUIPMENT
11780 MORTUARY EQUIPMENT
11850 NAVIGATION EQUIPMENT
11870 AGRICULTURAL EQUIPMENT

DIVISION 12—FURNISHINGS

12050 FABRICS
12100 ARTWORK
12300 MANUFACTURED CASEWORK
12500 WINDOW TREATMENT
12600 FURNITURE AND ACCESSORIES
12670 RUGS AND MATS
12700 MULTIPLE SEATING
12800 INTERIOR PLANTS AND PLANTERS

DIVISION 13—SPECIAL CONSTRUCTION

13010 AIR-SUPPORTED STRUCTURES
13020 INTEGRATED ASSEMBLIES
13030 SPECIAL PURPOSE ROOMS
13080 SOUND, VIBRATION, AND SEISMIC CONTROL
13090 RADIATION PROTECTION
13100 NUCLEAR REACTORS
13120 PRE-ENGINEERED STRUCTURES
13150 AQUATIC FACILITIES
13175 ICE RINKS
13180 SITE CONSTRUCTED INCINERATORS
13185 KENNELS AND ANIMAL SHELTERS
13200 LIQUID AND GAS STORAGE TANKS
13220 FILTER UNDERDRAINS AND MEDIA
13230 DIGESTER COVERS AND APPURTENANCES
13240 OXYGENATION SYSTEMS
13260 SLUDGE CONDITIONING SYSTEMS
13300 UTILITY CONTROL SYSTEMS
13400 INDUSTRIAL AND PROCESS CONTROL SYSTEMS
13500 RECORDING INSTRUMENTATION
13550 TRANSPORTATION CONTROL INSTRUMENTATION
13600 SOLAR ENERGY SYSTEMS
13700 WIND ENERGY SYSTEMS
13750 COGENERATION SYSTEMS
13800 BUILDING AUTOMATION SYSTEMS
13900 FIRE SUPPRESSION AND SUPERVISORY SYSTEMS
13950 SPECIAL SECURITY CONSTRUCTION

DIVISION 14—CONVEYING SYSTEMS

14100 DUMBWAITERS
14200 ELEVATORS
14300 ESCALATORS AND MOVING WALKS
14400 LIFTS
14500 MATERIAL HANDLING SYSTEMS
14600 HOISTS AND CRANES
14700 TURNTABLES
14800 SCAFFOLDING
14900 TRANSPORTATION SYSTEMS

DIVISION 15—MECHANICAL SYSTEMS

15050 BASIC MECHANICAL MATERIALS AND METHODS
15250 MECHANICAL INSULATION
15300 FIRE PROTECTION
15400 PLUMBING
15500 HEATING, VENTILATING, AND AIR CONDITIONING
15550 HEAT GENERATION
15650 REFRIGERATION
15750 HEAT TRANSFER
15850 AIR HANDLING
15880 AIR DISTRIBUTION
15950 CONTROLS
15990 TESTING, ADJUSTING, AND BALANCING

DIVISION 16—ELECTRICAL

16050 BASIC ELECTRICAL MATERIALS AND METHODS
16200 POWER GENERATION-BUILT-UP SYSTEMS
16300 MEDIUM VOLTAGE DISTRIBUTION
16400 SERVICE AND DISTRIBUTION
16500 LIGHTING
16600 SPECIAL SYSTEMS
16700 COMMUNICATIONS
16850 ELECTRIC RESISTANCE HEATING
16900 CONTROLS
16950 TESTING

ORGANIZATION OF SPECIFICATIONS

The best known use of MASTERFORMAT is for organizing specifications. Titles are provided in a logical sequence for almost all conceivable specification sections that might be required for a construction project. The specifications writer striving for uniformity should use the titles and numbers as shown. Sections can be written and reproduced at any time without fear they will be incorrectly placed in the project manual. This is one of the major advantages in the use of MASTERFORMAT. Assembly of the final document in numerical sequence assures the correct grouping of sections.

MASTERFORMAT has been developed to provide the specifier with a standard yet flexible system for organizing specifications. However, the titles do not necessarily relate to the work accomplished by a single trade or subcontractor. It is not the intent of MASTERFORMAT to define the work of individual trades since each contractor will subdivide the work differently among subcontractors.

Broadscope and mediumscope section numbers and titles are shown in MASTERFORMAT in their recommended sequence. When selecting a narrowscope title, a five digit number will need to be assigned since these titles are unnumbered in MASTERFORMAT. Users may select needed narrowscope titles or combine titles into a single section and assign their own numerically sequenced numbers. Numbers have been left unassigned throughout MASTERFORMAT to allow for numbering narrowscope titles and any additional titles that may be required on a project. When assigning additional numbers for new titles, the specifications writer should review MASTERFORMAT and assign unused numbers from groupings of subject matter closely related to the product being specified.

DATA FILING

The MASTERFORMAT system of numbers and titles also serves as a system for filing and retrieving technical data and product literature. Because it is the same as the system used for organizing specifications it is easy to relate the filed material to the specification sections being written for a project. MASTERFORMAT is a system for organizing construction publications of all kind on the shelves of a technical library; for filing information on products, methods, manufacturers, suppliers, and subcontractors; for inventory of construction materials; for coding data stored electronically; and numerous other information storage and retrieval activities.

COST CLASSIFICATION

The MASTERFORMAT titles and numbers also serve as the basis for a system for the accumulation and organization of construction costs. Since the same format is used for project manuals as for filing construction information, the benefits of uniformity and standardization are further increased. Familiarity with MASTERFORMAT allows users to easily relate a specification section with both product information and cost data. This simplifies the storage and retrieval of information.

A SERIES/OWNER-CONTRACTOR DOCUMENTS

A101	Owner-Contractor Agreement Form—Stipulated Sum (4/87) with instruction sheet wrapped
A101/CM	Owner-Contractor Agreement Form—Stipulated Sum—Construction Management Edition (6/80) with instruction sheet wrapped
A107	Abbreviated Owner-Contractor Agreement Form for Construction Projects of Limited Scopes (4/87) with instruction sheet wrapped
A111	Owner-Contractor Agreement Form—Cost Plus Fee (4/87) with instruction sheet wrapped
A117	Abbreviated Owner-Contractor Agreement Form-Cost Plus Fee (4/87) with instruction sheet wrapped
A171	Owner-Contractor Agreement for Furniture, Furnishings and Equipment (3/79) with instruction sheet wrapped
A177	Abbreviated Owner-Contractor Agreement for Furniture, Furnishings and Equipment (5/80) with instruction sheet wrapped
A191	Standard Form of Agreements Between Owner and Design/Builder(1985)
A201	General Conditions of the Contract for Construction (4/87)
A201/CM	General Conditions of the Contract for Construction—Construction Management Edition (6/80)
A201/SC	Federal Supplementary Conditions of the Contract for Construction (1990)
A271	General Conditions of the Contract for Furniture, Furnishings and Equipment (12/77) with instruction sheet wrapped
A305	Contractor's Qualification Statement (12/86)
A310	Bid Bond (2/70)
A311	Performance Bond and Labor and Material Payment Bond (2/70)
A311/CM	Performance Bond and Labor and Material Payment Bond—Construction Management Edition (6/80)
A312	Performance Bond and Payment Bond (12/84)
A401	Contractor-Subcontractor Agreement Form (5/87)
A491	Standard Form of Agreements Between Design/Builder and Contractor (1985)
A501	Recommended Guide for Bidding Procedures and Contract Awards (6/82)
A511	Guide for Supplementary Conditions (incorporates A512 6/87)
A511/CM	Guide for Supplementary Conditions—Construction Management Edition (3/82)
A512	Additions to Guides for Supplementary Conditions (12/89)
A521	Uniform Location Subject Matter (1981, Reprinted 7/83)
A571	Guide for Interiors Supplementary Conditions (3/82)
A701	Instructions to Bidders (4/87) with instruction sheet wrapped
A771	Instruction to Interiors Bidders (5/80) with instruction sheet wrapped

B SERIES/OWNER-ARCHITECT DOCUMENTS

B141	Standard Form of Agreement Between Owner and Architect (4/87) with instruction sheet wrapped
B141/CM	Standard Form of Agreement Between Owner and Architect—Construction Management Edition (6/80) with instruction sheet wrapped
B151	Abbreviated Owner-Architect Agreement Form (4/87) with instruction sheet wrapped
B161	Standard Form of Agreement Between Owner and Architect for Designated Services (11/77) with instruction sheet wrapped
B161/CM	Standard Form of Agreement Between Owner and Architect for Designated Services—Construction Management Edition (12/82) with instruction sheet wrapped
B162	Scope of Designated Services (11/77) with instruction sheet wrapped
B171	Standard Form of Agreement for Interior Design Services (3/79) with instruction sheet wrapped
B177	Abbreviated Interior Design Services Agreement (5/80) with instruction sheet wrapped
B181	Owner-Architect Agreement for Housing Services (6/78) with instruction sheet wrapped
B352	Duties, Responsibilities, and Limitations of Authority of the Architect's Project Representative (5/79)
B431	Architect's Qualification Statement (12/79)
B511	Guide for Amendments to AIA Document B141 (1990)
B727	Standard Form of Agreement Between Owner and Architect for Special Services (1988) with instruction sheet wrapped
B801	Standard Form of Agreement Between Owner and Construction Manager (6/80) with instruction sheet wrapped
B901	Standard Form of Agreements Between Design/Builder and Architect (1985)

C SERIES/ARCHITECT-CONSULTANT DOCUMENTS

C141	Standard Form of Agreement Between Architect and Consultant (4/87) with instructions wrapped
C142	Abbreviated Form of Agreement Between Architect and Consultant (4/87)
C161	Standard Form of Agreement Between Architect and Consultant for Designated Services (6/79) with instructions wrapped
C727	Standard Form of Agreement Between Architect and Consultant for Special Services (4/82) with instructions wrapped
C801	Joint Venture Agreement (6/79) with instructions wrapped

D SERIES/ARCHITECT-INDUSTRY DOCUMENTS

D101	Architectural Area and Volume of Buildings (1/80)
D200	Project Checklist (8/82)

F SERIES/ARCHITECT'S ACCOUNTING FORMS—MANUAL SYSTEM

F100	A set of accounting forms F101 thru F725 (Various editions from 1949 to 1972)
F101	Cash Journal—1949
F102	Cash Journal—1949
F103	Cash Journal—1949
F104	Cash Journal—1953
F105	Cash Journal—1949
F106	Cash Journal—1949[I]
F202	Payroll Journal—1949[I]
F203	Payroll Journal—1949
F301	Ledger Account Form—1949
F401	Job Expense Record Form—1953
F403	Fixed Assets Record—1949
F404	Note and Investment Record—1949
F501	Trial Balance Sheet—1953
F502	Balance Sheet—1953
F504	Indirect Expense Factor—1953
F601	Time Record Sheet—1971
F603	Expense Voucher Nonpersonel—1953
F701	Billing Extract—1972
F703	Aged Accounts Receivable—1972
F712	Project Payroll Cost Worksheet—1972
F714	Detail of Expenses—1972
F723	Project Progress Report—1972
F725	Project Progress Report—1972

F SERIES/COMPENSATION GUIDELINES FORMS AND WORKSHEETS

F800	A set of compensation worksheets from F810 through F860 based on AIA's Compensation Guidelines book (1978)

F SERIES/STANDARDIZED ACCOUNTING FOR ARCHITECT FORMS

F1000	A set of accounting forms from F1001 thru F5002 based on AIA's Compensation Guidelines book—1978
F1001	Cash Receipts Journal—1978
F1002	Cash Disbursements Journal—1978
F1004	Trial Balance—1978
F1006	Balance Sheet and Income and Expense Statement—1978
F2001	Expense Voucher—1978
F2002	Fixed Assets Record—1978
F3001	Time Record—(1978
D3002	Staff Expense Record—1978
F3003	Payroll Journal—1978
F3005	Staff Payroll Record—1978
F4001	Project Time Distribution
F5001	Billing Extract—1978
F5002	Invoice for Architectural Services—1978
F5003	Aged Accounts Receivable—1978
F6001	Ledger Account—1978
F6002	Journal—1978
F6003	Accounting Worksheet—1978
F6004	Accounting Worksheet—1978

G SERIES/ARCHITECT'S OFFICE AND PROJECT FORMS

G601	Land Survey Requisition (6/79) with instructions
G602	Geotechnical Services Agreement (8/83)
G605/606	Purchase Order and Purchase Order Continuation Sheet (1983)
G612	Owner's Instructions for Bonds and Insurance (1987)
G604	Professional Services Supplemental Authorization (3/79) with instructions
G701	Change Order (1987)
G701/CM	Change Order—Construction Management Edition (6/80)
G702	Application and Certificate for Payment (4/78, Rev. 5/83)
G702/CR	Continuous Roll for Application and Certificate for Payment (1983)
G703	Continuation Sheet for G702 (4/78, Rev. 5/83)
G703/CR	Continuous Roll Continuation Sheet for G702 (5/83)
G704	Certificate of Substantial Completion (4/78)
G706	Contractor's Affidavit of Payment of Debts and Claims (4/70)
G706A	Contractor's Affidavit of Release of Liens (4/70)
G707	Consent of Surety to Final Payment (4/70)
G707A	Consent of Surety to Reduction in or Partial Release of Retainage (6/71)
G709	Proposal Request (4/70)
G710	Architect's Supplemental Instructions (3/79) with instructions
G711	Architect's Field Report (10/72)
G712	Shop Drawing and Sample Record (10/72)
G714	Construction Change Directive (1987)
G722	Project Application and Project Certificate for Payment (6/80) with instructions
G723	Project Application Summary (6/80) with instructions
G801	Application for Employment (6/75)
G804	Register of Bid Documents (4/70)
G805	List of Subcontractors (4/70)
G807	Project Directory (4/70)
G809	Project Data (4/70)
G810	Transmittal Letter (4/70)
G811	Employment Record (11/73)
G813	Temporary Placement (1/74)

NOTE

Editions listed are the latest available from the AIA upon publication.

DOCUMENTS

OWNER - CONTRACTOR

DESIGN/BUILDER

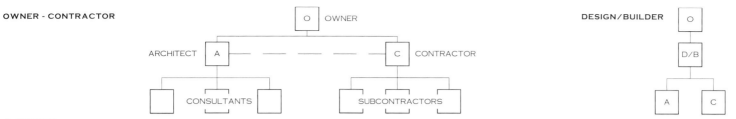

A SERIES

	STANDARD STIPULATED SUM	STIPULATED SUM - CM (ADVISOR)	STANDARD COST - PLUS A FEE	ABBREVIATED CONSTRUCTION CONTRACTS	STANDARD INTERIORS FIXED FEE AND EXPENSES	ABBREVIATED INTERIORS FIXED FEE AND EXPENSES	DESIGN	BUILD
Agreement	A101	A101/CM	A111	A107 A117	A171	A177	A191 Part 1	A191 Part 2
General Conditions	A201 A201/SC	A201/CM	A201 A201/SC	Included	A271	Included	N/A	N/A
Subcontractor	A401	A401	A401	A401	A401	A401	A491 Part 1	A491 Part 2
Contractor's Qualifications	A305	A305	A305	A305	A305	A305	N/A	N/A
Bidder's Instructions	A701	A701	A701	A701	A771	A771	N/A	N/A
Bonds	A310 A311 A312	A310 A311 A312	A310 A311 A312	A310 A311 A312	A310 A311 A312	A310 A311 A312	N/A	A311 A312
Guides (with model language)	A511	A511/CM	A511	A511	A571	A571	Assumed to be negotiated Contracts	

ARCHITECT - OWNER

DESIGN/BUILDER

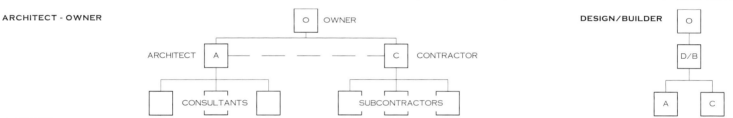

B SERIES

	AGREEMENT	SCOPE OF SERVICES	CONSTRUCTION MANAGER AGREEMENT	PROJECT REPRESENTATIVE	ARCHITECT'S QUALIFICATIONS		AGREEMENT
Standard Services	B141			B352	B431	B901 Part 1	B901 Part 2
Standard Services - CM	B141/CM	B801	B353	B431		N/A	N/A
Abbreviated Form	B151	(B162)		B352	B431	N/A	N/A
Designated Service	B161	B162	B161/CM	B352	B431	N/A	N/A
Interior Design Service	B171					N/A	N/A
Abbreviated Interiors	B177					N/A	N/A
Housing Service	B181	B162		B352	B431	N/A	N/A
Special Services	B727		B801	B352	B431	N/A	N/A
Guide	B511						

ARCHITECT - CONSULTANT

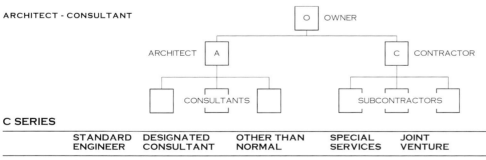

NOTE

The matrices on this page present AIA documents grouped in project delivery methods. The dominant method related to each matrix is also diagrammed above.

The terminology and provisions in the documents of each group are coordinated through parallel construction. This helps prevent gaps or laps in responsibilities from occurring which may even lead to life threatening disasters. It is important that the user, when making modifications to one of those documents, be aware of the impact on the other AIA documents in the grouping.

Generally, modifications will be necessary to adapt the standard AIA documents to the particular circumstances of a project. A helpful guide in making modifications is AIA Document A521, "Uniform Location of Subject Matter."

C SERIES

	STANDARD ENGINEER	DESIGNATED CONSULTANT	OTHER THAN NORMAL	SPECIAL SERVICES	JOINT VENTURE
Agreement	C141 C161		C431	C727	C801
Guide	(Coordinate with B511)9				

DOCUMENTS

PROFESSIONAL ASSOCIATIONS

Acoustical Society of America
500 Sunnyside Blvd.
Woodbury, NY 11797
(516) 349-7800 ext. 481

American Association of Certified Appraisers
800 Compton Road, #10
Cincinnati, OH 45231
(513) 729-1400

American Association of Cost Engineers
P.O. Box 1557
Morgantown, WV 26507-1557
(304) 296-8444

American Association of Design Drafting
5522 Norbeck Road, Suite 391
Rockville, MD 20853
(301) 460-6875

American Consulting Engineers Council
1015 15th Street, NW #802
Washington, DC 20005-2605
(202) 347-7474

American Institute of Architects
1735 New York Avenue, NW
Washington, DC 20006
(202) 626-7300

American Institute of Real Estate Appraisers
430 N. Michigan Avenue
Chicago, IL 60611
(312) 329-8559

American Planning Association
1776 Massachusetts Avenue, NW
Washington, DC 20036
(202) 872-0611

American Society of Architectural Perspectivists
320 Newbury Street
Boston, MA 02115
(617) 846-4766

American Society of Civil Engineers
345 E. 47th St.
New York, NY 10017-2398
(212) 705-7496

American Society of Consulting Planners
c/o Dennis Larkin, WBDC Group
2000 Town Center Suite 1390
Southfield, MI 48075
(313) 358-5080

American Society of Golf Course Architects
221 N. LaSalle Street
Chicago, IL 60601
(312) 372-7090

American Society of Heating, Refrigerating
And Air Conditioning Engineers, Inc.
1791 Tullie Circle, NE
Atlanta, GA 30329
(404) 636-8400

American Society of Interior Designers
1430 Broadway 22nd Floor
New York, NY 10018-3308
(212) 944-9220

American Society of Landscape Architects
4401 Connecticut Ave., NW 5th Floor
Washington, DC 20008
(202) 686-2752

American Society of Mechanical Engineers
1825 K Street, NW Suite 218
Washington, DC 20006
(202) 785-3756

American Society of Professional Estimators
11141 Georgia Avenue
Suite 412
Wheaton, MD 20902
(301) 929-8848

American Society of Safety Engineers
1800 East Oakton
Des Plaines, IL 60018
(708) 692-4121

American Society of Sanitary Engineering
30311 Clemens Road
Westlake, OH 44145
(216) 835-3040

American Subcontractors Association
1004 Duke Street
Alexandria, VA 22314
(703) 684-3450

Association of Energy Engineers
4025 Pleasantdale Road, Suite 420
Atlanta, GA 30340
(404) 447-5083

Association of Engineers Practicing in the Geosciences
8811 Colesville Road, Suite G106
Silver Spring, MD 20910
(301) 565-2733

Association of Professional Design Firms
685 High Street, Suite 5
Worthington, OH 43085
(614) 888-3301

Association of Specialists in Cleaning & Restoration
10830 Annapolis Junction Road, Suite 312
Annapolis Junction, MD 20701
(301) 604-4411

Association of Women in Architecture
911 Washington, Suite 225
St. Louis, MO 63101
(314) 621-3484

Illuminating Engineering Society of North America
345 E. 47th St.
New York, NY 10017-2304
(212) 705-7913

Industrial Designers Society of America
1142-E Walker Road
Great Falls, VA 22066
(703) 759-0100

Institute of Electrical and Electronics Engineers
345 E. 47th St.
New York, NY 10017
(212) 705-7900

Institute of Industrial Engineers
25 Technology Park/Atlanta
Norcross, GA 30092
(404) 449-0460

Interfaith Forum on Religion, Art, & Architecture
1777 Church Street, NW
Washington, DC 20036
(202) 387-8333

International Association of Lighting Designers
18 E. 16th Street Suite 208
New York, NY 10003
(212) 206-1281

International Facility Management Association
1 East Greenway Plaza, 11th Floor
Houston, TX 77046-1102
(713) 623-4362

National Association of Home Builders
15th and M Streets, NW
Washington, DC 20005-2802
(202) 822-0200

National Council of Acoustical Consultants
66 Morris Avenue
Springfield, NJ 07081-1409
(201) 379-1100

National Housing Conference
1126 16th Street, Suite 211
Washington, DC 20036
(202) 223-4844

National Multi Housing Council
1250 Connecticut Avenue, NW #620
Washington, DC 20036
(202) 659-3381

National Organization of Minority Architects
120 Ralph McGill Blvd., Suite 815
Atlanta, GA 30308
(404) 876-3055

National Society of Architectural Engineering
P.O. Box 395
Lawrence, KS 66044
(913) 864-3434

National Society of Professional Engineers
1420 King St.
Alexandria, VA 22314
(703) 684-2800

National Trust for Historic Preservation
1785 Massachusetts Avenue, NW
Washington, DC 20036
(202) 673-4000

Project Management Institute
PO Box 43
Drexel Hill, PA 19026
(215) 622-1796

Rehabilitation Engineering Society of North America
1101 Connecticut Avenue, NW #700
Washington, DC 20036
(202) 857-1199

Royal Architectural Institute of Canada
55 Murray Street Suite 330
Ottawa, Ontario Canada K 1N 5M3
(613) 232-7165

Society of American Registered Architects
1245 Highland
Lombard, IL 60148
(708) 932-4622

Society of Architectural Historians
1232 Pine Street
Philadelphia, PA 19107
(215) 735-0224

Society of Certified Kitchen Designers
124 Main Street
Hackettstown, NJ 07840
(201) 852-0033

Society of Glass and Ceramic Decorators
888 17th Street, NW
Brawner Building Suite 600
Washington, DC 20006-3959
(202) 728-4132

US National Society for the International Society of Soil
 Mechanics and Foundation Engineering
c/o Professor Harvey E. Wahls
CE Department, Box 7908
North Carolina State University
Raleigh, NC 27695
(919) 737-7244

TRADE ORGANIZATIONS

Air Conditioning and Refrigeration Institute
1501 Wilson Blvd.
Arlington, VA 22209-2403
(703) 524-8800

Air Distributing Institute
4415 West Harrison Street, Suite 242C
Hillside, IL 60162
(708) 449-2933

American Hospital Association
840 N. Lakeshore Drive
Chicago, IL 60611
(312) 280-6000

American Institute of Building Design
1412 19th Street
Sacramento, CA 95814
(916) 447-2422

American Insurance Association
1130 Connecticut Avenue, NW #1000
Washington, DC 20036-3904
(202) 828-7100

American Land Title Association
1828 L Street, NW
Washington, DC 20036
(202) 296-3671

American Lighting Association
435 N. Michigan Ave., Suite 1717
Chicago, IL 60611-4067
(312) 644-0828

American Society for Testing and Materials
1916 Race St.
Philadelphia, PA 19103-1108
(215) 299-5400

American Solar Energy Society
2400 Central Avenue B-1
Boulder, CO 80301
(303) 443-3130

DIRECTORY

American Welding Society
550 NW 42nd Avenue
Box 351040
Miami, FL 33135
(305) 443-9353

American Wood-Preservers Association
P.O. Box 849
Stevensville, MD 21666-0849
(301) 643-4161

Associated General Contractors of America
1957 E Street, NW
Washington, DC 20006
(202) 393-2040

Building Systems Institute
1230 Keith Building
Cleveland, OH 44115
(216) 241-7333

Construction Financial Management Association
40 Brunswick Avenue Suite 202
Edison, NJ 08818
(201) 287-2777

Cooling Tower Institute
Box 73383
Houston, TX 77273
(713) 583-4087

Federation of Societies for Coatings Technology
492 Norristown Road
Bluebell, PA 19422
(215) 940-0777

General Building Contractors Association
36 South 18th Street
Philadelphia, PA 19103
(215) 568-7015

Home Ventilating Institute Division of the Air
 Movement Control Association
30 West University Drive
Arlington Heights, IL 60004
(708) 394-0150

International District Heating and Cooling Association
1101 Connecticut Avenue, NW, Suite 700
Washington, DC 20036
(202) 429-5111

Industrial Fabrics Association International
345 Cedar Street
St. Paul, MN 55101
(612) 222-2508

Intelligent Buildings Institute
2101 L Street, NW, Suite 300
Washington, DC 20037-1534
(202) 457-1988

International Bank for Reconstruction and Development
1818 H Street, NW
Washington, DC 20433
(202) 477-1234

International Copper Association, Ltd.
708 Third Avenue
New York, NY 10017
(212) 697-9355

International Council of Shopping Centers
665 5th Avenue
New York, NY 10022
(212) 421-8187

International Facility Management Association
1 Greenway Plaza, 11th Floor
Houston, TX 77046
(713) 623-4362

Manufactured Housing Institute
1745 Jefferson Davis Highway, Suite 511
Arlington, VA 22202
(703) 979-6620

National Association of Industrial and Office Parks
1215 Jefferson Davis Highway - Suite 100
Arlington, VA 22202
(703) 979-3400

National Association of Miscellaneous,
Ornamental & Architectural Products Contractors
PO Box 280
10382 Main Street - Suite 200
Fairfax, VA 22030
(703) 591-1870

National Association of the Remodeling Industry
1901 North Moore Street, Suite 808
Arlington, VA 22209
(703) 276-7600

National Burglar and Fire Alarm Association
7101 Wisconsin Avenue, Suite 1390
Bethesda, MD 20814
(301) 907-3202

National Fenestration Council
3310 Harrison
Topeka, KS 66611
(913) 266-7014

National Fire Protection Association
1 Batterymarch Park
Quincy, MA 02269-9101
(617) 770-3000

National Landscape Association
1250 Eye Street, NW Suite 500
Washington, DC 20005
(202) 789-2900

National Parking Association
1112 16th Street, NW, Suite 2000
Washington, DC 20036
(202) 296-4336

National Solid Wastes Management Association
1730 Rhode Island Avenue, NW, Suite 1000
Washington, DC 20036
(202) 659-4613

The Post-Tensioning Institute
1717 West Northern Avenue, Suite 218
Phoenix, AZ 85021
(602) 870-7540

Society of Cost Estimating & Analysis
101 South Whiting Street, Suite 313
Alexandria, VA 22304
(703) 751-8069

Underwriters Laboratories
333 Pfingsten Road
Northbrook, IL 60062
(708) 272-8800

Urban Land Institute
625 Indiana Avenue, NW
Washington, DC 20004
(202) 624-7000

GOVERNMENTAL SERVICES

Bureau of the Census
Department of Commerce
Washington, DC 20233
(301) 763-7662

The Center for Building Technology
National Engineering Laboratory
National Institute of Standards
Building 226
Gaithersburg, MD 20899
(301) 975-5900

Department of Energy
1000 Independence Avenue, SW
Washington, DC 20585
(202) 586-5000

Department of Housing and Urban Development
451 Seventh Street, SW
Washington, DC 20410
(202) 708-1422

Environmental Protection Agency
401 M Street, SW
Washington, DC 20460
(202) 382-2090

Government Printing Office
North Capitol & H Streets, NW
Washington, DC 20401
(202) 275-3204

Office of Urban Rehabilitation
Department of Housing and Urban Development
451 Seventh Street, SW
Washington, DC 20410
(202) 708-1422

REGULATORY AND RELATED ORGANIZATIONS

Advisory Council on Historic Preservation
1100 Pennsylvania Avenue, NW, Suite 809
Washington, DC 20004
(202) 786-0503

American Arbitration Association
7301 Carmel Executive Park, Suite 110
Charlotte, NC 28226-8297
(704) 541-1367

American National Standards Institute
1430 Broadway
New York, NY 10018-3308
(212) 354-3300

The American Society for Nondestructive Testing
1711 Arlingate Lane
Columbus, OH 43228
(614) 274-6003

Building Officials and Code
   Administrators International
4051 W. Flossmoor Rd.
Country Club Hills, IL 60478
(708) 799-2300

Cold Regions Research and Engineering Laboratory
Army Corps. of Engineers
Hanover, NH 03755-1290
(603) 646-4100

Construction Specifications Institute, Inc.
601 Madison Street
Alexandria, VA 22314
(703) 684-0300

Historic American Buildings Survey
1100 L Street, NW
Room 6101
Washington, DC 20005
(202) 343-9604

International Conference of Building Officials
5360 S. Workman Mill Rd.
Whittier, CA 90601-2258
(216) 699-0541

National Association of County Planning Directors
440 First Street, NW
Washington, DC 20001
(202) 393-6226

National Bureau of Standards
Gaithersburg, MD 20899
(301) 975-2000

National Conference of State Historic Preservation Officers
444 N. Capitol Street, NW #332
Washington, DC 20001
(202) 624-5465

National Conference of States on Building Codes
 And Standards
505 Huntmar Park Drive, Suite 210
Herndon, VA 22070
(703) 437-0100

National Council of State Housing Agencies
444 N. Capitol Street, NW, Suite 118
Washington, DC 20001
(202) 624-7710

National Institute of Building Sciences
1201 L Street, NW #400
Washington, DC 20005
(202) 289-7800

National Register for Historic Places
National Park Service
P.O. Box 37127 (413)
Washington, DC 20013-7127
(202) 343-9536

National Standards Association
1200 Quince Orchard Blvd.
Gaithersburg, MD 20878
(301) 590-2300

Industry Specialist on Engineering and Construction
Department of Commerce
Washington, D.C. 20230
(202) 377-0132

EDUCATION, CERTIFICATION, AND RESEARCH

Accreditation Board for Engineering & Technical
 Development
345 East 47th Street
New York, NY 10017
(212) 705-7685

Architectural Research Centers Consortium
10008 Morningside Court
Fairfax, VA 22030
(703) 691-2551

Association of Collegiate Schools of Architecture
1735 New York Avenue, NW
Washington, DC 20006
(202) 785-2324

Building Research Board
2101 Constitution Ave., NW
Washington, DC 20418
(202) 334-3376

Earthquake Engineering Research Institute
6431 Fairmount Avenue, Suite 7
El Cerrito, CA 95430
(415) 525-3668

Forest Products Research Society
2801 Marshall Court
Madison, WI 53705-2257
(608) 231-1361

Institute for the Advancement of Engineering
P.O. Box 1305
Woodland Hills, CA 91365
(818) 992-8292

Intelligent Buildings Institute Foundation
2101 L Street, NW, Suite 300
Washington, DC 20037-1534
(202) 457-1988

National Council of Architectural Registration Boards
1735 New York Avenue, NW, Suite 700
Washington, DC 20006
(202) 783-6500

National Institute for Architectural Education
30 W 22nd Street
New York, NY 10010
(212) 924-7000

Reinforced Concrete Research Council
5420 Old Orchard Road
Skokie, IL 60077
(708) 966-6200

Research Council on Structural Connections
Dept. of Civil Engineering, ECJ 4.8
University of Texas
Austin, TX 78712 1076
(512) 471-7259

Roofing Industry Educational Institute
14 Inverness Drive East, Building H, Suite 110
Englewood, CO 80112-5608
(303) 790-7200

PRODUCT ASSOCIATIONS

Adhesive Manufacturers Association of America
401 North Michigan Avenue
Chicago, IL 60611-4267
(312) 644-6610

Aluminum Association Inc.
900 19th Street, NW #300
Washington, DC 20006-2168
(202) 862-5100

American Architectural Manufacturers Association
2700 River Road, Suite 118
Des Plaines, IL 60018-4104
(708) 699-7310

American Concrete Institute
22400 W. Seven Mile Road
P.O. Box 19150
Detroit, MI 48219-1849
(313) 532-2600

American Concrete Pipe Association
8300 Boone Blvd., Suite 400
Vienna, VA 22182
(703) 821-1990

American Fire Sprinkler Association
11325 Pegasus #S-220
Dallas, TX 75238
(214) 349-5965

American Floor Covering Association
13-154 Merchandise Mart
Chicago, IL 60654
(312) 644-1243

American Hardboard Association
520 N. Hicks Road
Palatine, IL 60067
(708) 934-8800

American Hardware Manufacturers Association
931 N. Plum Grove Road
Schamburg, IL 60173-4796
(708) 605-1025

American Institute of Steel Construction, Inc.
1 East Wacker Drive, Suite 3100
Chicago, IL 60601-2001
(312) 670-2400

American Institute of Timber Construction
11818 SE Mill Plain Blvd., Suite 415
Vancouver, WA 98684-5092
(206) 254-9132

American Iron & Steel Institute
1133 15th Street, NW, Suite 300
Washington, DC 20005
(202) 452-7100

American Plywood Association
7011 S. 19th St.
P.O. Box 11700
Tacoma, WA 98411-0700
(206) 565-6600

American Society for Concrete Construction
1902 Techny Court
Northbrook, IL 60062
(708) 291-1340

Architectural Precast Association
825 East 64th Street
Indianapolis, IN 46220
(317) 251-1214

Architectural Woodwork Institute
2310 S. Walter Reed Dr.
Arlington, VA 22206-1199
(703) 671-9100

Asbestos Abatement Council
1600 Cameron Street
Alexandria, VA 22314
(703) 684-2924

Asphalt Institute
Asphalt Institute Building
P.O. Box 989
College Park, MD 20740
(301) 779-9354

Asphalt Roofing Manufacturers Association
6288 Montrose Road
Rockville, MD 20852
(301) 231-9050

Association of Home Appliance Manufacturers
20 North Wacker Drive
Chicago, IL 60606
(312) 984-5800

Association of Wall and Ceiling International
1600 Cameron Street
Alexandria, VA 22314-2705
(703) 684-2924

Brick Institute of America
11490 Commerce Park Drive
Reston, VA 22091
(703) 620-0010

Builders Hardware Manufacturers Association, Inc.
355 Lexington Avenue, 17th Floor
New York, NY 10017
(212) 661-4261

Building Stone Institute
420 Lexington Avenue
New York, NY 10170
(212) 490-2530

Carpet and Rug Institute
310 Holiday Drive
Box 2048
Dalton, GA 30722-2048
(404) 278-3176

Cast Iron Soil Pipe Institute
5959 Shallow Ford Road, Suite 419
Chattanooga, TN 37421
(615) 892-0137

Ceramic Tile Institute
700 North Virgil Avenue
Los Angeles, CA 90029
(213) 660-1911

Certified Ballast Manufacturers
772 Hanna Building
Cleveland, OH 44115
(216) 241-0711

Cold Finished Steel Bar Institute
700 14th Street, NW, Suite 900
Washington, DC 20005
(202) 508-1030

Concrete Reinforcing Steel Institute
933 Plum Grove Road
Schamburg, IL 60173-4758
(708) 517-1200

Cultured Marble Institute
435 North Michigan Avenue, #1717
Chicago, IL 60611
(312) 644-0828

Deep Foundations Institute
P.O. Box 281
Sparta, NJ 07871
(201) 729-9679

Door and Hardware Institute
7711 Old Springhouse Rd.
McLean, VA 22102
(703) 556-3990

Expanded Shale, Clay and Slate Institute
2225 East Murray Holiday Road
Suite 102
Salt Lake City, UT 84117
(801) 272-7070

Expansion Joint Manufacturers Association
25 North Broadway
Tarrytown, NY 10591
(914) 332-0040

Fine Hardwoods/Veneer Association
5603 West Raymond, Suite O
Indianapolis, IN 46241-4356
(317) 244-3311

Flat Glass Marketing Association
White Lakes Professional Building
3310 Harrison Street
Topeka, KS 66611
(913) 266-7013

Hardwood Manufacturers Association
2831 Airways Blvd., Suite 205
Memphis, TN 38132-1100
(901) 346-2222

Hardwood Plywood Manufacturers Association
1825 Michael Faraday Drive
P.O. Box 2789
Reston, VA 22090-5304
(703) 435-2900

Industrial Heating Equipment Association
1901 North Moore Street, Suite 802
Arlington, VA 22209
(703) 525-2513

Insulated Steel Door Systems Institute
30200 Detroit Road
Cleveland, OH 44145-1967
(216) 899-0010

International Masonry Institute
823 15th Street, NW, Suite 1001
Washington, DC 20005
(202) 783-3908

Kitchen Cabinet Manufacturers Association
P.O. Box 6830
Falls Church, VA 22040
(703) 237-7580

Maple Flooring Manufacturers Association
60 Revere Drive, Suite 500
Northbrook, IL 60062-1563
(708) 480-9080

Marble Institute of America
33505 State Street
Farmington, MI 48335
(313) 476-5558

Masonry Institute, Inc.
4853 Cordell Avenue
Bethesda, MD 20814
(301) 652-0115

Metal Building Manufacturers Association
1230 Keith Building
Cleveland, OH 44115-2180
(216) 241-7333

Metal Lath Steel Framing Association
600 S. Federal Street, Suite 400
Chicago, IL 60605-1842
(312) 922-6222

Metals & Ceramics Information Center
2595 Yeager Road
West Lafayette, IN 47906
(317) 494-9393

National Association of Architectural Metal
 Manufacturers
600 South Federal, Suite 400
Chicago, IL 60605
(312) 922-6222

National Association of Mirror Manufacturers
9005 Congressional Court
Potomac, MD 20854
(301) 365-4080

National Concrete Masonry Association
P.O. Box 781
Herndon, VA 22070
(703) 435-4900

National Elevator Industry
185 Bridge Plaza North, Room 310
Fort Lee, NJ 07024
(201) 944-3211

National Forest Products Association
1250 Connecticut Avenue, NW, Suite 200
Washington, DC 20036-2603
(202) 463-2700

National Glass Association
8200 Greensboro Drive
McLean, VA 22102
(703) 442-4890

National Hardwood Lumber Association
P.O. Box 34518
Memphis, TN 38184-0518
(901) 377-1818

National Institute of Steel Detailing
1791 Tullie Circle
Atlanta, GA 30329
(404) 634-8424

National Kitchen and Bath Association
124 Main Street
Hackettstown, NJ 07840
(201) 852-0033

National Oak Flooring Manufacturers Association
P.O. Box 3009
Memphis, TN 38173-0009
(901) 526-5016

National Paint and Coatings Association
1500 Rhode Island Ave., N.W.
Washington, DC 20005
(202) 462-6272

National Particleboard Association
18928 Premiere Court
Gaithersburg, MD 20879
(301) 670-0604

National Precast Concrete Association
825 East 64th Street
Indianapolis, IN 46220
(317) 253-0486

National Ready-Mixed Concrete Association
900 Spring Street
Silver Spring, MD 20910
(301) 587-1400

National Retail Hardware Association
5822 West 74th Street
Indianapolis, IN 46278
(317) 290-0338

National Stone Association
1415 Elliot Place, NW
Washington, DC 20007
(202) 342-1100

National Terrazzo and Mosaic Association, Inc.
3166 Des Plains Avenue, Suite 132
Des Plains, IL 60018
(708) 635-7744

National Tile Roofing Manufacturers Association, Inc.
3127 Los Feliz Blvd.
Los Angeles, CA 90039-1506
(213) 660-4411

National Wood, Window and Door Association, Inc.
1400 E. Touhy Avenue, Suite G54
Park Ridge, IL 60018
(708) 299-5200

Northeastern Lumber Manufacturers Association, Inc.
272 Tuttle Road, P.O. Box 87A
Cumberland Center, ME 04021
(207) 829-6901

Plastic Pipe and Fittings Association
800 Roosevelt Road
Building C, Suite 20
Glen Ellyn, IL 60137
(708) 858-6540

Plastic Pipe Institute
Wayne Plaza II
155 Route 46 West
Wayne, NJ 07470
(201) 812-9076

Porcelain Enamel Institute, Inc.
1101 Connecticut Avenue, NW, Suite 700
Washington, DC 20036
(202) 857-1100

Portable Sanitation Association
7800 Metro Parkway, Suite 104
Bloomington, MN 55425
(612) 854-8300

Portland Cement Association
5420 Old Orchard Road
Skokie, IL 60077-1030
(708) 966-6200

Prestressed Concrete Institute
175 West Jackson Blvd.
Chicago, IL 60604
(312) 786-0300

Red Cedar Shingle & Handsplit Shake Bureau
515 116th Avenue, NE #275
Bellevue, WA 98004
(206) 453-1323

Resilient Floor Covering Institute
966 Hungerford Drive, Suite 12-B
Rockville, MD 20850
(301) 340-8580

Roof Coatings Manufacturers Association
6288 Montrose Road
Rockville, MD 20852
(301) 230-2501

Sealant, Waterproofing, and Restoration Institute
3101 Broadway, Suite 585
Kansas City, MO 64111
(816) 561-8230

Sealed Insulating Glass Manufacturers Association
401 North Michigan
Chicago, IL 60611
(312) 644-6610

Single Ply Roofing Institute
104 Wilmot Road, Suite 201
Deerfield, IL 60015
(708) 940-8800

Society of the Plastics Industry, Inc.
1275 K Street, NW #400
Washington, DC 20005
(202) 371-5200

Southern Cypress Manufacturers Association
2831 Airways Blvd., Suite 205
Memphis, TN 38132
(901) 346-2222

Southern Forest Products Association
P.O. Box 52468
New Orleans, LA 70152-2468
(504) 443-4464

Steel Deck Institute
P.O. Box 9506
Canton, OH 44711
(216) 493-7886

Steel Door Institute
30200 Detroit Road
Cleveland, OH 44145-1967
(216) 899-0010

Steel Joist Institute
1205 48th Avenue, North, Suite A
Myrtle Beach, SC 29577
(803) 449-0487

Steel Window Institute
1230 Keith Building
Cleveland, OH 44115
(216) 241-7333

Tile Council of America, Inc.
P.O. Box 326
Princeton, NJ 08542-0326
(609) 921-7050

Wallcovering Manufacturers Association
355 Lexington, 17th Floor
New York, NY 10017
(212) 661-4261

Western Red Cedar Association
P.O. Box 12786
New Brighton, MN 55112
(612) 633-4334

Western Wood Products Association
522 SW 5th Avenue
Portland, OR 97204
(503) 224-3930

Wire Reinforcement Institute
1760 Reston Parkway, Suite 403
Reston, VA 22090-3303
(703) 709-9207

Wood & Synthetic Flooring Institute
4415 West Harrison Street, Suite 242C
Hillside, IL 60162
(708) 449-2933

Wood Truss Council of America
401 North Michigan Avenue
Chicago, IL 60611-4267
(312) 644-6610

DECIMAL EQUIVALENTS

FRACTION	DECIMAL OF AN INCH	DECIMAL OF A FOOT
$1/64$	0.015625	
$1/32$	0.3125	
$3/64$	0.046875	
$1/16$	0.0625	0.0052
$5/64$	0.078125	
$3/32$	0.09375	
$7/64$	0.109375	
$1/8$	0.125	0.0104
$9/64$	0.140625	
$5/32$	0.15625	
$11/64$	0.171875	
$3/16$	0.1875	0.0156
$13/64$	0.203125	
$7/32$	0.21875	
$15/64$	0.234375	
$1/4$	0.250	0.0208
$17/64$	0.265625	
$9/32$	0.28125	
$19/64$	0.296875	
$5/16$	0.3125	0.0260
$21/64$	0.328125	
$11/32$	0.34375	
$23/64$	0.359375	
$3/8$	0.375	0.0313
$25/64$	0.390625	
$13/32$	0.40625	
$27/64$	0.421875	
$7/16$	0.4375	0.0365
$29/64$	0.453125	
$15/32$	0.46875	
$31/64$	0.484375	
$1/2$	0.500	0.0417
$33/64$	0.515625	
$17/32$	0.53125	
$35/64$	0.546875	
$9/16$	0.5625	0.0469
$37/64$	0.578125	
$19/32$	0.59375	
$39/64$	0.609375	
$5/8$	0.625	0.0521
$41/64$	0.640625	
$21/32$	0.65625	
$43/64$	0.671875	
$11/16$	0.6875	0.0573
$45/64$	0.703125	
$23/32$	0.71875	
$47/64$	0.734375	
$3/4$	0.750	0.0625
$49/64$	0.765625	
$25/32$	0.78125	
$51/64$	0.796875	
$13/16$	0.8125	0.0677
$53/64$	0.828125	
$27/32$	0.84375	
$55/64$	0.859375	
$7/8$	0.875	0.0729
$57/64$	0.890625	
$29/32$	0.90625	
$59/64$	0.921875	
$15/16$	0.9375	0.0781
$61/64$	0.953125	
$31/32$	0.96875	
$63/64$	0.984375	
1	1.00	0.0833
2		0.1667
3		0.2500
4		0.3333
5		0.4167
6		0.5000
7		0.5833
8		0.6667
9		0.7500
10		0.8333
11		0.9167
12		1.0000

SCIENTIFIC NOTATION

Scientific notation is used to abbreviate large numerical values in order to simplify calculations.

$4.2 \times 10^4 = 4.2 \times (10 \times 10 \times 10 \times 10) = 42{,}000$

$1.0 \times 10^1 = 1 \times 10 = 10$

$6.0 \times 10^{-4} = 6.0 \times (1 / 10 \times 10 \times 10 \times 10) = 0.0006$

MULTIPLYING AND DIVIDING POWERS

$$X^N X^M = X^{NM}$$

$$(X^N)^M = X^{NM}$$

$$\frac{X^N}{X^M} = X^{N-M}$$

$$X^{\frac{1}{N}} = \sqrt[N]{X}$$

PYTHAGOREAN THEOREM

$$C^2 = A^2 + B^2$$

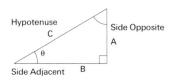

Hypotenuse C — Side Opposite A — Side Adjacent B — θ

BASIC TRIGONOMETRY FUNCTIONS

$$SIN\,\theta = \frac{OPPOSITE}{HYPOTENUSE} = \frac{A}{C}$$

$$COS\,\theta = \frac{ADJACENT}{HYPOTENUSE} = \frac{B}{C}$$

$$TAN\,\theta = \frac{OPPOSITE}{ADJACENT} = \frac{SIN\,\theta}{COS\,\theta} = \frac{A}{B}$$

$$COT\,\theta = \frac{ADJACENT}{OPPOSITE} = \frac{1}{TAN\,\theta} = \frac{B}{A}$$

RADIANS AND DEGREES

A radian is a way of measuring angles in addition to degrees. Radians are the primary unit of angular measurement used in calculations.

$$1 \quad RAD = \frac{180°}{\pi} = 53.7° \quad (APPROX)$$

$$1° = \frac{\pi}{180°} = 0.01745 \quad RAD \ (APPROX)$$

LINEAR DISTANCE

The distance **s** which a point **p** on the rim of a rotating wheel covers is called linear distance. The angle θ, the intercepting angle, is measured in radians.

$$S = R\theta$$

LINEAR SPEED

The linear speed **v**, of the point **p** around the rim of a rotating wheel, is the time taken **t** for point to travel the distance **s**.

$$V = \frac{S}{T}$$

ANGULAR SPEED

The angular speed ω, of the point **p** around the rim of a rotating wheel is the time taken, **t**, for the point to travel the angular distance, θ. The angular distance can be measured in degrees, revolutions, or radians. The resulting units of angular speed depend on the units used for angular distance and time.

$$\omega = \frac{\theta}{T}$$

LAW OF REFLECTION

A light ray reflects from a surface such that the angle of reflection equals the angle of incidence.

$$\theta'_1 = \theta_2$$

LAW OF REFRACTION

When a light ray traveling through a transparent medium strikes another transparent medium, part of the ray is reflected and part is refracted, entering the second medium. The angle of the refracted ray depends on the angle of incidence and the index of refraction of both mediums.

$$N_1 SIN\,\theta_1 = N_2 SIN\,\theta_2$$

TOTAL INTERNAL REFLECTION

When light attempts to move from a medium with a high index of refraction to a medium with a low index of refraction, there is a particular angle of incidence large enough that the angle of refraction reaches 90°. The transmitted light ray moves parallel to the surface of the first medium and no more light is transmitted.

This angle of incidence is called the critical angle and depends on the indexes of refraction of the two mediums. Any angle of incidence larger than the critical angle is reflected back into the first medium.

$$SIN\,\theta_C = \frac{N_2}{N_1}$$

Speed of Light in Medium

$$C_{MEDIUM} = \frac{C_{VAC}}{N_{MEDIUM}}$$

THERMAL EXPANSION OF LENGTH

An object of initial length L_o at some temperature. With a change in temperature of ΔT the length increases ΔL. The constant α is called the average coefficient of linear expansion for the given material.

$$\Delta L = \alpha L_o \Delta T$$

THERMAL EXPANSION OF AREA

An object of initial area A_o at some temperature. With a change in temperature of ΔT, the area increases ΔA. The constant γ is the average coefficient of area expansion for the given material.

$$\Delta A = \gamma A_o \Delta T \qquad \gamma = 2\alpha$$

THERMAL EXPANSION OF VOLUME

A mass of initial volume V_o at some temperature. With a change in temperature ΔT, the volume increases ΔV. The constant β is called the average coefficient of volume expansion for a given material.

$$\Delta V = \beta V_o \Delta T \qquad \beta = 3\alpha$$

USEFUL CONSTANTS

INDEXES OF REFRACTION (n)			
Air at 20°c, 1 atm.			1.000

Solids and liquids at 20°c			
Water	1.333	Polystyrene	1.49
Ice (H_2O)	1.309	Glass, crown	1.52

LINEAR EXPANSION COEFFICENTS (α)			
Aluminum	24×10^{-6}	Concrete	12×10^{-6}
Brass & bronze	19×10^{-6}	Lead	29×10^{-6}
Copper	17×10^{-6}	Steel	11×10^{-6}
Glass, ordinary	9×10^{-6}		

SPEED OF LIGHT IN A VACUUM	$C = 3.0 \times 10^8$ m/s
STANDARD GRAVITY	$g = 9.80$ m/s²

MATHEMATICAL DATA

FORMULAS NOMENCLATURE

E   Modulus of Elasticity of steel at 29,000 ksi.

I   Moment of Inertia of beam (in.^{4}).

M_{MAX} Maximum moment (kip in.).

M_1 Maximum moment in left section of beam (kip in.).

M_2 Maximum moment in right section of beam (kip in.).

M_3 Maximum positive moment in beam with combined end moment conditions (kip in.).

M_x Moment at distance x from end of beam (kip in.).

P   Concentrated load (kips).

P_1 Concentrated load nearest left reaction (kips).

P_2 Concentrated load nearest right reaction, and of different magnitude than P_1 (kips).

R   End beam reaction for any condition of symmetrical loading (kips).

R_1 Left end beam reaction (kips).

R_2 Right end or intermediate beam reaction (kips).

R_3 Right end beam reaction (kips).

V   Maximum vertical shear for any condition of symmetrical loading (kips).

V_1 Maximum vertical shear in left section of beam (kips).

V_2 Vertical shear at right reaction point, or to left of intermediate reaction point of beam (kips).

V_3 Vertical shear at right reaction point, or to right of intermediate reaction point of beam (kips).

V_x Vertical shear at distance x from end of beam (kips).

W   Total load on beam (kips).

A   Measured distance along beam (in.).

B   Measured distance along beam which may be greater or less than "A" (in.).

L   Total length of beam between reaction points (in.).

w   Uniformly distributed load per unit of length (kips per in.).

w_1 Uniformly distributed load per unit of length nearest left reaction (kips per in.).

w_2 Uniformly distributed load per unit of length nearest right reaction, and of different magnitude than w_1 (kips per in.).

X   Any distance measured along beam from left reaction (in.).

X_1 Any distance measured along overhang section of beam from nearest reaction point (in.).

Δ_{MAX} Maximum deflection (in.).

Δ_A Deflection at point of load (in.).

Δ_x Deflection at any point x distance from left reaction (in.).

Δ_{x1} Deflection of overhang section of beam at any distance from nearest reaction point (in.).

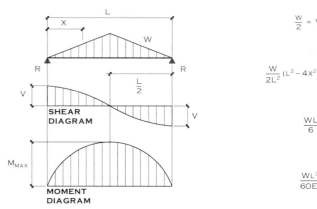

$$\frac{W}{2} = V = R$$

$$\frac{W}{2L^2}(L^2 - 4x^2) = V_x$$

$$\frac{WL}{6} = M_{MAX}$$

$$\frac{WL^3}{60EI} = \Delta_{MAX}$$

SIMPLE BEAM—LOAD INCREASING UNIFORMLY TO CENTER

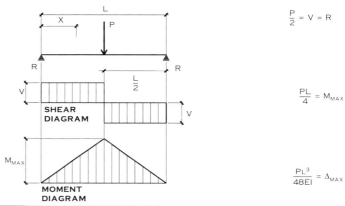

$$\frac{P}{2} = V = R$$

$$\frac{PL}{4} = M_{MAX}$$

$$\frac{PL^3}{48EI} = \Delta_{MAX}$$

SIMPLE BEAM—CONCENTRATED LOAD AT CENTER

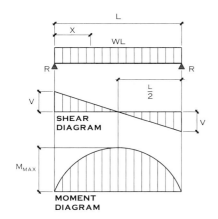

$$\frac{WL}{2} = V = R$$

$$W\left(\frac{L}{2} - x\right) = V_x$$

$$\frac{(WL)^2}{8} = M_{MAX}$$

$$\frac{5WL^4}{384EI} = \Delta_{MAX}$$

SIMPLE BEAM—UNIFORMLY DISTRIBUTED LOAD

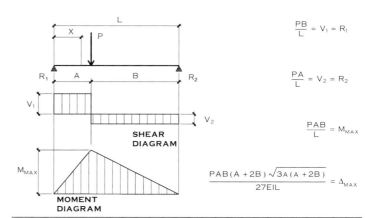

$$\frac{PB}{L} = V_1 = R_1$$

$$\frac{PA}{L} = V_2 = R_2$$

$$\frac{PAB}{L} = M_{MAX}$$

$$\frac{PAB(A+2B)\sqrt{3A(A+2B)}}{27EIL} = \Delta_{MAX}$$

SIMPLE BEAM—CONCENTRATED LOAD AT ANY POINT

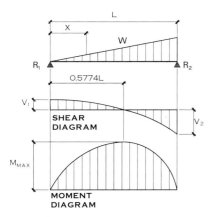

$$\frac{W}{3} = V_1 = R_1$$

$$\frac{2W}{3} = V_{2MAX} = R_2$$

$$\frac{W}{3} - \frac{Wx^2}{L^2} = V_x$$

$$\frac{2WL}{9\sqrt{3}} = M_{MAX}$$

$$0.01304\frac{WL^3}{EI} = \Delta_{MAX}$$

SIMPLE BEAM—LOAD INCREASING UNIFORMLY TO ONE END

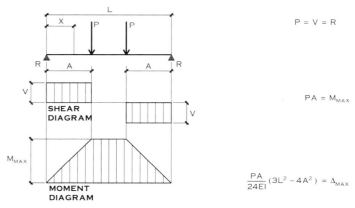

$$P = V = R$$

$$PA = M_{MAX}$$

$$\frac{PA}{24EI}(3L^2 - 4A^2) = \Delta_{MAX}$$

SIMPLE BEAM—TWO EQUAL CONCENTRATED LOADS SYMMETRICALLY PLACED

MATHEMATICAL DATA   Ⓐ

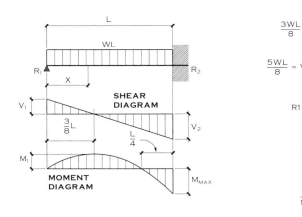

$$\frac{3WL}{8} = V_1 = R_1$$

$$\frac{5WL}{8} = V_{2MAX} = R_2$$

$$R_1 - Wx = V_x$$

$$\frac{WL^2}{8} = M_{MAX}$$

$$\frac{WL^4}{185EI} = \Delta_{MAX}$$

FIXED BEAM AT ONE END AND SUPPORTED AT OTHER—UNIFORMLY DISTRUBUTED LOAD

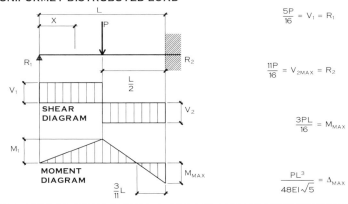

$$\frac{5P}{16} = V_1 = R_1$$

$$\frac{11P}{16} = V_{2MAX} = R_2$$

$$\frac{3PL}{16} = M_{MAX}$$

$$\frac{PL^3}{48EI\sqrt{5}} = \Delta_{MAX}$$

FIXED BEAM AT ONE END AND SUPPORTED AT OTHER—CONCENTRATED LOAD AT CENTER

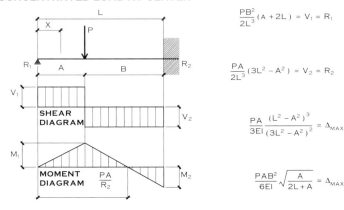

$$\frac{PB^2}{2L^3}(A + 2L) = V_1 = R_1$$

$$\frac{PA}{2L^3}(3L^2 - A^2) = V_2 = R_2$$

$$\frac{PA}{3EI}\frac{(L^2 - A^2)^3}{(3L^2 - A^2)^2} = \Delta_{MAX}$$

$$\frac{PAB^2}{6EI}\sqrt{\frac{A}{2L + A}} = \Delta_{MAX1}$$

FIXED BEAM AT ONE END AND SUPPORTED AT OTHER—CONCENTRATED LOAD AT ANY POINT

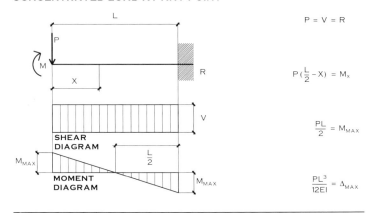

$$P = V = R$$

$$P\left(\frac{L}{2} - X\right) = M_x$$

$$\frac{PL}{2} = M_{MAX}$$

$$\frac{PL^3}{12EI} = \Delta_{MAX}$$

FIXED BEAM AT ONE END AND FREE TO DEFLECT VERTICALLY BUT NOT ROTATE AT OTHER—CONCENTRATED LOAD AT DEFLECTED END

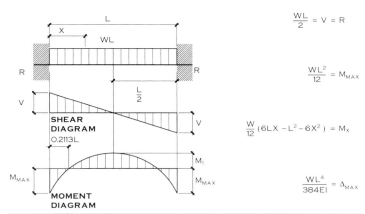

$$\frac{WL}{2} = V = R$$

$$\frac{WL^2}{12} = M_{MAX}$$

$$\frac{W}{12}(6LX - L^2 - 6X^2) = M_x$$

$$\frac{WL^4}{384EI} = \Delta_{MAX}$$

FIXED BEAM—UNIFORMLY DISTRIBUTED LOAD

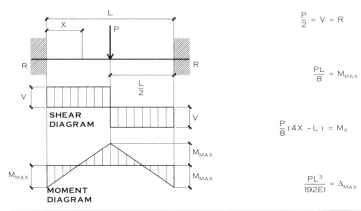

$$\frac{P}{2} = V = R$$

$$\frac{PL}{8} = M_{MAX}$$

$$\frac{P}{8}(4X - L) = M_x$$

$$\frac{PL^3}{192EI} = \Delta_{MAX}$$

FIXED BEAM—CONCENTRATED LOAD AT CENTER

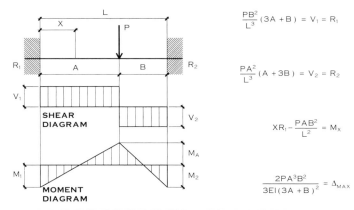

$$\frac{PB^2}{L^3}(3A + B) = V_1 = R_1$$

$$\frac{PA^2}{L^3}(A + 3B) = V_2 = R_2$$

$$XR_1 - \frac{PAB^2}{L^2} = M_x$$

$$\frac{2PA^3B^2}{3EI(3A + B)^2} = \Delta_{MAX}$$

FIXED BEAM—CONCENTRATED LOAD AT ANY POINT

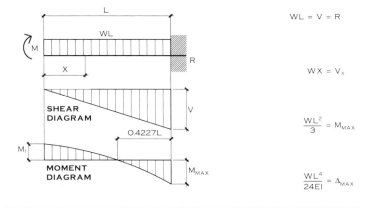

$$WL = V = R$$

$$WX = V_x$$

$$\frac{WL^2}{3} = M_{MAX}$$

$$\frac{WL^4}{24EI} = \Delta_{MAX}$$

FIXED BEAM AT ONE END AND FREE TO DEFLECT VERTICALLY BUT NOT ROTATE AT OTHER—UNIFORMLY DISTRIBUTED LOAD

 MATHEMATICAL DATA

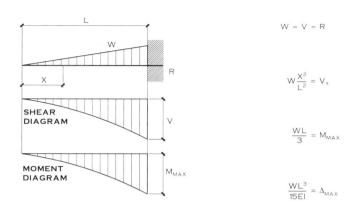

$$W = V = R$$

$$W\frac{X^2}{L^2} = V_x$$

$$\frac{WL}{3} = M_{MAX}$$

$$\frac{WL^3}{15EI} = \Delta_{MAX}$$

CANTILEVER BEAM—LOAD INCREASING UNIFORMLY TO FIXED END

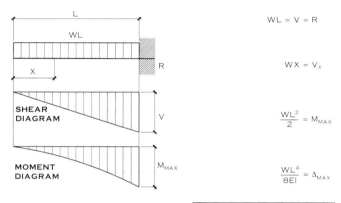

$$WL = V = R$$

$$WX = V_x$$

$$\frac{WL^2}{2} = M_{MAX}$$

$$\frac{WL^4}{8EI} = \Delta_{MAX}$$

CANTILEVER BEAM—UNIFORMLY DISTRIBUTED LOAD

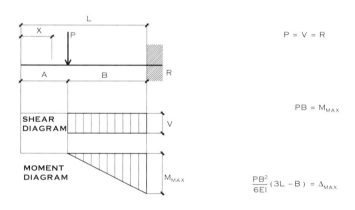

$$P = V = R$$

$$PB = M_{MAX}$$

$$\frac{PB^2}{6EI}(3L - B) = \Delta_{MAX}$$

CANTILEVER BEAM—CONCENTRATED LOAD AT ANY POINT

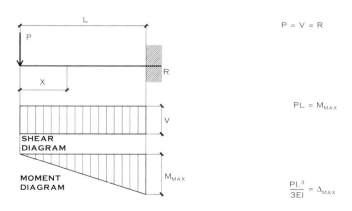

$$P = V = R$$

$$PL = M_{MAX}$$

$$\frac{PL^3}{3EI} = \Delta_{MAX}$$

CANTILEVER BEAM—CONCENTRATED LOAD AT FREE END

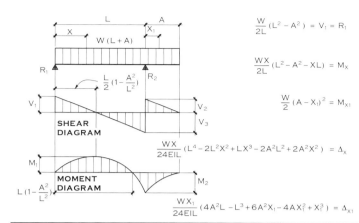

$$\frac{W}{2L}(L^2 - A^2) = V_1 = R_1$$

$$\frac{WX}{2L}(L^2 - A^2 - XL) = M_X$$

$$\frac{W}{2}(A - X_1)^2 = M_{X1}$$

$$\frac{WX}{24EIL}(L^4 - 2L^2X^2 + LX^3 - 2A^2L^2 + 2A^2X^2) = \Delta_X$$

$$\frac{WX_1}{24EIL}(4A^2L - L^3 + 6A^2X_1 - 4AX_1^2 + X_1^3) = \Delta_{X1}$$

BEAM OVERHANGING ONE SUPPORT—UNIFORMLY DISTRIBUTED LOAD

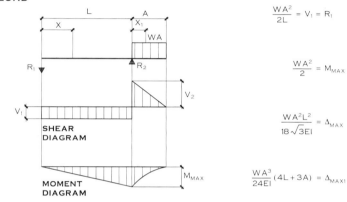

$$\frac{WA^2}{2L} = V_1 = R_1$$

$$\frac{WA^2}{2} = M_{MAX}$$

$$\frac{WA^2L^2}{18\sqrt{3}EI} = \Delta_{MAX}$$

$$\frac{WA^3}{24EI}(4L + 3A) = \Delta_{MAX1}$$

BEAM OVERHANGING ONE SUPPORT—UNIFORMLY DISTRIBUTED LOAD ON OVERHANG

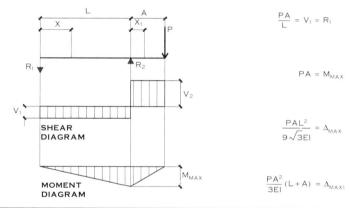

$$\frac{PA}{L} = V_1 = R_1$$

$$PA = M_{MAX}$$

$$\frac{PAL^2}{9\sqrt{3}EI} = \Delta_{MAX}$$

$$\frac{PA^2}{3EI}(L + A) = \Delta_{MAX1}$$

BEAM OVERHANGING ONE SUPPORT—CONCENTRATED LOAD AT END OF OVERHANG

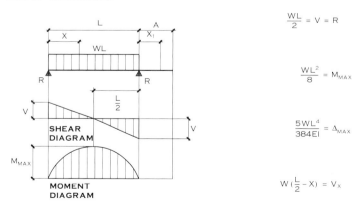

$$\frac{WL}{2} = V = R$$

$$\frac{WL^2}{8} = M_{MAX}$$

$$\frac{5WL^4}{384EI} = \Delta_{MAX}$$

$$W\left(\frac{L}{2} - X\right) = V_x$$

BEAM OVERHANGING ONE SUPPORT—UNIFORMLY DISTRIBUTED LOAD BETWEEN SUPPORTS

MATHEMATICAL DATA

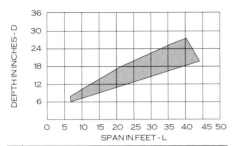

WOOD BEAM

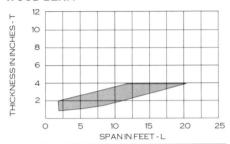

WOOD DECK

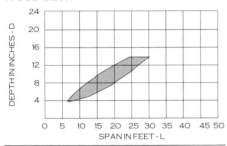

WOOD JOISTS

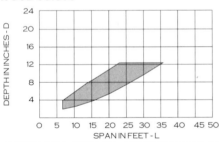

STRESSED SKIN WOOD

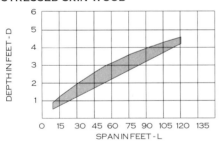

LAMINATED WOOD BEAM

GENERAL

These charts can be used to compare structural systems and estimate probable sizes early in the design process. They indicate the range of thickness and depth (or height) to span normally required for each of the systems indicated. Only the normal use of a single system is represented in these charts; they do not consider the extreme possibilities for either depth or span.

To use the charts, determine the span required for the design and choose a system appropriate to the design requirements. Read vertically from the appropriate span to the center of the range, then horizontally to the left of the chart to determine the normal thickness, depth, or height.

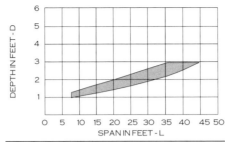

CONCRETE BEAM

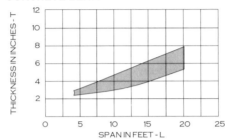

CONCRETE SLAB

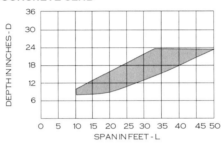

CONCRETE JOISTS

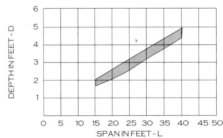

FLAT SLAB—CONCRETE

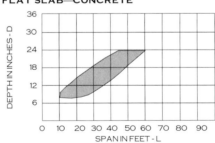

WAFFLE SLAB—CONCRETE

NOTE

Loads and spacing of members or supports determines whether to use the upper, middle, or lower portion of the chart's range. If, for example, greater than normal loads are anticipated or member spacing is great, the upper portion of the range should be used. If, however, loads are light or member spacing is closer than normal, the lower portion of the range should be used. The middle portion of the range is generally used for most designs.

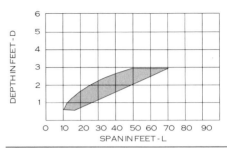

STEEL BEAM

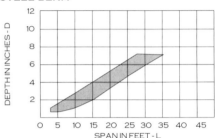

STEEL DECK

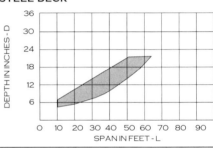

CORED CONCRETE DECK

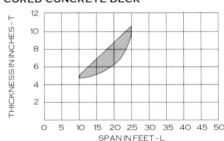

FLAT PLATE—CONCRETE

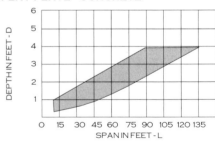

PRESTRESSED CONCRETE—T

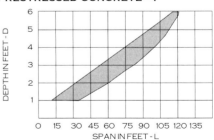

PRESTRESSED CONCRETE—I

 MATHEMATICAL DATA

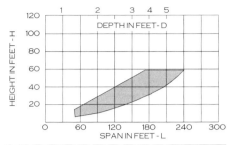

WOOD ARCH

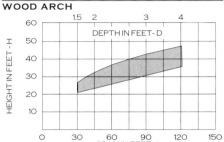

LAMINATED WOOD FRAME

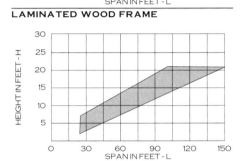

WOOD TRUSS—PITCHED

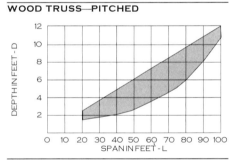

WOOD TRUSS—FLAT

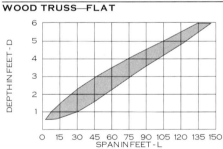

OPEN WEB JOISTS—STEEL

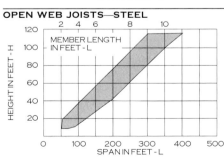

GEODESIC DOME

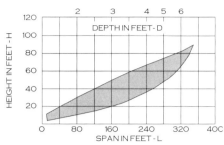

CONCRETE ARCH

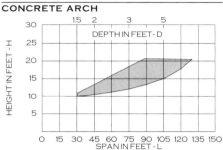

CONCRETE FRAME

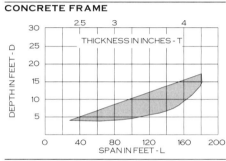

LONG BARREL VAULT—CONCRETE

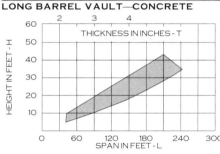

SHELL DOME—CONCRETE

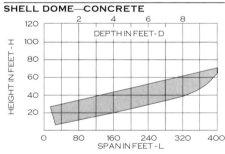

DOUBLE CURVED ARCH—CONCRETE

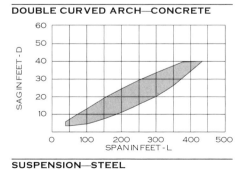

SUSPENSION—STEEL

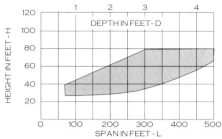

STEEL ARCH

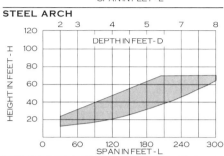

STEEL FRAME

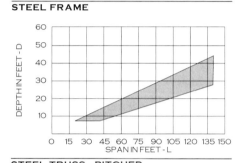

STEEL TRUSS—PITCHED

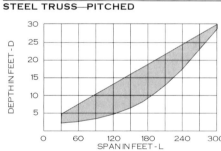

STEEL TRUSS—FLAT

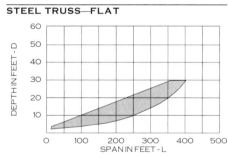

SPACE FRAME—STEEL, ALUMINUM

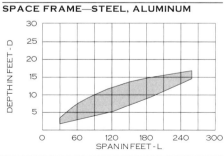

STRESSED SKIN—STEEL

MATHEMATICAL DATA

GENERAL

These charts are presented in two parts:

1. Structural supports that have an unsupported height of from 1 to 50 ft and primarily support only a roof or a one-story load.
2. Structural supports that have a normal one-story unsupported height and must support from 1 to 50 stories.

Each chart indicates the normal range of thickness or depth of independent or continuous vertical members.

Assume an unsupported height for vertical supports and from there read vertically to the center of the range, then horizontally to the left of the chart to find the required depth or thickness of the support.

Normal unsupported story height for these charts is from 8 to 12 ft.

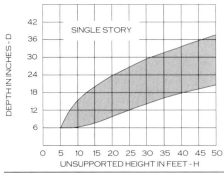

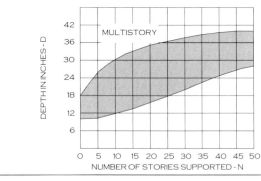

CONCRETE COLUMNS

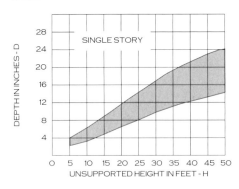

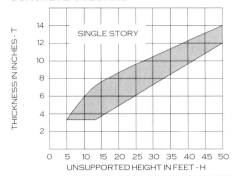

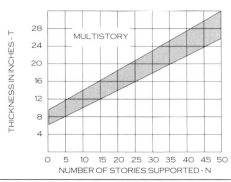

CONCRETE WALLS

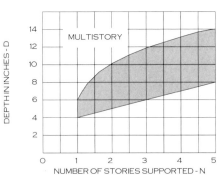

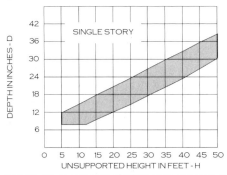

WOOD COLUMNS

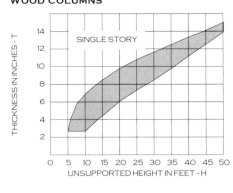

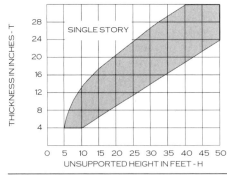

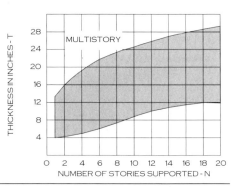

MASONRY PIERS

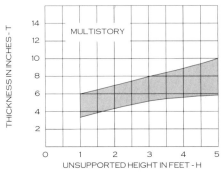

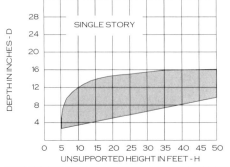

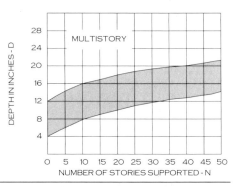

MASONRY WALLS

WOOD WALLS

STEEL COLUMNS

 MATHEMATICAL DATA

Index

GRINCH 3/91